THE AGE OF STATIC

THE AGE OF STATIC

HOW TV EXPLAINS
MODERN BRITAIN

PHIL HARRISON

MELVILLE HOUSE UK

LONDON

THE AGE OF STATIC

First published in Great Britain in 2020 by
Melville House UK
Suite 2000
16/18 Woodford Road
London E7 0HA

mhpbooks.com   @melvillehouse

A CIP catalogue record for this book is available from the British Library

ISBN 978-1-911545-52-1

ISBN 978-1-911545-53-8 (Ebook)

Printed in Denmark by Nørhaven, Viborg

Typesetting by Roland Codd

CONTENTS

INTRODUCTION

FROM CRAGGY ISLAND TO BREXIT ISLAND

Father Ted · Louis Theroux's Weird Weekends · Brass Eye
The Girlie Show · Our Friends in the North

TELEVISION ISN'T ALWAYS TAKEN as seriously as it deserves to be. In fact, it's often unfairly dismissed as the most disposable, least permanent of art forms. But television, perhaps more than any other art form, is political. Not always textually – regardless of intention, it's rare for a particular show to resonate widely enough to cause substantive change. Instead, the politics of television is contextual. It offers us a widescreen view of subtle and incremental social shifts; of building and subsiding currents. This applies particularly to the UK: there's an inescapability to British television, a universal quality which will persist for as long as the BBC, ITV and Channel 4 maintain public service duties. It remains an indispensable road map to the British psyche.

Accordingly, British television is often a battleground. It's one of the few places where we can't get away from each other, and in many ways, that's the genius of the country's broadcasting model. In

America, if they so desire, viewers can vanish down a Fox News or CNN rabbithole and never be confronted by uncomfortable ideas from an opposing perspective; here, television is a mirror into which we are all forced to look. Even people who rail furiously against the BBC and all they imagine it to stand for are, in their opposition, defined by it. Graphic novelist and writer Alan Moore posits the notion of Ideaspace: a sort of collective unconscious where psychic associations run free, apparently discrete ideas cluster in unlikely proximity, storms begin to brew and thoughts eventually take tangible forms. Thanks to its ubiquity and speed of turnover, television is a living, breathing, public example of this phenomenon.

I fell into writing about television in the summer of 2000. I wanted to be a culture journalist – and TV criticism turned out to be the easiest point of entry. *Time Out* magazine gave me my first break. Initially it was a slog: my work centred around the compilation of listings pages, and the torturous task of summarising the synopsis of an *EastEnders* episode in six words or less. Quickly, though, I realised how lucky I'd been; how unique and telling a medium television was. To sift and parse Britain's television is to investigate the country's collective mental evolution. For a variety of reasons, ranging from the often miserable winter weather to the totemic – and frequently well-deserved – reputation of the BBC, Britain is a TV nation in a sense that few if any other countries are. The British take television seriously – and, in both its best moments and its worst, television takes the British seriously too. Television is a palimpsest of the national mood.

Almost everything in the television firmament has changed between the end of the 1990s and now. But there's one document of the era that won't go away – and that's mainly because nobody in their right mind would want it to. Only three series were made of Graham Linehan and Arthur Mathews' peerless 1995 sitcom *Father Ted*, yet this Irish show is one of British TV's enduring glories; a proposition that can be tested almost every evening on More4. The show was showered in Bafta awards back in the 1990s. But its impact has been felt more widely than that, in a way that illustrates the soft power of the medium very satisfyingly. To this day, if you attend a protest march – almost regardless of the cause – you'll see banners reading 'Careful now' or 'Down with this sort of thing'. These almost incidental phrases from *Father Ted* which appeared during Ted and Dougal's reluctant protest against a risqué film have become a universal symbol, shorthand for a certain kind of charmingly absurdist gentility. The show has broken free from its moorings and become part of Britain's public language. From *Monty Python's Flying Circus* through to the various adventures of Alan Partridge, British television programmes have managed this trick with surprising regularity. They've identified archetypes and rendered them identifiably comic or tragic. They've become an intrinsic part of the way we view ourselves and each other.

Ian MacDonald concluded the monumentally gloomy introductory essay to his epic survey of The Beatles, *Revolution in the Head*, with the following statement. 'Far away from us, on the other side of the sun-flooded chasm of the 60s . . . The Beatles can still be heard singing their buoyant, poignant, hopeful, love-advocating songs.' Something similar can be claimed in relation to *Father Ted* and Britain in the 1990s. We all agreed on its brilliance, and on the basis of its regular appearance in both TV schedules and viewer-voted Best of . . . lists, we still do. In that sense, it feels like the last show of its kind – the final offspring of a lineage that also encompasses

Morecambe and Wise, *Only Fools and Horses* and *Fawlty Towers*. It's the generous, inclusive product of an era during which, despite pockets of unease, most of us were still able to sit down and laugh at the same things.

Who could possibly have imagined how rare and precious this consensus would seem twenty years later? Symbolically, even Graham Linehan is now a divisive figure, immersing himself in acrimonious debates about trans rights on Twitter. Think of the most successful post-millennium TV comedies. If your definition of success is commercial, it's hard to look beyond *Mrs Brown's Boys*. If critical acclaim is your yardstick, the *Comedy Vehicles* of Stewart Lee might be your strongest option. But those shows don't live in their own gentle, cartoonish bubble, like *Father Ted*. They divide, possibly deliberately. *Mrs Brown's Boys* feels proudly, almost militantly mindless – as if daring you to sneer at its antediluvian gormlessness. *Stewart Lee's Comedy Vehicle*, meanwhile, is deliberately and self-reflexively antagonistic. They are lightning rods; participants in a seemingly escalating culture war. They set urban against provincial. White collar against blue. They are both loved and hated. In the bitter, tribal Brexit era, they are no longer simply TV comedies, they are symbols. They feel a long way from the 90s.

The political scientist Francis Fukuyama famously described the fall of communism and the accompanying triumph of neoliberal capitalism at the start of the 1990s as 'the end of history'. So, in an apparently post-historical world, what defined British TV in the 90s? Much of it frolicked in the freedom afforded by that departed weight. For a while, anything went. In 1997, a programme called *The Girlie Show* introduced a feature in which women attempted to identify the penises of their partners as they poked – along with hopefully less familiar decoy members – through what were almost certainly the first glory holes to appear on British television. The feature, and indeed the show, was universally derided – but mainly because it was objectively terrible. Any taste issues were laughed off as slightly passé and quaint, and in the context of the deranged provocation, licentiousness and general havoc of much British TV in the 90s, that seemed par for the course. The 1970s-style moralistic proselytising of the likes of Mary Whitehouse felt anachronistic and distant; irrelevant and amusing to the point of kitsch.

This frivolity wasn't only a feature of light entertainment. Within the context of factual television, *Louis Theroux's Weird Weekends* also felt symbolically post-historical. These were shows whose tone wouldn't have fitted any decade prior to the 90s. They represented the beginning of a new kind of narrative technique, replacing drama with irony, and swapping scripted scenarios for the kind of real-life quirk and dysfunction which would become a staple of the constructed reality TV of the following decades. When viewers first encountered him, Theroux was a professional ingenue with charm to burn; a fourth-wall-breaking wink to camera in human form.

By way of his easy manner and shrewdly cultivated air of bafflement, Theroux elicited many minor revelations. But usually, his basic, underlying proposition was the same: that his subjects weren't serious people and therefore that their outlandish, sometimes troubling and occasionally dangerous ideas couldn't possibly be taken seriously either. Instead, they were amusing curios – mere grist to the entertainment mill. These trips into oddity haven't aged brilliantly. Notably, they often showcased the kind of people – white supremacist survivalists, conspiracy theorists and hardcore

Christian evangelists – whose context was about to alter dramatically in the age of Donald Trump.

Theroux – along, in fairness, with virtually everyone else in the British television industry – later applied a similarly soft pedal to Jimmy Savile. Savile now represents a symbolic warning encoded within British TV's DNA: everything is subtext, and nothing is ever quite what it seems. Theroux's subsequent journey towards 2020 feels emblematic of the road we've all travelled during this period. In his latest, often impressive, guise as a serious documentarian, he has put away childish things. Every film he makes feels like a kind of *mea culpa*. Earnest sincerity wasn't the done thing when Theroux began his career; flippancy and irony were very late-90s modes of expression. Now, in the midst of more serious times, they often feel like decadent luxuries that we can no longer afford.

It was hard to discern much in the way of moral rigour within Theroux's early wanderings. But more adventurous writers and performers interpreted the decade's tone and texture more thoughtfully. Chris Morris's 1997 landmark comedy series *Brass Eye* simultaneously embodied the freedoms of the era and held its frivolity up to the light. *Brass Eye* is one of a small band of shows that actually altered broadcasting conventions; twisted reality to force it to accommodate a particular creative vision. Its edge-walking audacity led to the introduction into the Broadcasting Code of a new clause allowing the misleading of interviewees for satirical purposes.

Morris was lucky to be operating at a historical sweet spot – after the tense, polarised 1980s and before the smorgasbord of paranoia, cultural sensitivity and dysfunction heralded by the triple whammy of 9/11, the Iraq War and the financial crisis. While the show railed against the triviality and banality of the era, it also contained a paradox in that it might not have been green-lit at any other time. Even at its daftest, it carried unmistakable moral weight. What kind of society, it asked, allows its agendas to be driven by tabloid hysteria and political quick fixes? In this sense, *Brass Eye* was, like much of the very best TV satire, both a document of its era and a warning of what might lie ahead. As we shall see, it would return a few years later to help answer its own implied question.

The new socio-political settlement affected everyone in different ways. For every example of post-historical playfulness, there was a serious attempt to make sense of the times. Self-evidently, 1996's brooding, generation-spanning drama *Our Friends in the North*, written by Peter Flannery, occupied very different territory to *Brass Eye* – not to mention *The Girlie Show* and the documentaries of Louis Theroux. But by exploring a loss of agency, purpose and existential certainty, it was part of the same current, another ripple of the past reaching the shore. What these shows had in common was that they had the air of responses to a newly materialised vacuum.

Our Friends in the North was a masterfully constructed, self-consciously portentous journey through the previous three decades' worth of hot button issues. Its characters' political explorations encompassed wet-behind-the-ears 1960s radicalism, the fierce militancy of the 1970s and the bruising, pivotal class conflicts of the 1980s. Eventually, the quartet landed, bewildered but more or less intact, in the compromised managerialism of the 1990s.

Britain's then prime minister John Major claimed that the general election of 1992 had 'killed socialism in Britain', and however you felt about the implications of that statement, it was hard to argue that it didn't carry the ring of truth. The travails of *Our Friends in the North*'s central characters seemed to signify that some sort of endpoint had been reached; that the battle of ideas was done and dusted. The right had won the economic war; the left had won the cultural one. This was where we were, and it was almost certainly where we'd stay.

Still, there was an underlying restlessness to *Our Friends in the North*; a sense that the tectonic plates would keep shifting, albeit less perceptibly. This gave the drama its power and prescience. It remains a resonant work to this day, partly because as it concluded the sense lingered that the generation of baby boomers at its heart hadn't quite finished their upheavals. Two decades later – at the EU referendum in June 2016, to be precise – this suspicion would prove to be well founded. The referendum would probably have split the four friends down the middle: Nicky and Mary were surely Remainers to the bone, but it's easy to imagine Geordie and Tosker succumbing to the blandishments of Messrs Farage, Johnson and Gove. Certainly, each of them seemed like a potent archetype whose identity crises were on hold but far from settled, even within the political context of 1996. This is what television can do at its best – the quartet felt like living, breathing representatives of us, as we grappled with the dilemmas of the era.

Is there anything linking these shows that makes them fittingly representative of 90s television and, in a wider sense, indicative of Britain's national identity as the millennium approached? There was a certain playfulness to the mid to late 90s, a sense of ballast being shed. But with that loss of anchorage came drift. What began to manifest itself was a growing elasticity of meaning and purpose. This came partly via emergent technology. It was also due to the politics of the era, which were increasingly underpinned by the assumption that free market liberal democracy would simply thrum away noiselessly in the background as the population detached itself from anything as old-fashioned as overt ideology. We began to atomise, to shoot off in different directions. Coming together again in more serious times would prove tricky.

And in some ways, this is where we now find ourselves. These shows capture British television – and by extension, British society – just before the beginning of a very different chapter in our national story. They exemplify their era while also offering subtle hints regarding our future direction of travel. In the early years of the following decade, it became abundantly clear that history hadn't ended after all. The 1990s had seemed a calm, even complacent interlude. But in reality, British society had begun to Balkanise. In terms of wealth, culture, education, expectations, even diet, Britain was becoming a less unified place.

To an extent that only became inarguable in retrospect, London and its surrounds had become the country's cultural and economic driver to an unhealthy extent. In 1997, London was responsible for 18.7 per cent of GDP; by 2015, that figure had risen to 22.7 per cent. Meanwhile, industrial decline, hastened by the Conservative governments of the 1980s and accepted as irreversible by their Labour successors, had left parts of the Midlands and the North denuded of both economic heft and, crucially, collective identity. The generally favourable economic conditions (Britain as a whole had recovered strongly from its early 90s recession, enjoying a remarkable forty successive quarters of growth up to 2008) had done a decent job of masking these uncomfortable facts.

But like most facts, they couldn't be dismissed for ever. Thanks to the political and economic upheavals of the first decade of the new century, various conflicts imagined to be settled have flared again with the kind of intensity that makes a mockery of any idea of closure. The terrorist attacks of 2001 on the World Trade Center and the Pentagon, and of 2005 on London's public transport system, shattered our collective sense of security. The shoddily conceived and dubiously conducted invasion of Iraq in 2003 removed any sense that Britain occupied the moral high ground. And the financial crisis of 2008–9 undermined the notion that our system was worth protecting in the first place. As a result of these successive disorientations, a series of temporarily pacified behemoths have lurched up again from the depths. The concept of multiculturalism is freshly disputed. Notions of sexual freedom and gender parity are contested fiercely. Nativist poison has infected discussions relating to national identity. And capitalism itself is coughing and wheezing; its workings demonstrably fail to offer either sustainability in the long term or prosperity and equality in the short.

One of the effects of Fukuyama's 'end of history' moment was that neoliberal capitalism ceased to be regarded as simply one way of ordering the world. Instead, it was seen by many as the only way. The Cold War period was characterised by what John Lanchester, in his book *Whoops! Why Everyone Owes Everyone and No One Can Pay*, describes as 'a beauty contest' between statism and private enterprise. Capitalism's triumph was partly predicated on the assumption that it would deliver social justice as well as economic growth – which serves to some extent to explain enlightened and progressive projects like the construction of social housing and the maintenance of that storied symbol of popular socialism, the NHS. Since 1990, this idea has been quietly sidelined in favour of privatisation and the relentless drumbeat of market forces. We've seen exactly what the unfettered free market does to our institutions, our public services, our personal relations, our entertainments, and even our collective and individual sanity. Something is wrong, and everybody knows it.

Britain's decision to leave the European Union in 2016 was part of a proxy battle, almost incidental to what was really under discussion. It's often characterised as a revolt against elites, but this isn't even superficially true. It's a revolt against the established order only in the sense that taking hallucinogens is a revolt against sober and rational decision-making. It is a scrambling, distorting and self-sabotaging act. Whether it's viewed in cold, hard economic terms or in the context of social cohesion, Brexit seems fundamentally irrational. Therefore, it's clear that its roots must lie not in logic but in emotions, instincts, feelings somewhere deep in our collective gut. They lie in the conversations we have, our relationships with each other and our surroundings, our work, our leisure and the entertainment we consume. Theresa May's 'Brexit means Brexit' mantra was a construction of perfect vapidity, but it also told an unconscious and profound truth. For many people, Brexit is a belief system and an end in itself. What it ultimately means in practical terms is, for the time being at least, less important than how it feels.

So how do we, as a nation, discuss these issues? What is the figurative watercooler around which we can gather? Often, it's culture. It's films, books, music, advertising and perhaps most illuminatingly, television. It pokes and prods us in certain directions, anticipates our feelings and provokes them too. It is cause but it's also effect. Television is a good place in which to explore societal currents because it's a sort of cultural clearing house. Everything ends up on television: high culture and low; fact and fiction; music and politics; sport and shopping. It's a noosphere; a realm of thought, a place where ideas are mulled over, pursued, discarded. Whether it's reacting to events, setting the scene for them or both, the evolution of British television since the turn of the century offers any number of revealing routes backwards and forwards through our developing tumult. Via television, it is possible to construct an illuminating alternative history of our last two decades. How did we get here?

Examining British television – and the political and cultural context in which it was produced – suggests some answers. How did television help enshrine class deference? How did reality TV influence populist politics? Did the BBC's interpretation of 'balance' jeopardise its ability to report current affairs effectively? From *Big Brother* to *Downton Abbey*, from *Detectorists* to *Top Gear* and from *The Apprentice* to Adam Curtis, the recent history of British TV can be read as both a struggle with the past and a series of signposts towards the future. How can modern Britain awaken from its nostalgic small-screen dreams and face the future? Brexit Island feels like a long way from Craggy Island, and there's no obvious escape route at hand. Perhaps, to move forwards, we first need to retrace our steps.

1

REALITY TV REALITY

Big Brother · The Apprentice · Britain's Hardest Workers
The Office · The Thick of It · Have I Got News for You

IN BIG BROTHER 17, which took place in the summer of 2016, housemate Lateysha Grace was given the task of being a news reporter. As luck would have it, she didn't have to dig for a lead – a big story dropped into her lap on her very first day in the job. 'The UK has voted to leave the European Union,' she announced to the group. 'I didn't even know that was a thing,' she continued. 'Anyway, over and out.'

As it turned out, after an initial burst of uncomprehending but performative astonishment, the news was received with the kind of nonplussed bewilderment that one came, in later years, to associate with the inhabitants of the *Big Brother* house. And yet it was still an oddly telling moment. The housemates instinctively understood that this was kind of a big deal. But at the same time, they weren't quite sure why. Scoff if you will, but this response mirrored rather neatly the reaction of many inhabitants of the country at large. It hit all of us in different ways, but there was one largely common factor: Britain's decision to leave the EU was something that, whether we received the news in joy or desolation, most of us felt rather than fully understood. Drew Westen notes, in his book *The Political Brain*, that the 'political brain is an emotional brain. It is not a dispassionate calculating machine, objectively searching for the right facts, figures and policies to make a reasoned decision.' Voters, though often well-informed and politically aware, think 'with their guts'.[1] By 2016, British public life, like British television, was all about the feels.

The idea that *Big Brother* would reflect some aspect of British society infused the show from the moment of its launch back in 2000. But exactly what version of Britain *Big Brother* – and the many other reality shows which appeared in its wake – reflected was subject to constant evolution. The show's tropes burst from their bounds; stopped merely dramatising our behaviour and embedded themselves within it. Almost every aspect of life – from the eternal search for love to the more era-specific search for reliable and fairly remunerated employment – has since become grist to the reality TV mill. Accordingly, to watch the opening series of *Big Brother* now is to be reminded of the incremental nature of change; the way in which seemingly tiny and insignificant developments are compounded over time. Barely perceptible in isolation, they eventually gather to form a dramatically altered overall picture.

Darren Ramsay quit his job at the Millennium Dome to appear on the first season of *Big Brother*. His career change both date-stamps the show and straddles two cultural eras very satisfyingly. It was the first year of the twenty-first century. The past had been celebrated and – for the time being – left behind. Now it was time to go somewhere new. That somewhere was a large, open-plan, one-storey house on an industrial estate in Bow, east London.

From the vantage point of 2020, the first series of *Big Brother* looks genuinely quaint; nothing dates as fast as the first iteration of a brand new thing. The contestants are sheepish and bashful and strikingly human. There are chickens in the garden of the house and it's suggested, rather optimistically, given the time frame involved, that the housemates might try and grow their own vegetables. The voiceover is sober: this show, it seems, imagines itself as much a social experiment as a TV entertainment. And the atmosphere surrounding the show seems positively austere to jaded modern eyes – the now-familiar pseudo-gladiatorial hype and hoopla is conspicuously absent. No one is milking cheers or boos from an assembled crowd, because the crowd is mainly comprised of the participants' friends and family members.

Initially, *Big Brother* was as jarringly strange to watch as it must have been to work on, either in front of or behind the cameras. With only one season of the show's Dutch forerunner to use as a reference point, the production team were on as much of a journey of exploration as the audience and the housemates. Channel 4 took to running a fixed-camera live feed during its hours of program-ming downtime, so that all through the night, lonely or obsessive viewers could, if they wished, watch over their new virtual avatars as they slept. Early *Big Brother* was that rarest combination of things: both genuinely populist and audaciously experimental. But the show's frequent longueurs were undeniable – most of the time, the contestants didn't appear to know what to do with themselves. That great broadcasting taboo, dead air, became a surprisingly regular feature. In fact, it contributed to the aesthetic of the show, becoming a signifier of rarefied realness; the lack of a script was the selling point.

The first batch of housemates were, by reality TV's later standards, a varied group. Tongues loosened by alcohol and truth games, a few details began to emerge. Sada was a hippie. Tom was a softly spoken Irish farmer who appeared to have wandered into the wrong show by mistake while looking for the set of *Countryfile*. Craig was a bluff, earnest Scouse builder. There was a computer programmer and a teacher; a marketing manager and a psychologist. They were a likeable, relatable and, in the kindest possible sense, very average bunch.

There was, however, a human time bomb lurking in the group, holding the key to the show's – and arguably, the entire genre's – subsequent development. Broker Nick Bateman, it turned out, was both a man on a mission and a scheming and ruthless rulebreaker. His attempts to manipulate the nominations process were discovered by Darren and Craig, with eventually explosive results. Viewed in isolation, the downfall of 'Nasty Nick' was a vivid, quietly dramatic and, eventually, cheering morality play in which honesty, decency and collective solidarity triumphed over sneaky, gameplaying duplicity.

The conversation in which Nick's cheating is revealed remains fascinating. It's unembellished and lengthy. Cameras zoom into troubled, incredulous and guilty faces and stay there. It works like an authored narrative reveal; the climax of a drama during which pretences fall away and a character is stripped bare in front of us. Even at a couple of decades' remove, it's gruelling to watch – a mercilessly dark moment of extremely personal, but now very public crisis. It's also impossibly compelling and as such, marks the moment when the format took flight, became inexorable, earned its stripes. It became clear that at its best, this stuff had what it took to compete with, and possibly even surpass, scripted fiction. Yet at the same time, it feels unpleasantly, prophetically voyeuristic, establishing simplified narratives of vice and virtue, playing out real-life conflict in the context of prime-time entertainment. In his post-eviction conversation with the show's host Davina McCall, Bateman mused: 'I think perhaps this kind of environment has brought out the worst in me.' He wouldn't be the last participant to feel this way.

In truth, Bateman had made a beginner's mistake. At the time, he was widely condemned for his cynicism – but if anything, he was naive. It was 2000, but his behaviour was very last century. He'd acted as if he was simply a contestant on a game show. He'd strate-gised towards winning *Big Brother*'s cash prize and ignored the bigger picture. He'd attempted to manipulate the inhabitants of the house, but had forgotten how his behaviour appeared to the outside world. Subsequent contestants would realise that in order to milk optimum potential out of the platform, precisely the opposite approach was required. Through the opportunity for identity creation enabled by the *Big Brother* house, individuals could self-brand. Viewers could be enlisted as supporters. You didn't play the game; instead, you played the cameras, the producers, the directors, the tabloid press and therefore, the audience.

Big Brother was instantly addictive, thanks to its rawness and occasional extremity. But as with any addiction, the buzz needed to be ramped up on a regular basis. As contestants began to realise what was required of them, so did those responsible for casting and editing the show. Series by series, a certain streamlining, homogenising and codifying was taking place. Some of the societal developments reflected – and arguably hastened – by the show were unequivocally positive. The house was, in its own peculiar way, a liberal and inclusive environment. Bullying or dishonesty was rarely rewarded, and divides of race and class were challenged. The formative years of *Big Brother* saw victories for a gay man (series two's Brian Dowling) and a transgender woman (series five's Nadia Almada). The pressurised environment was unerringly revealing of character, in ways that were often uncomfortable, but sometimes uplifting too.

In 2002, a dental nurse from Bermondsey called Jade Goody made her *Big Brother* bow and the format's evolution took its next quantum leap. Goody was a polarising figure from the start: did her ignorance of the existence of asparagus, and her insistence that Rio de Janeiro was a person not a place, make her refreshingly unpretentious, or a symbol of a new and poisonous strain of ignorance? The debate raged pointlessly for some time, but ultimately wasn't very illuminating, beyond revealing the class prejudices of the debater. More significant was the emergent culture that, thanks to the likes of Goody, was soon walking in lockstep with *Big Brother* and other shows like it.

Reality shows were diversifying and multiplying. Soon, a greasy pole was in place that the most rapacious and marketable contestants could scramble their way up. An embryonic career structure became established – reality TV was now part of a self-reinforcing, self-perpetuating and self-sustaining celebrity ecosystem comprising TV, magazines, tabloid newspapers and eventually, the hyper-accelerating and disorientating churn of social media. This network allowed a new breed of celebrity to either initiate or sustain a career, more or less in a vacuum. But the process wasn't forgiving, and the toll it took on participants' wellbeing often wasn't pretty. Worse still was the suspicion that the psychological wear and tear of such a career was now part of the spectacle. Dysfunction was becoming a grimly marketable commodity. Real-life failure, trauma, disgrace and despair were simply plot points in an ever more familiar narrative arc that, for entertainment purposes, would previously have been the exclusive domain of fictional creations.

Kerry Katona is an instructive example of a celebrity who, for a while, appeared to be living her entire life at the point where a constructed, TV-ready character, and a more troubling personal reality, intersected to the point of indistinguishability. Katona initially found fame as a member of girl group Atomic Kitten, but from 2001 onwards she eagerly threw herself into the ravenous maw of celebrity culture. She won 2004's jungle endurance reality show *I'm A Celebrity . . . Get Me Out of Here*. In 2009, she was rejected by *Celebrity Big Brother* after failing psychological tests but remarkably, was admitted to the show the following year – presumably, in the intervening period, she'd conquered her demons to the production team's satisfaction.

She was briefly the face of budget supermarket Iceland, and then of short-term loans company Cash Lady. She lost a sponsorship deal after photographs of her taking cocaine in her own bathroom were sold to the newspapers – but even these apparent setbacks could be put to work. They led to her becoming the subject of a raft of MTV reality shows, one of which explored her struggle with bipolar disorder. She was declared bankrupt in 2013. In short, modern celebrity was a hell of a ride, but one often predicated on a willingness to submit to situations which surely only compounded already existing problems. In a 2018 interview on ITV's *This*

Morning, Katona recalled her suicidal thoughts and extensive drug use during this period and said, 'I felt ashamed and embarrassed. I was lost and I didn't know who I was as a person.'

If Katona often gave the impression of careering out of control, Jade Goody appeared to have a reasonably firm grasp on her direction of travel. *Celebrity Big Brother* had initially tested the water as a one-off in conjunction with 2001's *Comic Relief* charity telethon. It was so self-evidently a good idea (not least because compared to scripted drama, which required writers and demanding and expensive professional performers, these shows were so cheap and easy to make) that the series soon became an annual fixture. By 2007, Goody, who had spent the previous four years finessing her first *Big Brother* appearance into what gave every impression of being a viable ongoing career, made it into the house again. By now, Jade, remarkably, had turned herself into a celebrity.

At this point, everything went south. To observe the unfolding of the 2007 *Celebrity Big Brother* racism scandal was to observe Jade Goody forgetting the Golden Rule of reality TV. As Nick Bateman had failed to understand, being successful in the context of these formats wasn't about manipulating – or indeed, befriending – your fellow participants. Indeed, these relationships were all but irrelevant. It was about making a connection with the watching public. Could Jade Goody's behaviour be construed as racist? It's hard to know what else anyone was expected to read into her addressing of fellow contestant Shilpa Shetty as 'Shilpa Poppadom'. Were Goody's comments as overt as those of fellow mean girls Danielle Lloyd and Jo O'Meara? Certainly there was nothing quite as unpleasant as O'Meara's reaction to Shetty's undercooked chicken dinner ('That's why they're all thin, because they're sick all the time, because they're ill'), or Lloyd saying that she didn't like Shetty touching her food because she didn't 'know where her hands had been'. It's also worth noting that Goody herself hailed from a mixed-race background. Essentially, she just didn't like Shetty, and expressed her animosity in a way that suggested she'd become so accustomed to her environment that she'd forgotten anyone was watching.

Tellingly, at the height of the row, Shetty told Goody 'the only thing you're famous for is this'. She was, of course, entirely correct. But even so, the quip was probably not quite so wounding as Shetty would have liked to imagine. After all, trying to make a living in this way was, by 2007, becoming normal and indeed, vaguely aspirational to a subset of young British people. Goody knew perfectly well where the roots of her fame lay and was fine with the arrangement. Like Shetty, she was an actor. She destroyed, on prime-time TV, her own constructed character by allowing herself to forget the basis of her success. And even if she partly rebuilt her persona with a penitent – albeit tragically curtailed – appearance on *Big Brother*'s Indian iteration, Jade Goody remains reality TV's most striking cautionary tale. She's also arguably its foundational figure. From tests of endurance in Australia, to talent shows with the Christmas number one single up for grabs – indeed, in any public popularity contest where success or failure could be determined by one's ability to appeal to the wider world – Jade's Golden Rule continued to apply. Eventually, it spread further than anyone could possibly have imagined.

Within a couple of years of its launch, the implications of *Big Brother*'s success were beginning to resonate through television's commissioning corridors of power. This was a basic formula that lent itself to almost infinite adaptation. It could shape-shift; be tweaked and adapted; be dismantled and reassembled to cross demographic boundary lines. Reality TV didn't have to involve simply a bunch of attractive youngsters drinking, arguing and flirting in a house. As the emergence of *I'm A Celebrity . . . Get Me Out of Here* had proved, they could be drinking, arguing, flirting – and eating kangaroo anuses into the bargain – in the Australian jungle. But really, there were no limits. The fundamentals of the format could go anywhere. In America, this process had already begun. In early 2004, professionally rebarbative real estate magnate Donald Trump was launched into the ether with consequences that proved eventually to be absurdly far-reaching. He was installed at the helm of a show called *The Apprentice*, in which a dozen or so furiously ambitious business bots scrambled to win the favour of the rich, powerful man in the plush executive chair, and were eliminated one by one.

Initially, the British version of the show seemed an unlikely pitch, with gruff north London tycoon Alan Sugar playing the Trump role. But *The Apprentice* is still going strong, and its continued success – and the glut of philosophically related 'business TV' that followed in its wake – is another illuminating small-screen route into the heart of Britain in the early twenty-first century. More and more, reality TV started to feel like our lives.

Cultural critic Mark Fisher's *Capitalist Realism* was published in 2009. The book's central thesis was that it was now easier to imagine the end of the world than the end of the world's dominant economic organisational principle: neoliberal capitalism. Its ethics, priorities and assumptions had embedded themselves so completely into our work, our play, our value systems, our entertainment and even our emotional lives that its hegemony had caused a failure of imagination, a stagnation of our capacity to even conceive of alternatives.

During the period in which Fisher was writing his book, the process it described was being dramatised by the ever-multiplying varieties of business-orientated reality television. *The Apprentice* was putting down strong roots. And it was being joined in the TV schedules by the likes of *Dragons' Den*, *Undercover Boss* and *Mary Queen of Shops* – all of which merged manipulated versions of an increasingly subjective 'reality' with the constructed narrative arc which was becoming a comfortingly familiar feature of prime-time sofa-fodder.

The UK iteration of *The Apprentice* arguably marked a sea change in the treatment of ordinary members of the public on television. Thanks in part to the precedent set by *Big Brother*, their foibles were now fair game. In early series of the show, viewers were encouraged to luxuriate in lashings of weapons-grade schadenfreude as the programme's production and editing teams set the controls for maximum ludicrousness. The show had about as much to do with genuine business practices as *Big Brother* had to do with a group of friends having a few drinks together. The contestants' on-screen personas were manipulated shamelessly. After elimination, they were allowed a public decompression chamber courtesy of *The Apprentice: You're Fired*, which prepared them for their inevitable return to the small software business in Swindon they'd spent the previous month pretending was the next Apple. But these aftermath shows – in which the rejected apprentices redeemed themselves by manifesting a certain degree of humility and normality – simply illustrated the extent to which they were caricatured in the show's edit for our appalled entertainment.

In TV, things don't always finish exactly where they started. Shows both cause and reflect incremental shifts. As was the case with *Big Brother*, business TV eventually slithered out of its box in the corner of the living room and mounted a hostile psychic takeover. *The Apprentice*, like the later seasons of *Big Brother*, showcased a particular personality type. The contenders were unselfconscious. They were largely lacking in self-awareness and humour. They were terrifyingly ambitious. They were narcissistic, paranoid, needy and desperate for constant reassurance. Gradually, the show normalised them.

Over the course of a decade and a half, the inhabitants of the real world have become more and more like *Apprentice* contestants. In a perfect illustration of the theory of Capitalist Realism writ small, the world of the show, its behavioural standards and its implied values has expanded to internalise us – subtly altered our wiring, codified what once seemed like extremity, infused us all with the crass, slightly desperate essence of contestants like overbearing alpha male Rory Laing and the relentlessly confrontational Melissa Cohen. At first, we mocked. But to mock, we imitate, to imitate we assimilate and after assimilation, we adopt. Have the show's contestants become more run-of-the-mill in recent seasons? Maybe. But it seems likelier that we've just got tired of fighting them; stopped noticing their preposterousness because our culture as a whole has drifted in their direction.

Anyone who doubts that *The Apprentice* is a show for its times should consider what's happened to the job market and the wider economy over the duration of the show's run. Whether by coincidence or design, the world of work as we currently experience it has come to mirror the torched, brutal and unforgiving landscape of *The Apprentice*. Jobs for life have become rarer and rarer. Hirings and firings have become more seemingly arbitrary. Paranoia reigns in a buyers' job market characterised by precarity, part-time and temporary work and zero-hours contracts. The holes in the safety net have widened. Of course, Britain's changing economic circumstances over this period cannot be blamed on a TV show. But the way we as a nation have dealt with these changing realities feels revealing of an attitudinal shift.

According to a 2016 investigation by the *Guardian*, the number of UK workers in positions which they could potentially lose at short or no notice had grown by almost two million over the previous decade. Meanwhile, TUC figures suggested that trade union membership fell from a peak of 13.2 million in 1979 to just 6.2 million in 2015–16. Workplace solidarity, the increasingly quaint notion of collective bargaining, of workers facing down unfair bosses, has become a thing of the past. Like most competitive reality shows, *The Apprentice* revelled in and inevitably reinforced the 'last person standing' trope which was also showcased in successful films of the era like *The Hunger Games*; the notion that sharp-elbowed competitiveness was the only feasible route to personal fulfilment. This was the TV embodiment of the brutality of a capitalist-realist society, in which humiliation is endured as a necessary evil, ruthlessness is rewarded and there are, ultimately, many, many more losers than winners.

When *Apprentice* candidate Stuart Baggs described himself as 'the brand', the nation howled with laughter. But really, Baggs was a pioneer of sorts. Because during this period, we've all begun to brand ourselves – via Facebook and Twitter, Instagram and LinkedIn. As a greater percentage of our lives has come to be lived online, we've become able to construct and then direct a curated persona outwards towards friends, families, potential employers and, quite a lot of the time, random strangers. Accordingly, we strive to demonstrate heightened versions of societal norms; to project basic, obvious signifiers of success and happiness.

But the more we've branded ourselves, the less we've managed to stand out. Paradoxically, the ultimate effect of this notionally individualistic capitalist-realist epoch has been flattening and homogenising. This has become evident in many of our collective choices. A combination of rising educational costs and the harshness of the graduate job market has begun to drive young people away from rarefied areas of academia and into the arms of cookie-cutter study briefs with no purpose beyond the conventional straight and narrow of working life. Accordingly, what has evolved seems to be a narrower, more vocationally angled curriculum with less room for the abstract, the arcane and the quixotic; education that is a means to an end rather than its own reward.

Since tuition fees made higher education in the UK a privilege not a right, and much study became essentially transactional, there's been a corresponding change in student priorities in UK universities. Between 2004 and 2015, there was a 6.7 per cent decrease in the number of students embarking on courses centred around historical and philosophical subjects, and a massive corresponding increase (15.9 per cent) in take-up for courses related to business and administration. The hyper-acceleration of rewards for those working in business, and especially in finance, have made vocational career choices like science, teaching or medicine less attractive. A certain philistinism is evident in the *Apprentice* generation. None of the contestants on *The Apprentice* are stupid, exactly. But many of them are profoundly ignorant and worse still, utterly incurious. They appear strangely deracinated – remember Michael Sophocles from series four; a self-described 'good Jewish boy' who, it turned out, didn't know what the word 'kosher' meant?

In America, *The Apprentice*'s coarsening and simplifying of business practice gave a platform to a future president in Donald Trump. So far, Britain hasn't been quite as unfortunate: the show's gifts to British public life thus far have comprised series two winner Michelle Dewberry – who ran unsuccessfully for Parliament on a pro-Brexit platform in 2017 – and Katie Hopkins. It would be unfair to blame even a show as dispiriting as *The Apprentice* for the latter's rise, but her trajectory does exemplify an aspect of an emerging media culture with reality TV at its heart.

In classic reality TV style, it was unclear whether Katie Hopkins ever truly wanted to win *The Apprentice*. She too had the Rule of Jade in mind. After all, she declined Alan Sugar's offer of a place in the final stages of series three, citing problems over childcare arrangements – problems which mysteriously hadn't prevented her from managing the commitments demanded by the show up to that point. It soon became apparent that she had her eyes trained beyond her immediate surroundings, on much bigger prizes.

Instead of spending the next few years running errands for Sugar, Hopkins embarked upon a media career that arguably began to look like a deliberate and escalating anti-charm offensive. She appeared on ITV's *This Morning* to state that she would stop her children from playing with schoolmates bearing names like Chantelle and Chardonnay: 'A name, for me, is a short way of working out what class that child comes from,' Hopkins said. 'There's a whole set of things that go with children like that. They are quite a disruptive influence at school. That's why I don't like those sort of children.'[2] She gained weight in order to prepare for a show called *My Fat Story* on digital channel TLC, in which she aimed to prove that overweight people were to blame for their obesity – one notable lowlight included Hopkins telling 57-stone interviewee Nicki that 'one of your boobs is bigger than my head'.[3]

Then it got worse. In a column in the *Sun* in April 2015, she called migrants 'cockroaches' and suggested the UK should deploy gunboats against them.[4] She was eventually sidelined by the *Daily Mail*, the *Sun* and radio station LBC as her views became ever more outlandish.[5] And while it's hard to imagine that Katie Hopkins would ever willingly allow her children to play with the offspring of Kerry Katona, in reality the pair aren't so different. In fact, their frenzied jags through the British print and broadcast media are strikingly similar – except, of course, that Katona's destination involves manifesting a measure of tranquility on various daytime TV sofas, whereas Hopkins has ended up on the fringes of far-right politics. But essentially, they've both walked a tightrope by monetising their neuroses; initially parlaying some coarsened and abstracted version of their 'real' personalities into an ongoing career, before overplaying their hands. Neither will be anything more than a footnote in television history, but they do illustrate both the infinite adaptability of reality TV, and its fatal flaw. While the world will never run out of people willing to rubberneck at individual dysfunction, pandering to voyeurism requires a degree of constant escalation that isn't sustainable for long.

One solution to the moral qualms often induced by reality TV has often been to dress the format up as something else entirely. If the original *Big Brother* could be marketed as anthropological exploration as much as entertainment, perhaps a version of the format could work as a phantom limb of the BBC's current affairs department too? Or perhaps not. In 2016, reality TV intersected with the sharp end of the British labour market's descent into austerity and precarity in the grimmest way imaginable. Here was a lesson for commissioning editors everywhere: just because you can, it doesn't necessarily follow that you should. It's not impossible that social historians of the future will pore over BBC One's *Britain's Hardest Workers* and come to regard it as one of the more shameful documents of the age. This was where we had suddenly found ourselves, and it wasn't pretty.

Sceptical viewers often sniggered at the pyrrhic nature of triumph in *The Apprentice*. As it turned out, in terms of hollow victories, we hadn't seen anything yet. There was a time when the escalating crisis of an economy churning out jobs characterised mainly by low wages and a shocking degree of workplace insecurity would have merited a serious and penetrating documentary on the BBC. Instead, it got what presenter Anita Rani described as 'a unique social experiment', and what anyone with a brain and a conscience might have described as a tone-deaf mismatch of format and content.

Britain's Hardest Workers was a competitive reality show with a difference. And the difference was a massive, deeply unsavoury overload of reality. In it, actual minimum wage workers did actual minimum wage jobs and were eliminated from the process, one by one. The prize, for the last person standing, was £15,000. And for the rest? Back to the job centre and the food bank, presumably. The show was given a touch of window dressing here and there. Occasionally, Rani took a few moments to talk to an economist or a trade union representative (sample question: 'Aren't some jobs so basic that actually, they don't deserve to have higher pay?').

But these fig leaves didn't do much to disguise the unedifying nature of the whole. What we were actually learning from this 'experiment' was that people could earn as little as £24 for nearly four hours of sorting through excrement-strewn rubbish, picking broccoli or cleaning, against the clock, hotel rooms recently vacated by stag parties – and still get the sack at the end of it. Of course, this wasn't news to hundreds of thousands of potential viewers: according to the Office of National Statistics, almost one million people reported that they were on zero-hours contracts in the period from October to December 2016. What may have come as more of a shock to them was learning that their travails – and by implied extension, the travails of anyone just about getting by in this punishing environment – could be corralled into a reality TV format and repurposed as infotainment.

Maybe we should have seen *Britain's Hardest Workers* coming. As we've already observed, TV viewers had long since become accustomed to television that reduced psychological dysfunction to the level of spectacle. In the spirit of capitalist realism, it should have come as no surprise that it was now doing the same to dysfunction of an economic, political and social variety. Since the financial crisis of 2008 replaced credit-driven consumerist frivolity with cold hard dread, echoes of the reality genre had been creeping into the realm of politics. And politics had begun to respond.

In 2011, Mary Portas – whose 2007 BBC Two series *Mary Queen of Shops* had been shown rationalising various struggling retail outlets with a no-nonsense blend of expertise and tough love – was commissioned by Britain's then-prime minister David Cameron to lead a review into the future of Britain's high streets. Rather more troubling was the case of welfare-to-work company A4e. The company reached out into the world of reality TV in 2010 via Channel 4's *The Fairy Jobmother*, in which its domineering employee Hayley Taylor encouraged and cajoled unemployed people back to work. A4e's chairman Emma Harrison had been appointed families advisor by Cameron that same year. The company – it's now been rebranded as PeoplePlus – faced fraud allegations, lost customer data and became the subject of an efficiency investigation into various public contracts they'd been awarded.[6] Eventually, MP and chair of the Commons public accounts committee Margaret Hodge damned A4e's 'abysmal' returns on the public money it hoovered up.[7] Despite her patchy record, Harrison walked away with a dividend of £1.375 million.[8]

So, in truth, reality had been beginning to bite for some time. Via the dubious voyeurism of the emergent *Big Brother* industry, the rapacious ruthlessness of *The Apprentice* and the curtain-twitching moralising of shows like *The Fairy Jobmother*, the quotidian aberrance of *Britain's Hardest Workers* was a destination we appeared to have been speeding towards for a while. But when we finally arrived it still came as something of a shock.

Small-screen fiction faced challenges as a result of reality TV's increasing commissioning heft and stylistic influence. One creative solution was to incorporate its tropes into various forms of meta-drama. Ricky Gervais and Stephen Merchant's sitcom *Extras* was patchy but periodically inspired; its 2007 climax played out as a critique of needy Z-list celebrity culture, centred around lead character Andy Millman's appearance on *Celebrity Big Brother*. *Extras* was, of course, the follow-up to the pair's wildly successful comedy *The Office*, which told its hilarious and eventually poignant story via the medium of a spoof fly-on-the-wall documentary.

The Office was arguably as close as the era came to a classic workplace – and maybe even working-class – sitcom. It reflected the reality that the nature of the working class had changed – David Brent and friends were white-collar wage slaves, and their working lives were all the more frustrating for their lack of grit and substance. Tellingly, the show barely bothered with the minutiae of their working activity at all. Instead, what mattered was the spoof documentary element, rendering the show deeply human while parodying the now familiar tropes of the curated and mediated self. Brent only became sympathetic and redeemable once he dropped his guard, stopped trying to speak to his imagined wider public audience, and faced directly what was in front of him. One of the reasons *The Office*'s climactic 2003 Christmas special struck such a chord was because it featured a man rediscovering himself by unlearning the lessons imposed by aspirationalism and media saturation.

TV audiences had been soaking up these lessons for years. The vérité documentary style had deeper roots than the various reality experiments which had begun to proliferate as far back as the 1970s. But thanks to the burgeoning appetite – partly fuelled by the likes of *Big Brother* – for 'normal people' on TV, it had truly hit its stride since the turn of the century. It was as successful as it was ripe for fictional exploitation. In 2005, with a timely combination of genre parody and political comedy, another show began to do exactly that.

Created by Armando Iannucci, *The Thick of It* was a scabrous, pseudo-fly-on-the-wall imagining of a contemporary British politics that seemed to exist in a space only marginally beyond reality. When *The Thick of It* premiered, the centrist Labour government of Tony Blair was in power but becoming increasingly unpopular, limping towards obsolescence. It was tainted by the catastrophic invasion and subsequent occupation of Iraq from 2003 onwards. And, more importantly from the perspective of the show, it was perceived as having surrendered to spin; sacrificing any notion of ideological credibility on the altar of image-maintenance and crisis management. However, 2005 was also the year that David Cameron, who according to former Tory cabinet minister Kenneth Clarke privately referred to Blair as 'the master', became leader of the Conservative Party, and began to modernise it along similarly post-ideological and managerial lines.[9] This was fertile ground for satire, and it seemed telling that Iannucci's chosen format was the deceptive chaos of the reality documentary. The style allowed for the blurring of boundaries, for a sense of dislocation and organised confusion to overwhelm clarity, creating its own internal logic.

There's a freeform, hyperreal quality to *The Thick of It*. The show is a disorientating whirl of movable principles, bad faith and even worse language. The format allows viewers the sense of eavesdropping, of gaining access to a secret world. In fact, the naturalistic acting often feels a good deal less performative than the kind of thing you might witness in an average episode of *Big Brother*. The perpetually jerky and restless filming style lends an almost seasick aspect to the experience; there's an entirely appropriate sense of the ground constantly shifting under the feet of viewers and characters alike. Which, of course, it is. No one here is to be trusted beyond the next reshuffle or major policy announcement. There's no situation that can't be gamed for maximum political advantage; no alliance that represents anything more than convenience.

The ecosystem of the show is a closed loop – it depicts politicians as the inhabitants of an airless, self-sustaining yet self-cannibalising environment; effectively a Big Brother house of politics. They're entirely detached from the people they've been elected to serve, so encounters with the public are inevitably excruciating. At one stage

Roger Allam's Conservative dinosaur Peter Mannion is chided by an aide who suggests that he 'can't say the public are horrible'. 'Yes I can,' Mannion replies. 'I've met them.' From the cleaners in government buildings to distressed mothers upset about failures in care provision, every encounter between the show's governors and governed reveals the former's ineptitude and crassness.

At the heart of the grotesque parade of chancers, dimwits and career bullshitters that comprise the show's cast – and by some distance, the most powerful figure viewers come to know intimately – is Peter Capaldi's Malcolm Tucker. Said to be based loosely on Tony Blair's fearsome press secretary, spokesman and all-round consigliere Alastair Campbell, Tucker – described within the show by *The Spectator* as 'Iago with a BlackBerry' – is political spin made craggy, cynical flesh. His performance is distinguished by some of the most gleefully inventive invective ever committed to film. And yet there's a poignancy to Tucker; certainly a sense of the mask eating the face but also the implication that, regardless of the damage it might be doing us, his aggression, duplicity and obsession with optics is the only way that politics can now work in a media-saturated age. It's tempting to wonder whether, for all its undoubted brilliance, *The Thick of It* might have done serious harm to the British public's perception of modern politics. Probably not: disenchantment with politicians is surely as old as politics itself. But in terms of both effect and intent, the murderous environment of the show is a world away from the bumbling gentility of previous prime-time political comedies like *Yes, Minister*.

In the penultimate episode, while giving evidence at the climactic enquiry into the death of a public sector worker bullied to the point of suicide by the state, Tucker is allowed something close to a soliloquy. On a narrative level, his words are a contemptible exercise in self-justification. But they also serve as a moment of authorial editorialising; an overview of the cultural climate which both created him and allowed him to thrive. Touching on social media, reality television and the jarring excesses of celebrity culture, Tucker communicates his pugnacious yet gloomy insights. 'The whole planet's leaking,' he claims. 'Everyone's spewing up their guts onto the internet. We've come to a point where there are millions of people who are quite happy to trade a kidney in order to go on television . . . How dare you blame me for this! Which is the result of a political class which has given up on morality and simply pursues popularity at all costs.'

Much like reality TV, politics, when all is said and done, is a public popularity contest. The word 'popularity' is, of course, massively flexible in this context. In political terms, it can mean anything from personal charisma to a capacity for stirring oratory to (just very occasionally) a programme of persuasive policy. But ultimately, political success is about convincing enough of the electorate that you have the right stuff. The popularity contests played out in *The Thick of It* feel like a glance at the inner workings of the Golden Rule of Jade Goody. A party or politician attempts to appeal to a faceless wider public, paying no heed to the havoc they might wreak upon their immediate surroundings. The public, in this context, are simultaneously all-powerful and hopelessly unaware of the real nature of their choices. As ideological differences between the two main British parties dwindled and capitalist realism solidified, a sort of vacuous elasticity became the strategic political norm. Politics now was all about presentation and crisis management.

And yet somehow, there's a certain distance about Malcolm Tucker now; a sense that he and his ilk are disappearing in our collective rear-view mirror. The perceived inauthenticity he – and by implication, the real-life likes of Alastair Campbell – were seen to epitomise has been replaced by something arguably even more pernicious. Nudging aside the hyper-managerialism and triangulation of the Blair/Cameron era, a cross-generational cluster of politicians has risen to prominence trading on an ersatz version of the opposite. Authenticity has returned – but in the bitterest of ironies, it's now a brand in itself, and comes surrounded by quotation marks. It's a reaction all right – but not one that seems likely to herald a bright new future.

'Famous for being famous' was a scornful yet rather trite insult that was heard frequently during the mid to late 2000s. Kerry Katona probably was. Jade Goody definitely was. But they weren't the only public figures to deserve such summary dismissal, and they weren't the least sympathetic ones either. The celebrity circus was becoming harder to ignore. In 2007, the then-prime minister Gordon Brown had found it necessary to have an opinion on the *Big Brother* racism scandal – which at one point, thanks to the understandable offence taken by many people in India, looked like it might turn into a genuine diplomatic incident. A politician like Brown was too gruffly maladroit to survive for long during this hypersensitive, emotion-driven era. Once you've been caught calling an old lady a 'bigoted woman'[10] on an effects microphone during an election campaign, the clock is ticking.

But the political world was starting to produce figures who, despite emerging from manifestly more gilded and privileged backgrounds than the likes of Katona and Goody, were copying a few of their moves. Some of these figures were beginning to gain some influence. Labour Party fringe rabble-rouser George Galloway had tested the waters of *Celebrity Big Brother* in 2006, and found that even pretending to be a cat and lapping imaginary milk from the hands of Rula Lenska wasn't a barrier to a continuing political career. The likes of Boris Johnson and Nigel Farage didn't go so far as to venture into the *Big Brother* house, but the (presumably) unconscious employment of reality TV strategies permeates their political careers like writing through sticks of seaside rock.

Boris Johnson has comprehensively absorbed the Golden Rule of Jade. Johnson has rarely let reliable or consistent behaviour towards his professional responsibilities distract him from using the media to woo his wider public. He likes to keep us guessing: just like the producers of a reality show, with their carefully calculated casting decisions and mutable storylines, Johnson tweaks his own persona – and accordingly, public perception – for maximum effect. From his artfully mussed hair to a range of gaffes that are, in all likelihood, nothing of the sort, Johnson is a vision of perfectly calibrated sloppiness. He is also playing a game – in fact, his whole political career sometimes feels like the result of a prank that got out of hand. Given that an article he wrote arguing the case for Britain to remain in the EU surfaced in several papers in autumn 2016,[11] what was Boris Johnson's support for Brexit other than a pure and careful calculation of where he needed to position himself to gain the job of Prime Minister?

But, as detractors will endlessly point out in relation to the bigger stars of celebrity culture, at the heart of Boris Johnson there's a void. Much as reality TV trajectories are completely detached from any artistic or cultural aspirations (making music, acting, or promoting a perfume or a fashion line is simply a means to an end), so is Johnson's political trajectory completely detached from any distinct ideology. He is broadly of the right, but that's where precise definition ends: he was as comfortable manifesting himself as cheerful, liberal, multicultural Boris (for the purposes of his London mayoral bid) as he is in the current guise as patrician, nationalistic, Brexit Boris.

Ultimately though, Boris Johnson, like Jade Goody before him, is simply famous for being famous. He made his name by writing waggish but factually flimsy newspaper columns and being vaguely amusing on TV panel shows. His multiple appearances on current affairs comedy quiz *Have I Got News for You* showcase his now familiar rhetorical techniques in embryonic form. Consciously or not, he is honing his gift for obfuscation and deflection; for undercutting seriousness with humour; for sidestepping responsibility for his own past actions. He's familiarising us with his modus operandi. As with Jade Goody's various acts of public personality projection, it's a process underpinned by considerable self-awareness – like Goody, Johnson is an actor playing a part based on, but not anchored by, a notional personal reality. Both resulted in sustained performances for which audiences were willing to suspend their disbelief. Of course, this is no more the fault of the show itself than the Trump presidency is the fault of the producers of *The Apprentice*. But it does emphasise the increasing interplay between television, identity creation and politics during this era. Somehow, Johnson parlayed this performance into the highest position of office. He is the blond, scruffy, quotable embodiment of political clickbait. People recognise him and vote accordingly. And with the whole concept of voting having been tweaked – and arguably devalued – by the weekly, orchestrated, push-button choices facilitated by reality TV, is it any wonder that, in certain moods, the public will give their backing to funny Boris off the telly?

Nigel Farage is, on the face of it, a more substantial political figure than Boris Johnson. In fact, on his own terms, it could be argued that he's among the most successful politicians in Britain's post-war history. And yet how often the mask slips – his neediness manifests itself constantly. Despite having apparently achieved comprehensive political fulfilment in June 2016, in early 2018 he went onto Channel 5's *The Wright Stuff* and suggested that another EU referendum might now be needed. It appeared a very peculiar position for Farage to be adopting, until one considered how close the summoning of Brexit left him to self-inflicted oblivion. As much as any reality star, and as much as Boris Johnson, he's an actor – albeit one playing to a slightly different crowd.

Farage, it could be argued, is a simulacrum, a right-wing Tory's fantasy construct of the politician who should have taken over from Margaret Thatcher in 1990. And he inhabits this persona perfectly. The 'authenticity' manifested by Farage's public character is self-devised and self-ordained. Just as reality series are cast with roles in mind (the gobby one, the sexy one, the boring one, the outrageous one), so has Farage curated his character. He's 'a man of the people'. He's at war with elites. Like his target audience, he's opposed to bureaucracy and red tape and political correctness. He's just enjoying a pint and a fag while saying what everyone's thinking. For an electorate beginning to tire of managerial politics, his tub-thumping brand of Home Counties 'common sense' was just the ticket.

Of course, he was able to make all this fly because there was a vanishingly small chance of him having to deal, in any practical sense, with the forces he unleashed. Instead he was able to simply light the fuse and retreat to the margins, where, until early 2019, he still lurked; policing his own particularly nebulous version of Brexit via regular media appearances, and keeping his fanbase on a slow, angry simmer. When he did return, he decided that actually publishing a manifesto behind which his new Brexit Party would fight the European Parliament elections would be a concession too far. Never mind the policy, Farage assumed that the electorate would respond to an emotional offer. And he was entirely correct: despite being only a few months old, the Brexit Party was the largest party, winning 30.5 per cent of the vote.

Speaking to the *Observer*'s Carole Cadwalladr, Labour MEP Richard Corbett offered a fascinating insight into Farage's modus operandi in the European Parliament. Despite multiple attempts, Nigel Farage has never succeeded in becoming an MP. Instead, he has found a new way of building a power base. Like other successful political reality stars, he also follows the Golden Rule of Jade. He ignores his immediate surroundings in favour of reaching a wider audience. 'Farage turns up once a month, and often what he talks about has absolutely nothing to do with what's being discussed,' said Corbett. 'You think, what's going on? And then you realise it's got nothing to do with the parliament. It's just for his social media output. Sometimes he doesn't even hang around for the answers. Two minutes later, he's back on the Eurostar and gone.'[12] This is pure reality show politics, scorning the niceties of conventional democratic or social process in favour of precisely targeted appeals to a receptive crowd. The twin behemoths of social media and all-access streaming sites like YouTube have made nurturing and sustaining a political career using techniques like this ever more possible. Up to a point, Farage knows how to win popularity contests.

In September 2018, the *Guardian* produced a series of short films reporting from the heart of Brexit Britain. In the final film, journalist John Harris extracted a remarkable and telling off-the-cuff quote from Farage as he was enjoying a pre-speech cigarette at a Vote Leave event. Farage called Brexit 'an emotional decision'. That's a big and significant shift given that he and his UKIP colleagues were casting Brexit as the purest essence of common sense back in 2016. It might, in fact, be the most honest thing Farage has ever said. Because, just like every other politically successful reality TV contestant before him (including, most notably, his friend Donald Trump in the White House), and just like the *Big Brother* contestants when they heard the result of the referendum, Nigel Farage understood he was trafficking in feelings. Trump's success has empowered fringe players all over the world: his Twitter outbursts have begun to stretch the boundaries of acceptable political discourse, meaning that half-truths from the likes of Johnson and Farage begin to seem tame in comparison. They produce an elasticity of intention and meaning which becomes self-perpetuating. Fictional stories can unleash powerful, deeply felt and genuine emotions with wide-ranging, real-world consequences.

Johnson and Farage aren't the only ones. Further down the political food chain, ersatz authenticity is everywhere. The desperation of younger British voters to find a handrail to grasp in the midst of the darkness of modern British economic and political life was real and understandable. But what is Jeremy Corbyn if not the bewildered symbol of a misty-eyed exercise in left-wing nostalgia; a waking dream of resolute old-school socialist values? And Tommy Robinson? Even his name is ersatz: Stephen Yaxley-Lennon is a man who took his *nom de guerre* from a former Luton Town football hooligan, a man with convictions for both violence and fraud who has piggybacked his way into the fringes of far-right political discourse by means of pure opportunism.

Twenty-first-century political populism and reality TV have developed in parallel. But it's hard to argue that either of them has brought out the best in us as a nation. Thanks partly to the shows discussed in this chapter, lines have blurred like never before. The line between politics and showbiz. The lines between fiction and constructed reality; between truth and artifice; between acting and being yourself; between fictional characters based on real ones (Malcolm Tucker) and 'real' characters based on fictional constructs (Boris Johnson, Nigel Farage, Jade Goody).

Around the end of the first decade of the century, the crossover between fiction and reality gathered ominous pace. The plot of an episode of Charlie Brooker's future-shock anthology drama *Black Mirror* ('The National Anthem', in which a fictional prime minister was forced to have sex with a pig to save a minor royal from a kidnapper) became conflated with a real-life fiction involving a pig and David Cameron. This was Reality TV Reality: a place where all that was solid melted into air, and all that was insubstantial suddenly became tangible, real and potent. Somewhere along the line, a situation arose where a reality TV star found himself in the White House – and where Boris Johnson became prime minister of the United Kingdom.

'This isn't a reality TV contest!' yowled Defence Minister Tobias Ellwood, as the Conservative leadership race clicked into gear in May 2019 following the departure of Theresa May – a politician who really didn't seem to understand the extent to which politics is a battle for popularity. But by this time, he was fooling nobody, least of all, one suspects, himself. It was nothing beyond a reality TV contest. At the very moment when the British government was engaged in the most difficult operation to face any administration in the last seventy years, the contest was a pure vacuum of meaning, a policy void, a contest over who could conjure the prettiest unicorn out of thin air. Finally, Boris Johnson had exactly what he'd always wanted. Famous for being famous, representing nothing but his own empty ambition, Johnson was revelling in pure, blank spectacle.

During her first run on *Big Brother*, the *Sun* launched an anti-Jade Goody campaign around the phrase 'Vote out the pig!'[13] After the racism scandal and before her death in 2009, there was, briefly, a Facebook group called 'Yay! Jade Goody has Cancer!' In all sorts of ways, this can be read as an early warning: about the kind of online disinhibition that's led to the poisonous discourse that surrounds Britain's current politics, and about the kind of weaponised cruelty that can be enabled by the anonymity of social media. But most of all, it warned of the nature of collective suggestibility; about the madness that this ever-expanding bedlam of signifiers was capable of unleashing. Jade Goody rolled the dice and experienced both sides of this hyperstimulated environment. She came from a humble background and saw a chance of having some fun and making a few quid. For a while, it paid off. Who, really, can blame her? Forgiving Boris Johnson and Nigel Farage might not be quite so easy.

2

HOW THE OTHER HALF LIVE

Little Britain · Shameless · Relocation, Relocation
Jamie's School Dinners · The Secret Millionaire
The Jeremy Kyle Show · Benefits Street · Fleabag

SOMETIMES, THE COMEDY OF the past ages like a fine wine. But often, it turns to vinegar. For example, the cultural historians of the future will probably look fondly upon the likes of *Monty Python's Flying Circus* and *Father Ted*. The brand of humour – and, most importantly, the spirit of the humour – means that these shows will be regarded as universal but pointed; inclusive, original and notable for their ability to endure, to unite and to transcend their era of origin. Time may not be quite so kind to *Little Britain*. Our hypothetical cultural critics will note Matt Lucas and David Walliams's undeniable chemistry and their gift for physical comedy. Other aspects of their creation may prove more problematic.

What, for example, will they make of Lucas's grotesque delinquent Vicky Pollard? Will she seem as dubious to future generations as a show like *Love Thy Neighbour*, whose central conceit was simply the inevitable hilarity prompted by a West Indian couple moving in next door to a white racist? It's not impossible. What, after all, is anyone to make of two privately educated men sending up the behaviour, appearance, language and cultural assumptions of a working-class teenage girl? Was there really a point at which the BBC thought it advisable to commission a show in which this class-based caricature swaps her baby for a Westlife CD? Then again, it's possible that even at a few decades' remove, no one will much mind. After all, there are fault lines and antagonisms within British society that seem as hardily perennial as royalty, rain and milky tea. Our attitudes towards race, gender and sexual orientation have evolved over time. Class, on the other hand, is different. Form is temporary but, in British public life at least, class is permanent.

Generally in Britain, once the Labour and Conservative parties get behind the same idea, that idea becomes the only game in town. Britain's version of liberal democracy has come to prioritise choice – but choice, in this context, is a weasel word. Even as consumer choice was widening, the parameters of political choice started to seem vanishingly narrow during the final years of the twentieth century. In 1990, Conservative prime minister John Major proclaimed his desire to 'make the whole of this country a genuinely classless society'. In 1997, his Labour successor Tony Blair went further, claiming that 'the class war is over'. Simply saying something, however, doesn't make it so. Instead, it causes cognitive dissonance; makes the gap between idea and reality yawn more confoundingly than ever. Was the class war really over? If so, who had won? And why did the eternal issue of class still feel so inescapable? Britain, we're often told, is a meritocracy. But meritocracy only bears logical scrutiny if everyone starts from roughly the same place. If that isn't the case, then the proclamation of a classless society isn't merely a fantasy, but also a cruel confidence trick; a form of political gaslighting. It implies that anyone who finds themselves at the bottom deserves to be there, and is simply occupying their rightful place. It begins to invalidate even the discussion of class as a potential determinant of success or failure.

In 2004, Channel 4 launched a new series which vividly dramatised Britain's class divide. Paul Abbott was a fierce and fluent writer who, on the face of it, seemed to be a poster boy for meritocracy. He'd come up the hard way; his childhood in Burnley had featured extreme poverty, family breakdown, sexual abuse and two suicide attempts. And yet Abbott had dragged himself outwards and upwards: first writing radio plays for the BBC, and then spending over a decade as a script editor and writer for *Coronation Street*.

Eventually, he struck out alone, launching a series of solo small-screen ventures which confirmed him to be a writer of unusual wit, depth and versatility. In 2000, BBC One launched *Clocking Off*, an exploration of workers' lives at a Manchester textile factory, and eventually showered with Baftas. The impossibly twisty and complex political thriller *State of Play* (2003) saw him transcend what some might have regarded as the limitations of his background. It was, as he told the *Hollywood Reporter* in 2011, 'written as a tantrum. A journalist called me white bread. So I wanted to show him I could make something posh, to show it wasn't my upbringing that lets me write like this. It's fucking talent.'[14]

By the time *Shameless* lurched unsteadily into view, Abbott was a made man; an individual who had refused to allow his gifts to be constrained by anything as trifling as upbringing. *Shameless* proceeded to emphasise how bumpy his road had been. Based loosely on Abbott's own father (but apparently a more benign version), Frank Gallagher was the addled patriarch of a barely functional family living on a council estate in Manchester. Even their address – 2 Windsor Gardens, Chatsworth Estate – felt pointed; a scornful nod to aristocracy with an implicit suggestion that there are chancers and freeloaders at both the top and bottom of society. While David Threlfall's Frank stumbled around drunk, his oldest daughter Fiona (Anne-Marie Duff) picked up the considerable slack, becoming everything from breadwinner to surrogate mother to the rest of the extensive Gallagher clan.

The show was bawdy, fast-paced and funny with a lingering undertow of tragedy. It made no apologies for the lives it drama-tised, and its leavening humour acted as something of a Trojan horse for the examination of issues including addiction, benefits dependency and social exclusion. It offered nuance and uplift too – an insight into the humanising resilience of community life in difficult circumstances. As Abbott told the *Hollywood Reporter*: 'I wanted to sneak in a sitcom that would force the audience to watch our underclass, to watch British poverty as it really is. But I remember things that were beautiful – I was remembering things from my past that were pretty horrific and sitting, at the same time, with a smile on my face. I wanted to tell a story about poverty by having something beautiful.'

Shameless really snapped into focus when Steve McBride arrived. Portrayed with rakish energy by James McAvoy, Steve was cheer-fully downwardly mobile, an articulate and charismatic middle-class lad who had run from his apparently comfortable destiny. Was Steve to be an avatar aimed at accommodating viewers for whom this world was a mystery? Abbott was too smart for that.

The Gallaghers demanded to be taken as they were found – by Steve, and by the show's audience too. Steve's romantic pursuit of Fiona had strings attached, and their relationship was convincingly complex from the start. Steve wasn't allowed to be a class tourist and Fiona refused to be a charity case. At times, her stubbornness threatened to become self-sabotaging. In the second episode, after a clash with Frank, Steve revealed that he had turned his back on a possible career in medicine to become a car thief – in search, he said, of 'some personality that wasn't a carbon copy of my father's'. Fiona was understandably furious. 'And you say it's my dad who's a waste of organs? Given the choices you've had, it's a bit rich that you don't like other people living with theirs.'[15]

This exchange was, in the context of the show's early days at least, the essence of *Shameless* – and in some ways, the era which spawned it – laid beautifully bare. Choice was our new god. It was fetishised; in personal morality, in the reform of public services, in broadcasting, in consumerism. It was among the key drivers of the post-industrial British economy, which relied to an ever greater extent on credit-fuelled consumption. But choice functioned as a negative too. Choice, and the ways in which it was exercised, became a stick with which to beat people – frequently, people like the Gallagher family. This was an era in which a gap was re-established between the 'deserving' and 'undeserving' poor. Implied within that distinction was the suggestion that choice was a key determinant of dysfunctional lives as well as functional ones. Because that, we were told, is how meritocracy works. In *Shameless*, Paul Abbott, speaking from the perspective of someone who knew, turned the notion neatly on its head. Not everyone has a choice. Because choice – like wealth, ability and privilege – isn't equally distributed.

The 1970s are often lazily posited as Britain's post-war nadir. They were, according to received wisdom, the decade in which the centrally planned and paternalistic dreams of Clement Attlee's visionary 1945 Labour government ran out of steam. They were a decade in which choice was stifled, in which unionised labour held the nation repeatedly to ransom. They were a decade of dowdy, dingy beiges and browns; frustration and football hooliganism; punk, power cuts and powerlessness. They were the decade that spawned a thousand ill-considered clichés, the most misleading of which was that they represented Britain's darkest hour before the Thatcherite dawn.

What is sometimes overlooked is that modern Britain has never been closer to being an actual, literal meritocracy than in the 1970s. The Gini coefficient is a measurement aimed at quantifying the degree of material inequality within a country's population. According to Britain's Gini coefficient, the share of income going to the top 10 per cent of the population fell by more than 13 per cent between 1938 and 1979 while the share reaching the bottom 10 per cent rose, albeit fractionally, over the same period. According to this measure, Britain in 1979 came as close as it's ever been to equality. Subsequent decades have seen inequality rise sharply.

In *Estates*, her superb history of social housing in modern Britain, Lynsey Hanley pondered the theories of French architect and urban planner Le Corbusier – who, she wrote, 'envisaged that, in the blankness of the machine-home, people would turn away from thoughts of individual improvement and instead, concentrate on mutual improvement; that, in the absence of opportunities to assert superiority to one's neighbour, man's spiritual nourishment would start to come from within, rather from without'.

Le Corbusier had reckoned without Margaret Thatcher. In the 1980s, Thatcher began a transformative programme. It was centred around housing and would change for ever our relationships with our homes and, therefore, with each other. Launched in 1980, the Conservative government's Right to Buy initiative was an audacious piece of social engineering. By giving all socially housed secure tenants the right to purchase their dwellings (at impressive discounts), it effectively privatised huge chunks of social housing. Michael Heseltine, the minister responsible for implementing the policy, reflected that 'no single piece of legislation has enabled the transfer of so much capital wealth from the state to the people.'[16]

This may well have been true. But the policy had multiple secondary effects. A percentage of the money accrued from the sales went back to councils. But they were prevented by central government from using the money to replenish social housing stocks. This inevitably resulted in a significant decline in the quantity and quality of housing available, as Thatcher attempted to draw a line between the statist past and the privatised, entrepreneurial future. Furthermore, it separated the occupants of council estates into new categories: upwardly mobile strivers and rut-dwelling skivers. Running alongside the crushing defeat for the unionised British working class that was the miners' strike, it paralleled the decade's other privatisations of state provision and function; fuelled the notion that Britain should become an individualistic, share-owning democracy.

In 1979, almost half the British population lived in social housing. By 2016, less than 8 per cent were housed by their local authority.[17] The administrators of social housing had, by this time, been forced to abrogate any of their aspirations towards promoting community cohesion via state-subsidised accommodation. Instead, social housing had become a last resort – the places where the real-life Frank Gallaghers and their families were dumped. In the private sector, things were very different. The housing market was going nuclear, and there was money to be made. But the place of housing in recent British cultural history is about much more than simply money.

If any one TV presenter could be said to have internalised the spirit of Margaret Thatcher and then projected it outwards, it would be Kirstie Allsopp. What's more, she would probably take that description as a compliment. The daughter of the 6th Baron Hindlip, Allsopp dropped her title for the purposes of her TV career, which began in earnest with Channel 4's 2000 series *Location, Location, Location*. The show followed Allsopp and her screen partner, former surveyor Phil Spencer, as they attempted to find the perfect properties for house hunters.

Allsopp and Spencer displayed a flirty chemistry that led to much (unfounded) speculation about the nature of their relationship. But when it came to property, they were brisk, efficient and businesslike. They were selling the dream very seductively. It was vicarious escapism; a bubble with an Aga in the corner. You could set your watch by the show's narrative structure, which reliably did an excellent job of simplifying and mediating the messy, difficult business of life. Everything was sorted inside an hour. Aspiration was followed by quest – generously undertaken on behalf of participants by Allsopp and Spencer. Generally, there was some sort of problem, usually centred around a recalcitrant estate agent, a bothersome property chain or an unsightly structural feature. But eventually, there was resolution.

The show was an immediate success. And as home ownership in Britain reached its peak in 2003, with 71 per cent of people owning their homes, it was followed by a much more problematic spin-off, *Relocation, Relocation*. Here, the focus wasn't on getting onto the property ladder; being on it already was a precondition of appearing on the show. The emphasis was on diversifying your existing assets: speculating, stretching out, cashing in. If you'd been lucky enough to buy at the right time, the world was now your oyster, and a second home a real prospect.

These – and the multitude of other property shows that followed in their wake – were confoundingly easy programmes to watch uncritically; to slide into like a comfort blanket. 'You can live the dream', proclaimed the introduction, 'by making your property work for you.' Imagine what your life could be like if you owned your London flat. As the very first couple to appear on the show proved, you could potentially afford to swap it for a cottage overlooking Loch Lomond and a crash pad in Glasgow.

This was TV for society's arbitrarily selected winners. It didn't concern itself with what life was like for anyone on the wrong side of the property divide. These televised investment missions constituted a brutal dose of status anxiety for many viewers. From the perspective of anyone locked in the increasingly vicious rental market, they seemed almost dystopian. Furthermore, they commodified the home, continuing the process set in motion a couple of decades earlier by the Right to Buy scheme. In *Relocation, Relocation*, home was no longer just a place to live: it was an embryonic investment opportunity. Yet for an alienated – and significantly large – chunk of the population, these notions of home were unrecognisable. For them, property was starting to create and reinforce a hierarchy.

Relocation, Relocation fed into and interacted with other national divides too. Thanks to a dearth of demand for property in the north (partly due to the de-industrialisation hastened by the Thatcher years), participants were frequently amazed by how far their money went in less economically buoyant parts of the country. However, Allsopp and Spencer didn't just advise on prime locations; they warned against apparently undesirable ones too. In 2007, the mayor of Middlesbrough complained to Ofcom after an edition of *Location, Location, Location* suggested his city was the worst place to live in the UK.[18] Meanwhile, the corresponding dearth of supply (and the resulting wild price inflation) in southern England financially underwrote the whole queasy exercise.

The show also illuminated the incipient intergenerational schism which has been compounded exponentially over time. The original *Relocation, Relocation* crash-pad generation will be pushing fifty by now and presumably, most will be delighted with the returns their investments have accrued since the early 2000s. Whether their millennial successors will ever enjoy similarly rosy prospects seems highly debatable. Like Right to Buy itself, the circumstances surrounding the first generation of property TV now look like a one-generation deal. Property shows have multiplied and diversified, ranging from the practical, such as *Property Ladder* and *To Buy or Not to Buy*, to the outlandish – like the astonishingly durable *Grand Designs*, which emphasises the innovative and aesthetic components of architecture. Whether many people watching a couple with a half-million-pound budget attempting to construct a triple-glazed eco barn in Dorset feel anything other than alienated is unclear.

These shows now feel like a momentary gaze into a hermetically sealed world, beyond normal experience or comprehension. Meanwhile, back in reality, an English housing survey report in 2017 revealed that the private rented sector has doubled in size since

2004 – almost half of all people in England aged between 25 and 34 are paying a private landlord for their accommodation.[19] According to the Nationwide Building Society, a typical 20 per cent deposit in London was, as of 2018, hovering around £80,000 – almost three times the national median wage.[20]

Housing in the UK is a mess. Freedom of Information data analysed by the *Guardian* in early 2019 paints a damning picture of the aftermath of Right to Buy. Forty years have passed since the original policy initiative. And just as lucky buyers are counting their profits, local authorities are counting the cost. They are being forced to spend millions of pounds on renting former council homes from private landlords to shelter ever-increasing numbers of homeless families. Many councils have repurchased their former properties at more than six times the amount they were originally sold for. Hundreds of private landlords now own five or more former Right to Buy properties in several London boroughs, and more than half the houses sold through the scheme are no longer owner-occupied, but have found their way into the hands of private landlords. Stories abound of former family homes being carved up and portioned out to multiple households by unscrupulous landlords eager to squeeze in as many tenants as possible. In early 2019, official government figures for the end of the previous year reported that on a single night in autumn, 4,677 people slept either on the streets, or in sheds and tents.[21] This was a rise of 165 per cent from 2010, and charities suggested the figures were likely to be an underestimate.

The Thatcherite dream of a property-owning democracy lies in tatters. This mess wasn't directly created by TV property shows. Property shows weren't responsible for Right to Buy, or indeed for its ultimate failure. Neither were they directly responsible for the

2008 economic crash or for our current dearth of genuinely afford-able housing. But, like so much UK television, these programmes vividly reflected and influenced the tone of their times. They interacted with social, political and cultural trends; were part of the push and pull of popular thought; provided a legitimising and galvanising effect. They helped to normalise property speculation as a mainstream, middle-class aspiration, to promote the concept of the home as commodity, to enable the return of landlordism and to encourage the mushrooming of buy-to-let investments.

Our living environments help to define us; we project our hopes and fears onto them. One of the earliest and most daringly utopian ideas associated with social housing was the notion that it would break down conventional and stubborn barriers of class. Former Labour health minister Aneurin Bevan spoke of the positive benefits of 'the living tapestry of a mixed community'. He envis-aged doctors, teachers and manual labourers living together on the same street, and through proximity and some measure of equality growing to understand each other's lives – and correspondingly the vital contributions to society made by each. What has since transpired is almost the complete opposite of that idealistic vision. A gaping material gulf accentuates an equally wide gulf of under-standing. Today, the people we now describe as 'the underclass' are not so much housed as warehoused in the last, tatty remnants of Britain's original social housing stock; out of sight and often out of mind. That doesn't mean we never see them on TV any more. But the contexts in which they're often presented would be unrecognis-ably aberrant to anyone dropping in unannounced from the shabby but equitable 1970s.

* * *

Every era of recent British social history has drawn a corresponding, class-related response from television. In the 1960s, *The Likely Lads* exemplified a certain perky, chippy northern working-class attitude, while *Cathy Come Home* explored, in forensic detail and with great compassion, the downward spiral of a family as they fell through society's safety net. In the 1970s, shows like *The Good Life* and *The Fall and Rise of Reginald Perrin* managed to combine comedy with a surprisingly subversive undertow. These were shows whose middle-class protagonists were fumbling in the dark, casting around for alternatives to lives that were beginning to disappoint them.

The polarities of the 1980s found expression in multiple small-screen forms. Derek Trotter from *Only Fools and Horses* was an uncannily timely creation: a Tory-curious working-class south Londoner who instinctively and correctly understood Right to Buy as a stroke of luck for those in a position to get on board; simply a nifty, short-term way of 'making a bit of bunce'. The lads from *Auf Wiedersehen, Pet* responded to the privations of Thatcherism by decamping to continental Europe in search of work. Meanwhile, a more overtly politicised and anguished take on the era was offered by *Boys from the Blackstuff*, a feverish and furious transmission from recession-hit Liverpool. Much TV of the 'post-historical' 1990s looked inwards: less obviously political and more individualistic, shows like *This Life* and *Cold Feet* seemed less concerned with wider society and more concentrated on families, friends, workplaces, emotional issues, intimate support structures. Tellingly, even the best British television from this particular era rarely felt rigorous or serious.

So how did the TV of the 2000s respond to Britain's new social settlement? Shows like *The Office* and Phil Bowker's wildly under-rated suburban high street retail comedy *PhoneShop* explored, hilariously, what were in some regards fresh yet also timeless aspects of workplace misery. But all too often, TV looked back. The soaps continued to churn out melodrama of variable quality. But they now felt set in amber; locating idealised and anomalous working-class communities in the kinds of areas where such cohesion had long since vanished, at the hands of property developers and gentrifica- tion. There was a gathering wave of nostalgia. *Rock & Chips* was an underwhelming *Only Fools and Horses* prequel while the likes of *Minder*, *The Fall and Rise of Reginald Perrin* and *Steptoe and Son* were faithfully rebooted, to negligible effect. *Life on Mars* and *Ashes to Ashes* dealt rather more inventively with the relationship between past and present, using nostalgia for the 1970s and 80s as a way of examining changing attitudes towards race and gender via the unusual format of the time-travelling police procedural. These shows were underpinned by a certain wistfulness about the changing nature of working-class life; they often felt like TV reimagined as a series of sepia photographs of your grandad going to work down a mine. Different times and fond memories, no doubt. But you wouldn't necessarily want to go back there. The era's best and most convincing slice of fictionalised reality came from a show which spanned the 1990s and 2000s: *The Royle Family*. Caroline Aherne's creation was both witty and pointed, capturing the love and longueurs of family life in a way that felt both specific and universal.

Running parallel to these shows was, of course, reality TV in all its proliferating incarnations. These were the new working-class dramas – not just the likes of *Big Brother*, but constructed reality; shows like *The Call Centre*, which often felt like a bizarre attempt to recreate the fictional universe of *The Office* using real people. So it was probably inevitable that Britain's growing inequality would be examined via variants of this genre too. Despite the best efforts of *Shameless*, the most socially illuminating TV of the era was non-fictional, ranging from the ineffectually well-intentioned to the downright mendacious. It was also frequently bleaker than anything *Shameless* could ever approach.

There was something disturbingly binary about the attitude developing in Britain towards society's less fortunate. The tabloid newspapers overflowed with stories about 'benefits cheats'. Phrases like 'sink estate' became commonplace as descriptions of poor urban environments. In 2004, Labour Home Secretary David Blunkett announced measures to extend the use of anti-social behaviour orders, aka ASBOs, which were designed to limit delinquent behaviour, but became a peculiarly passive and yet invasive means of social control. There was a distinct trajectory too, a clear direction of travel. In the early 2000s, Britain had established itself as a deregulated, largely privatised society – but it was basking in relatively tranquil economic waters, a situation which masked underlying structural economic and social problems.

Conceptually, there was absolutely nothing wrong with *Jamie's School Dinners*, Jamie Oliver's 2005 attempt to improve the diets of Britain's children. All he wanted was 'a better, cooler, cleverer, healthier nation'. And who in their right mind wouldn't agree with those objectives? The scale of the problem Oliver was attempting to address was immediately clear. Back in 1980, the Conservative government had deregulated the school system via the Education Act. A few years later in 1988, the Local Government Act saw the introduction of compulsory competitive tendering, which obliged local authorities to subject school meals to a bidding process. Inevitably, this prioritised economies above quality of provision and, in some cases, led to a race to the bottom. As soon as Oliver arrived at Kidbrooke School in south-east London, the problems were rendered graphically tangible. At one point, the chef visited a paediatrician who reported having to treat five-year-old children whose digestive systems were so clogged with saturated fats that they had essentially ended up vomiting semi-formed faeces. This was what a budget of 37 pence per meal bought you.

Jamie's School Dinners was often darkly amusing. Initially, the kids voted with their feet, clustering protectively around their beloved Turkey Twizzlers, visibly horrified by the unappetising lumps of vegetable matter suddenly polluting their previously pristine culinary environment. At one point, they even organised a small demonstration against this incursion of health-giving nonsense. And after all, these were, lest we forget, just kids. Regardless of their background, kids generally prefer chips to casseroles. Who wants to be told to eat their greens?

But then again, how many kids actually want to go to school? That doesn't mean they shouldn't have to, just that the environment should reflect the practical priorities surrounding their education. There's often a gap between what we want and what we need. Oliver's crusade attracted a certain amount of hostility, not least from the people he was trying to help. Reactions to the show became stratified along class lines. There was considerable middle-class pearl-clutching over the spectacle of parents passing junk food through the school railings to their kids at Rawmarsh School in Rotherham after Oliver rolled his scheme out more widely. The mothers involved were dubbed 'sinner ladies' in newspapers ranging from the *Guardian* to the *Daily Mirror*.[22] But perhaps the incident – and the ambivalence towards the scheme in general – was more complex than it seemed.

Sam Walker, who passed food to her child, told the *Guardian*, 'this isn't about us against healthy food. It's about how people change the rules.'[23] What was presumably a genuine desire to help was being lost in translation, interpreted as condescending or patronising. In a perverse sort of way, the hostility to the scheme was about choice and who did and didn't get to make it.

Oliver's campaign was by no means a complete failure. At the very least, he raised awareness of the importance of nutrition in early development, catching the attention of senior politicians along the way. But there were measurable benefits too. In 2011, Oxford University research indicated a 6 per cent improvement in the number of children reaching a high level in English tests and an 8 per cent improvement in science in schools where his healthier meals were eaten. There was also a marked decrease in children taking sick days. In 2012, a report by the Children's Food Trust showed a considerable fall in the proportion of teenagers consuming chips or starchy food and a corresponding rise in the consumption of vegetables.

Nevertheless, the chef himself was disappointed by the outcome. Eventually, he concluded that the problem was essentially one of class. In September 2015, he told the *Radio Times*: 'In Britain, eating well and feeding your kid right and being aware about food is all considered very posh and middle class.'[24] He may have been half right. But actually, this fed into larger issues surrounding agency and state intervention. Working-class British people were being cut adrift. In many media portrayals, they were at the mercy of society's judgment. And yet the shrinking of the state had created a problem. Working-class people were now expected to pull themselves up by their bootstraps, while the structural apparatus to help them do so no longer existed. There wasn't much of a ladder any more, and neither was there much of a safety net. No wonder cosmetic attempts to present these issues as entertainment were resented by some.

British TV had begun a dalliance with the idea of the privileged or successful reaching down, demonstrating noblesse oblige; helping out of the goodness of their heart. During the course of *Jamie's School Dinners*, Oliver, in understandable moments of exasperation, frequently said things like 'I don't need to be doing this.' And fair enough: he absolutely didn't. But this posed a bigger question. Why was someone like him having to? And what if he hadn't? Shouldn't a ministerial equivalent have been getting involved, long before the situation turned so critical? Someone offering less in the way of rococo profanities and a tantalising way with a tray-baked artichoke – and more in the way of funding, systemic overhaul and departmental lobbying? Oliver's show shone a light on systemic failure; simply tackling the symptoms of this failure wasn't going to be enough.

Perhaps inevitably, Oliver's initiative was ultimately at the mercy of vacillating government mood, as his subsequent tangles with Michael Gove (over food standards in free schools and academies) and Theresa May (over plans to axe free school meals for infants) showed. As much as TV occupied a unique place in British life, there was only so much it could do. However, as long as the ratings held up, that wasn't going to stop it from trying.

'Charity', declared Clement Attlee in 1920, 'is a cold, grey, loveless thing. If a rich man wants to help the poor, he should pay his taxes gladly, not dole out money at a whim.' But as we've already seen, the policies of Attlee's post-war government were at odds with emerging British values in the twenty-first century. Televised charity was now very much a thing, and not just in the once-a-year, Comic Relief sense. But you wouldn't exactly call Channel 4's series *The Secret Millionaire* cold, grey and loveless; more overheated, hypersaturated and emotionally incontinent.

Beginning in 2006, *The Secret Millionaire* showed the rich covertly infiltrating the lives of the poor. The security gates of their mansions would creak open and the participants would move, temporarily, into troubled neighbourhoods. They would adopt some sort of cover story – usually that they were charitable volunteers – get their hands dirty in the area and along the way, ponder the situations and characters of the people they met. Eventually, they would shower some of them with money. To be clear, in many respects, critiquing *The Secret Millionaire* doesn't sit right. No one is entitled to impugn the characters or motives of the show's subjects, who almost without exception were thoroughly admirable: selfless, brave, resourceful and kind. As with Jamie Oliver's school dinner initiative, it seemed churlish to doubt the good intentions of any of those involved. And yet whose catharsis was this? Superficially, the show was satisfying – but it became formulaic, too. And when a formula involves the exploitation of such emotional rawness for the purposes of entertainment, it's hard not to wince. There's also a particular power dynamic that is unique to charity as opposed to unrewarded civic virtue or state aid. 'It gives you such an amazing feeling inside,' reported entrepreneur Ben Way, the first millionaire to take the journey.[25] It was hard to avoid the impression that, sometimes, *The Secret Millionaire* was more about the givers than the receivers.

Charity, by definition, is about choice; it's arbitrary. As Britain became more unequal, the nature of choice began to change – and this was what became troubling about *The Secret Millionaire*. For many of those involved, the climactic moment at which the true intentions of their visitors were revealed will have been the first true lucky break of their lives. Accordingly, it was logical for viewers to assume that such people existed – unheralded and unhelped – plugging away in every struggling community across the country. The show couldn't help but flag up gaping holes in Britain's social provision. Yet there was no political or polemical dimension to *The Secret Millionaire*; no interrogation of systemic failure, no sense of anger about closing youth clubs, unaffordable cancer treatments, shoddy housing or lonely, impoverished pensioners. It remained studiously neutral.

The dubious power dynamic wasn't always entirely symbolic either. On at least a couple of occasions, it was all too tangible. By the time the show reached the editing suite, the power had shifted entirely as the producers set about turning whatever had unfolded into a neat, self-contained fifty minutes of small-screen entertainment. Choices were also made at this point; choices that risked leaving participants feeling betrayed. For example, Colin Biggs, who ran a disability charity in Barrow-in-Furness, decided to return £10,000 donated by entrepreneur Rob Calcraft in the light of the show's negative portrayal of his home. 'They ripped Barrow and Barrow Island to bits,' he told the *Telegraph*. 'I have a shop on the island and it is a lovely community that didn't deserve this. I feel so let down by the production crew. They reassured us that the programme would not portray Barrow in a negative way, and we said we would pull out of the programme if that was the case.'[26]

Arguably more worrying still was the case of Kervin Julien, a reformed drug addict who, by the time *The Secret Millionaire* arrived, had got clean, begun working for the benefit of his community and was planning to sell his home to open a drug rehabilitation centre in Coventry. His benefactor Sue Stone's gift had strings attached. According to Julien, after the cameras stopped rolling, she began to veto his suggestions for spending the money.[27] Her money, you might argue. But surely, true gifts are unconditional? Stone wasn't starting a business with Julien, she was helping him to help others. By making her gift conditional, she was imposing her will and in doing so, using her money to compromise his autonomy. She was exercising a choice that he, and the people who relied upon him for assistance, didn't have.

These, it should be stressed, were isolated incidents. Over-whelmingly, the show guaranteed satisfyingly neat happy endings. But the neatness was part of the problem. *The Secret Millionaire* uncovered an apparently limitless number of microcosmic, isolated tragedies which surely added up to a much greater whole. The show didn't make a case for more charity, it made a case for more and better-enforced taxation and increased public spending. But its positioning as entertainment rather than polemic meant it could never make this entirely valid argument anything more than implicit. A 2012 Reuters analysis of official data suggested that despite a jump in profitability, big companies were consistently paying less tax than in 2000. Meanwhile, in 2017, a public accounts committee report examined HMRC's specialist unit, which collects tax from high net-worth individuals. As quoted in the *Guardian*, it discovered that 'the amount of tax paid by this very wealthy group has actually fallen by £1 billion since the unit was set up' in 2009. Over the same period, overall tax receipts rose by £23 billion.

Doubtless, if there was still an appetite for *The Secret Millionaire*, the production company would be making it to this day. That they aren't is more to do with changing times and the circadian rhythms of prime-time TV than the sense that anything has been solved; quite the opposite, in fact. There weren't enough sticking plasters to go around. And as long as they're applied so selectively and on a voluntary basis, there never will be. We weren't running out of devastated or impoverished communities to feel sad about or heartrendingly virtuous local heroes to celebrate – we were running headlong into something else. Something that would lead to another step change in TV's attitude towards the disadvantaged.

The financial crisis of 2008 arrived as a huge, jolting correction after a long period of prosperity. It was caused, overwhelmingly, by the excesses of the very wealthy – from gamblers in high finance to deregulators in government. But once it had been established that certain institutions were too big to fail, vast sums of money had to be found for a mass defibrillation of the banking system. With a Conservative prime minister taking office in 2010, this was never likely to play out well for those most reliant on public services (and least responsible for the crisis). And sure enough, it didn't. As austerity bit, appallingly difficult decisions had to be made.

Initially, there were a number of thoughtful and affecting TV contributions to the national debate about where the axe should fall. For example, BBC Four's *The Year the Town Hall Shrank* was a frequently devastating series documenting the impossible choices being made (in Stoke-on-Trent, but it could have been anywhere) between hospices and swimming pools, social housing and Sure Start schemes. BBC One's *Poor Kids* was similarly compassionate and brutal – a child's eye view of the practical and emotional effects of poverty as experienced in the context of consumerist, neoliberal democracy.

In his 1972 book *Stone Age Economics*, Marshall Sahlins wrote, 'Poverty is not a certain small amount of goods, nor is it just a relation between means and ends; above all it is a relation between people. Poverty is a social status . . . it has grown as an invidious distinction between classes.' *Poor Kids* showed the lived reality of that statement. It wasn't just that you didn't have enough to eat. It was also that you looked like you didn't have enough to eat. You had the wrong trainers, so the other kids took the piss. Your mum had been forced to cut your hair and send you to school in the tatty old coat your big sister had grown out of. These tiny, daily indignities suffered by the most vulnerable added up to an almighty punch to the solar plexus. The documentary showed that society, with its eagerly internalised material aspiration and entrenched inequality, had begun to enforce its own hierarchies, and in doing so, had devised a particular kind of hell for these helpless, heartbreakingly charming youngsters.

But something uglier was in the air too. And we knew this because it had been bubbling under for years – pre-dating, in latent form, the post-crash justification of spending cuts by deciding precisely which poor people deserved state assistance. Since the mid-2000s, there had been accumulating evidence of a climate of scorn and contempt towards Britain's 'underclass'. It was manifest in TV characters like Vicky Pollard and in websites like the deeply unpleasant Chavscum – whose creators branched out into publishing in 2004 with a book called *Chav! A User's Guide to Britain's New Ruling Class*. The final four words of that title were significant. 'Britain's New Ruling Class'? They spoke to the absurd but prevalent notion that somehow, these not-quite-people were playing the game and winning; lowering the tone, taking us all for a ride and getting away with it.

As is the British way, this phenomenon spawned a confoundingly successful TV arm. ITV launched *The Jeremy Kyle Show* in 2005, and it ran until 2019, when it was cancelled due to the suicide of a guest. Its longevity also suggested that there were plenty of viewers who enjoyed starting their day with a censorious yet guiltily voyeuristic twitch of their televisual curtains.

The Jeremy Kyle Show specialised in provoking titillating confrontations – sorry, addressing complex interpersonal issues – between estranged friends, lovers, family members and work colleagues. The participants were drawn, almost without exception, from working-class Britain. The titular host adopted an infuriating tone: half ingratiating wheedle, half moral scold, as he roamed around, and sometimes basked upon, the studio set, shadowed at all times by a posse of mountainous, buzzcut security guards. He'd introduce a guest and inform them that, for example, their boyfriend had got their best friend pregnant. And then, one at a time, for maximum dramatic effect, he would introduce the other protagonists. A frank exchange of views reliably followed.

While his demeanour was arguably provocative, Kyle also cast himself as the voice of reason. He was the self-appointed moral arbiter of the show – yet Jeremy Kyle hardly ever actually helped. Nor did he try to truly understand. Instead, he took sides – and therefore, so did the show's viewers. In fact, ethically, the show appears to have been even worse than it seemed during its run: a Channel 4 *Dispatches* documentary aired after the cancellation alleged that staff on the show were taught psychological priming techniques known as 'talking up'.[28] They would be encouraged to ramp up the intensity; feed the guests' anger. The show was about conflict resolution – therefore the participants needed to be in conflict. The documentary also alleged that some guests were plied with alcohol and even, in some cases, encouraged to take drugs.[29]

It was the divide between the 'worthy' and 'unworthy' poor, dramatised before our eyes. Audience members, of course, were allowed a free pass; their effective permission to enjoy the spectacle was given by Kyle's apparent imposition of this binary divide. He was judging, so they could too. The show's 'baddies' deserved whatever they got. People went on the show voluntarily, after all. So, the reasoning went, they knew what they were getting themselves into. In truth, the guests often appeared in the hope of sorting out relationship issues using the show's lie detectors; to sift the good from the bad, the show relied heavily on technology which is often flawed, particularly when subjects are experiencing stress.[30] A 1997 survey of 421 psychologists estimated the average accuracy of polygraph tests at around 61 per cent, making them unreliable at best and, at worst, little better than chance.

The guests were selected to inspire fear, hatred, contempt and superiority in the show's viewers. There was often something strikingly authoritarian about the spectacle: 'You won't get past him,' goaded Kyle on one occasion, as an angry guest was restrained by security, 'he could do you with his little finger.' Impotent, desperate rage constantly bumped up against a greater physical force – cruelly mirrored, of course, by the real-life lack of agency, of choice, of opportunity, of simple ability. Just as impoverished people struggle with managing money and debt, they also struggle with less tangible traps; with reasoning, with understanding, with the ability to perceive escape routes and possibilities. On *The Jeremy Kyle Show*, they were not being helped; they were being further stigmatised.

Until recently, a quick glance at YouTube bore this impression out. But when the show reached its moment of reckoning in May 2019, ITV removed its range of helpfully labelled and compiled clips. With titles like 'Most Vicious and Shocking Fights!' and 'Rudest, Most Offensive Guests', these highlights packages appeared designed to help potential viewers decide what kind of poverty porn fix they fancied on a particular day. Despite the show's veneer of sanctimony, the ringmasters knew exactly what people wanted, and had been willing to provide it. The effect was shocking but eventually desensitising; the obvious next step for the audience was to ask themselves why they should care about these people. And, by extension, to wonder why they should have public money spent on them.

A judge in Manchester described *The Jeremy Kyle Show* as 'human bear-baiting' during a prosecution resulting from a violent incident on the show.[31] And it was hard to disagree. But it was also hard to challenge the suspicion that, particularly while austerity decimated services in the communities least equipped to cope with it, the show was, consciously or otherwise, serving a political purpose. In late 2013, prime minister David Cameron suggested that austerity would become 'permanent', that even once the nation's structural deficit had been eliminated, government spending would not return to pre-crash levels. As if to add a witty, indeed almost self-satirising touch of black comedy to this ominous news, he made the announcement at the Lord Mayor of London's banquet, rising from a golden chair to place his speech notes upon a golden lectern. With optics like those, he was clearly going to need some help with selling this gloomy prospect to the nation.

Fortunately for Cameron, British TV was ever more willing to punch down. Early the following year, *Benefits Street* arrived. Fans of awkward, class-based juxtaposition might be amused to learn that *Benefits Street* was made by Love Productions, the same company responsible for the consolatory, bunting-strewn bun bacchanalia, *The Great British Bake Off*. Unlike its prim middle-class cousin, *Benefits Street* was instantly controversial – which was presumably the point. Set on Birmingham's James Turner Street, it explored the lives of the bereft, the sick, the petty criminal and the benefits-dependent.

Benefits Street appeared to know exactly the kind of responses it was aiming for, and how to elicit them without overt editorialising. Instead, it played with signifiers: barbed wire, litter, gloomy music. We tended to meet only the most entertainingly picaresque or most obviously damaged members of this community. We saw the shop-lifting, the fags and the cans of Kestrel Super. We heard the proud boasts about how much money could be extracted from housing benefit and income support. There was no serious discussion of actual routes out of poverty, or of the problems that undoubtedly bedevilled the area, just 'evidence' of endless system-gaming.

But what did we really learn? Only that powerlessness compounds, like interest in a tax avoider's offshore savings account. The almost jaunty tone was nauseating. The vast majority of these people were, quite simply, victims. We met Fungi, an addict and a survivor of child abuse. Already his difficulties were so palpable that he was forced to ask 'mum of the street' White Dee to speak to social services on his behalf, because he couldn't understand the forms. What was television like this doing, other than inviting viewers to wallow vicariously in his misery?

Social media had, by now, become a powerful tool in the TV creative's armoury – and rarely was it deployed more effectively than in conjunction with *Benefits Street*. The show's hashtag would sporadically materialise on screen, but somehow its appearances always coincided with a moment seemingly designed to elicit rage, contempt or disdain. Someone discussing the government's widely loathed bedroom tax in the context of the small cannabis farm they've set up in their house? Hashtag. Someone flogging some clothes they've just nicked from a department store in town? Hashtag.[32] Whether by accident or design, television was playing perfectly to Cameron's agenda.

In a startling 2003 essay in the *New York Times*, Helen Epstein wrote about a phenomenon she dubbed Ghetto Miasma. It was a study of disastrous public health issues in impoverished neighbourhoods of urban America. 'Some of these neighborhoods have the highest mortality rates in the country, but this is not, as many believe, mainly because of drug overdoses and gunshot wounds,' she wrote. 'It is because of chronic diseases – mainly diseases of adulthood that are probably not caused by viruses, bacteria or other infections and that include stroke, diabetes, kidney disease, high blood pressure and certain types of cancer.'[33] What was causing this heightened susceptibility was a matter for debate, but stress was a persuasive explanation. Arline Geronimus, a professor of public health at the University of Michigan, suggested that the experience of constant poverty has a 'weathering' effect. There are knock-on effects for all areas of individual health.

For example, the need to produce hormones which the brain and body release to combat stress can have physical side effects in terms of diet, nudging stressed people in the direction of fatty, sugary foods. These foods have been shown to inhibit temporarily the release of the brain chemicals which cause stress responses. Could poverty, and the anxiety which often accompanies it, therefore be connected to diabetes and heart disease? Does the need to keep children inside due to fears associated with living in a dangerous neighbourhood lead to obesity or asthma – conditions commonly associated with spending long periods of time in low quality housing? What does seem clear is that the segregation and warehousing of poor people is contributing to a vicious cycle; to problems that speak more of victimhood than moral turpitude. In both cause and effect, programmes like *Benefits Street* and *The Jeremy Kyle Show* are the dramatisation of Ghetto Miasma – they mine its symptoms for titillation while doling out binary moral lessons to their viewers. But we're only given a superficial glimpse; these lives are generally viewed through the prism of crime, drug abuse and generalised bad choices. We're not encouraged to consider how it would feel to live a lifetime with the miasma in our lungs. Nor are we encouraged to join the dots, to think about exclusion and poverty in the context of wider power structures.

In *Estates*, Lynsey Hanley writes movingly about 'The Wall in the Head'. It's a concept whose origins lie in the reunification of Germany after the fall of the Berlin Wall in 1989. In the following years, and in the aftermath of a lifetime of externally imposed boundaries and limitations, many East Germans found it psychologically difficult to come to terms with the new set of possibilities that presented themselves. They were bewildered by the multitudinous, unpredictable sprawl of their new lives. They were confounded by choice. Hanley, who grew up on a council estate herself, describes something similar in terms of her early life. How do you get from here to there? How do you even understand the value of a possible escape route if its potential isn't being fully explained? Hanley ponders the lengthy and sometimes fortuitous process by which she was able to transcend the apparent limitations imposed by her background. But at the time she wrote the book, a route out, however torturous it might be, was still just about available. Is the road harder for the children of Jeremy Kyle, the kids from *Benefits Street*? Has permanent austerity killed our politicians' dreams of a classless society for a generation?

And what are the implications for our politics? In the 2016 EU referendum, much was made of the significant working-class vote for Leave, particularly in parts of the country eviscerated by the deindustrialisation of the Thatcher years. The result seemed to reflect a generalised, almost directionless sense of rage; the idea that any change was desirable; that wherever we ended up, it would surely be better than where we currently found ourselves. The vote wasn't an endorsement of any particular future vision of Britain, but instead a pure and furious rejection of the preceding three decades of politics and economics as perpetuated by both main parties. It was at least in part, a reflection of powerlessness.

What seems to have become rarer in television focusing on working-class life during this century are depictions of agency. Director Penny Woolcock's remarkable *Tina* films for Channel 4 are some of the most singular explorations of 'underclass' life in recent memory. They're fictionalised accounts of real lives, performed by inhabitants of the Leeds estates upon which they are set. They are at once naturalistic and highly contrived, often unbearably bleak but always penetrating – and occasionally, oddly magical in their depiction of communities that operate by their own implacable internal logic. In 2001's *Tina Takes a Break*, Woolcock conjures a striking image. Night is falling and a manic, impromptu street party is raging. The party is right at the point at which drunken high jinks have the potential to topple over into violence and chaos. In the midst of it all, a tiny girl heaves herself onto the top of an ice-cream van and simply surveys the scene. It oddly foreshadows the opening credits of *Shameless*, in which Frank Gallagher is master of ceremonies at an outdoor gathering centred around a burning car.

These are both scenes that could appropriately be played for either humour or horror. What they share is a certain proud ambiguity; a sense of nuance. Crucially, there's something thoroughly unapologetic about both. Neither the *Shameless* crowd nor the cast of *Tina Takes a Break* are acquiescing to respectability, and no one is telling them that they must. They are subject to what we might call the Middle-Class Gaze, but they don't care. They still, as the saying goes, dance as if no one is watching. There's something defiant, even triumphant about both scenes. Either consciously or subconsciously, there's a refusal to succumb to the gaslighting of meritocracy. This isn't victimhood or villainy: in its own messy way, it's community. These might not be good choices, but the scenes don't represent powerlessness either.

Do we see enough working-class lives on television? Is the TV industry – both in front of and behind the camera – another manifestation of British society's tendency to impose invisible boundaries on the horizons of certain of its citizens? In 2018, a report from community arts organisation Create London and the foundation Arts Emergency found that only 12.4 per cent of people working in film, TV and radio had origins that could be described as 'working class'. Black and minority ethnic people fared even worse, at just 4.2 per cent.[34]

Representation of non-white Britons feels like a particular area of failure for British television. Rather shamefully, Channel 4's Peckham barber's shop sitcom *Desmond's* – which premiered as long ago as

1989 – still feels like something of a beacon. Speaking to the *Guardian* at the beginning of 2019, creator Trix Worrell observed that 'when I started out, they made braver choices in television'. What *Desmond's* managed to achieve was deceptively difficult: this was a show that managed to convincingly and simultaneously evoke both cultural specificity and universality. 'I wrote it for white people so they could see how black people really are,' recalled Worrell. The answer seemed to be: in every fundamental way, pretty much the same.

What has emerged in the television of twenty-first-century Britain has sometimes looked worryingly like a normalising of difference. Growing paranoia with respect to apparently self-contained BAME communities (and particularly, in the wake of the Tube bombings of July 2005, around Muslims) has led to an upsurge of dramas in which racial and religious identities are signifiers of conflict with 'mainstream' society. In 2008, the BBC screened its White Season. It was controversial even before broadcast, thanks to its trailer ident which showed a white face being gradually obscured by layers of writing proclaiming 'Britain is changing' in a multitude of different languages. At the heart of the season was Abi Morgan's drama *White Girl*, the story of a white working-class family, unsteadily headed by a single mother, forced to flee an abusive relationship. They end up in the Muslim enclave of an unspecified English city where, to her mother's intense chagrin, eleven-year-old Leah (Holly Kenny) finds solace in the acceptance of her new neighbours.

In many ways, *White Girl* was a fine drama, dealing compassionately with both the struggles of a particular family, and a sense of dislocation and identity loss which felt deeper and wider. But the Muslim characters are underdeveloped, perhaps deliberately. The family are portrayed as strangers in their own land; what this narrative possibly underplays is that what 'their own land' means has changed. British Muslims are now a part of Britain, just as Catholics, Jews and Rastafarians are.

The economics of the past forty years have been an attack on working-class people of all ethnicities – it's just that racial and religious minorities are accustomed to being attacked and have had ample practice at developing survival strategies and alternative support structures. Shows like *White Girl* dramatise the struggles of the white working classes when faced with the removal of identities previously taken for granted. But they don't tell us much about the functionality (or otherwise) of BAME families and communities, or clearly make the point that, while, in terms of systemic disadvantage, white and non-white working class people are often in the same boat, there's an extra layer of jeopardy and alienation for members of ethnic and religious minorities.

Parts in serious dramas for BAME Brits have remained a bone of contention. In 2019, Ronan Bennett's excellent BAME-led crime drama *Top Boy* returned, having been axed by Channel 4 in 2013. The show was revived via a strange and fortuitous route; partly due to the public intervention of Canadian rapper Drake, but mainly thanks to the willingness of streaming giant Netflix to back a previous winner. It was hard, though, to escape the impression that the show had been denied the chance to fully tell its story. Bennett certainly thought so: at the 2019 premiere of the third season, he said the cancellation had felt like 'a slap in the face to the community it was representing'. There's been a trend towards black British actors (among others David Harewood, Eamonn Walker and Idris Elba) departing for America in search of their big break. Instead, BAME representation has often been limited to light-hearted, culturally specific comedies like the cheerful sketch shows *Goodness Gracious Me* and *Famalam*, and the well-meaning but hackneyed sitcom *Citizen Khan*. One of the more interesting recent explorations of BAME Britishness came from the sitcom *PhoneShop* which explored, hilariously, the all-conquering tropes of multiculturalism in the context of a suburban high street.

Crucially, *PhoneShop* didn't feel forced. It wasn't a polemic: it didn't have much of an agenda beyond being funny. It simply dealt with modern British society as it found it. Accordingly, it managed to feel more real and more telling than any self-consciously serious attempt to explore Britain's changing identity. Like *Desmond's*, it wore lightly whatever cultural significance it might have carried. Reflecting on the success of *Desmond's*, Trix Worrell suggests that nothing much has changed in thirty years. 'Unless your name's Toby or Ben, it's really difficult for black writers to get commissioned.' Inevitably, BAME representation will only change when TV hierarchies do. What happens in front of the camera will be influenced by the emergence of non-white commissioners, controllers, executives, directors and even director generals. We may be waiting a while.

Clearly, the Arts Emergency/Create London figures suggest the existence of wider systemic issues relating to education and social mobility. A lack of representation in the arts is a symptom of wider inequality. But the problems they illuminate are dramatised on television with clockwork regularity. What reaches our screens aren't necessarily working-class lives as they are actually lived; instead they're the kinds of working-class lives that resonate in television terms. The template for working-class drama usually involves trauma, often horror, almost always a certain powerlessness. There's regularly a shortage of moral ambiguity and a tendency towards absolutes.

Dramas like Jimmy McGovern's 2017 *Broken* document – with a great deal of sympathy and genuine compassion – the effects of poverty and desperation on blameless individuals and families. There's no shortage of good intention underpinning the creation of a show like *Broken*; there's no lack of skill in its realisation either. But we aren't hearing a sufficiently wide variety of voices. Paul Abbott still sticks out like the proverbial sore thumb. And by doing so, he still gives the lie to the notion of Britain as a classless society. If that were true then, by now, Abbott should be notable only for his talent, not for his background. Sadly, not only does he remain an outlier, but his success and the freshness of his authorial voice feels more singular than ever.

What is lacking in televisual representations of working-class people mirrors what is lacking in society itself. Working-class people aren't allowed many failures or much in the way of agency. They don't get soft landings. Over the course of the century to date, the social contract has weakened and – via benefits cuts and educational culls – society has become less forgiving. Equally significant is the psychological dimension: working-class people don't grow up with the benefits of entitlement. They know from experience that the world doesn't owe them a living. Sometimes, a good way of considering what's missing from television representations of modern working-class life is to examine one rooted in the opposite perspective.

Phoebe Waller-Bridge's *Fleabag* is a truly remarkable sitcom. It's a show that manages to say profound, honest and moving things about sexuality, grief and identity while remaining genuinely hilarious. And yet, in terms of narrative evolution, it's somehow very easy to imagine how a working-class equivalent of the titular character might be treated in television terms. She'd face harsh consequences for her choices. She'd probably get pregnant. She'd probably have an unsympathetic boss whom she couldn't afford to upset. She'd struggle with precarious living conditions. She almost certainly wouldn't end up accidentally running a small business in spite of her chaotic lifestyle. If she was allowed a happy ending, it would be clear and morally edifying. She'd have changed her ways. She'd have found the love of a good man. She'd have been unambiguously redeemed.

This is not a criticism of *Fleabag*. The show never pretends to be anything it isn't. Phoebe Waller-Bridge has her own valid truths and she tells them with uncanny wit and skill. Furthermore, those truths are not exclusive to the class or social background of the characters in the show – most of them are precisely and perceptively expressed enough to be universal. For that reason, it's possible to relate to Fleabag's travails across class, race or gender divides. But it is a criticism of the social and television context from which *Fleabag* emerged. More than that, it's a reflection on the non-Fleabags; the similarly messed-up working-class women whose parents don't own an enormous London pile which at some stage, they will inherit. Fleabag is allowed a degree of nuance that would almost certainly be denied to a working-class counterpart. But more than ever, we need to hear those other stories. They need their shades of grey too.

They'll need to be written by working-class Phoebe Waller-Bridges, many of whom – singular as her talent undoubtedly is – will be out there somewhere. These women will need to be nurtured from a young age. They'll need to be made aware of the possibilities and helped to get started. They'll need to be allowed and encouraged to try again when they fail. They'll need to see other women like them making progress. They'll need to believe that what they've created has value and deserves to be seen. And finally, they'll need to be allowed access to the inner circle once they've produced something of worth. If space can be found for these voices then maybe, once again, we'll be able to talk hopefully about meritocracy, and dream of a classless society. But it's a long road, which will have carried us far away from Vicky Pollard and Jeremy Kyle. These women will need help to demolish the wall in the head. Then, maybe, we'll get some new perspectives on how the other half live.

3

CULTURE WAR

*Top Gear · Brass Eye Special · The Great Global
Warming Swindle · Has Political Correctness Gone Mad?
British Workers Wanted · HyperNormalisation*

ON 20 MARCH 2015, outside new Broadcasting House in
London, a man in a white jumpsuit and helmet disembarked from
a tank whose gun turret was pointing squarely at the heart of the
British broadcasting establishment. He was dressed as The Stig, the
anonymous racing driver from *Top Gear*, and he was carrying a
petition that bore almost one million names. The subject of the
petition was the suspension of presenter Jeremy Clarkson from
what, by this time, had become the BBC's flagship Middle England
outreach programme. By 2015, *Top Gear* had burst its boundaries.
It was no longer just a programme about cars. It wasn't even simply
a daft TV institution in which grown men behaved like adolescents
for the edification of other men whose own teenage recklessness was
a distant memory. *Top Gear* – and its main presenter in particular
– was now a cause. The fans of *Top Gear* were, to coin an as yet
undefined phrase, Taking Back Control.

Shortly afterwards, former *Top Gear* presenter Quentin Willson appeared on the BBC's *Today* programme to discuss the affair. 'Jeremy is a massive global talent,' he claimed. 'A hugely distinctive voice in a world of creeping political correctness and health and safety. And that's why the show is so popular.' On the one hand, it was hard to argue with this thesis. Clarkson had indeed become a line in the sand; a symbol of defiance; the last bastion of a particular strain of British character. Yet the scale of the furore seemed utterly bewildering. What was the source of this incoherent – yet apparently widely held and deeply felt – anger?

Top Gear had begun life in 1977 as a mild-mannered motoring magazine show. In its first incarnation, a typical segment might feature presenter Angela Rippon driving from London to Birmingham, reporting on conditions along the way as she went. It covered automotive minutiae including speed traps, traffic jams and the nuances of car insurance. It wasn't, as you might have gathered, a programme to set pulses racing, nor was it designed as such. In varying shades of inertia and bathos, the original format ambled on until late 2001. Then, revolution arrived. It was wearing a fur-lined leather flight jacket and boot-cut jeans, it was puffing on a Marlboro Red – and its name was Jeremy Clarkson.

Clarkson and producer Andy Wilman's 2002 revamp completely transformed *Top Gear*. Speeding foot-to-the-floor away from its mousy origins, with the window rolled down and a mid-period Genesis album blaring, the show became an object lesson in trusting the instincts of the talent. Clarkson, along with eventual co-presenters Richard Hammond and James May, was given licence to be himself. This was a mixed blessing. But amid the crashes, stunts, amusingly blunt car reviews and disdain for cultural sensitivity, one thing *Top Gear* could never be accused of was lack of commitment to its own concept. What it offered went well beyond cars: it represented the Platonic ideal of traditional male friendship, all piss-taking and pathological competitiveness and uncomfortable punches to the upper arm. The show became unfeasibly and internationally huge.

But that in itself doesn't entirely explain how *Top Gear* became a cultural and even political football. How did a situation arise whereby, upon his dismissal, Clarkson could claim that 'the BBC have fucked themselves,'[35] and that statement could appear anything other than ludicrous? The answer lay in the era's context. A culture war was beginning to rage and, like all culture wars, it needed its symbolic battlefields. By now, as Quentin Willson hinted, political correctness and its much-mocked, adopted little brother health and safety was, in some quarters, perceived to have gone mad. This endlessly summoned bogeyman – ritualistically and theatrically denounced by right-wing tabloids and their readers – moved inelegantly in lockstep with another slippery concept; that of 'banter'. Somewhere between the two lay a version of Britain that everyone might be able to agree on. But neither side was giving much ground. *Top Gear* in general, and Clarkson in particular, found itself central to this battle.

Political correctness and banter are sworn and mortal enemies. They appeal to opposing human instincts – to our angels and our devils. To its critics, political correctness is a joyless, prissy irrelevance at best, and an attempt to limit free speech at worst. What advocates might regard as a desire to recognise that structural hierarchies related to race, nationality, gender, class and sexual orientation exist and lead to systemic discrimination, opponents might simply characterise as a remorseless war on irreverence and humour. As Archie Bland wrote, in an excellent article on the subject in *The Guardian* (surely the national organ of anti-banter), 'political correctness asserts that a racist joke is primarily racist, whereas banter asserts that a racist joke is primarily a joke'. Political correctness is as elastic as it is elusive: it can encompass everything from the imagined 'policing' of language to equally imaginary municipal outrages, such as – at least as alleged by the tabloids – the 'banning of Christmas' in the late 1990s by Birmingham City Council.

The conflation of health and safety with political correctness is one of the more bizarre developments of the last couple of decades. It arose as an attempt to satirise an excess of red tape, but the phrase is now regularly invoked as a catch-all complaint against any well-intended but cumbersome bureaucracy. In fact, if you follow any piece of health and safety legislation back far enough, you'll usually bump into some sort of avoidable tragedy: presumably anyone who has lost a loved one to asbestos poisoning will deeply regret that the issue wasn't 'politicised' earlier. Banter rails against these twin tyrannies by refusing to take anything seriously. Accordingly, the problem with banter (or its hidden superpower, depending on your point of view) is that it's hard to argue with effectively. Banter maintains its strange hegemony because it is tricky to oppose without looking like a sour, hyper-sensitive hand-wringer. However, if left unchallenged, it expands to impose its own values on the banteree. For all the recent mockery of the liberal, progressive concept of the safe space, banter is itself a safe space – a place with automatically activating defences against censure; a place where troubling assumptions go unchallenged, where accusations of racism, sexism or homophobia double back into nothing and lose their traction. Because after all, it's just banter.

Banter's year zero was probably 1994, the year that saw the birth of both pioneering lad mag *Loaded*, and Frank Skinner and David Baddiel's TV show *Fantasy Football League*. Banter was a good fit for the relatively apolitical 1990s – it was typically cushioned by several layers of irony and underpinned by the assumption that many of the battles surrounding race, gender and sexual orientation were already sufficiently settled to allow a certain irreverence towards them. It remains notable, however, that the vast majority of the masters of the form have been straight, white males. To be fair to both banter and banterers, it was, as Bland wrote, simply 'the name for what British men already regarded as their natural tone of voice'. Banter as a conversational mode was nothing new. But its identification and codification was. Banter was sanctified. It acquired legitimacy.

In a television context, many banterers have been called but few chosen. That's because, as purveyed in public life, banter is deceptively difficult to get right. Banter can be rather sad – Channel 4's excellent 2011 student sitcom *Fresh Meat* featured the resonant character JP. Played by Jack Whitehall, JP was the dark heart of banter; a self-styled 'Bantonio Banteras', a young adult so consumed, embodied and possessed by the cultural imperatives of banter that when its potential is removed, he shrivels to a husk; finds himself crying in the shower, embracing a dying horse and even, most transgressively of all, being honest and open about his crippling emotional blockages.

Banter is also frequently too unpleasant for mainstream acceptance. Football commentators Richard Keys and Andy Gray, for example, came a cropper in 2011 when they were recorded off-air making distasteful comments, initially in relation to a female match official and then later, an unnamed woman with whom, it was suggested, one of the studio guests may have enjoyed sexual relations. Keys later described it as 'prehistoric banter', an inadvertently amusing turn of phrase suggesting that banter is as ancient and British as mysterious stone circles or white chalk drawings of well-endowed men on hillsides. As anyone who has ever visited that apex of National Trust-endorsed banter, the Cerne Abbas Giant in Dorset, will confirm, that may indeed be true. But in this case, the bants was decidedly grim, and carried too unmistakable an undertone of misogyny to be allowed to stand. Keys and Gray lost their jobs. A similar fate would later befall hapless character comedian Dapper Laughs, aka Daniel O'Reilly. The street-level, lads-on-the-pull banter of his mercifully short-lived 2014 ITV2 show now looks merely pathetic – banter as a signifier of all-pervasive inadequacy. Tellingly, however, the controversies surrounding Keys, Gray and Dapper Laughs did, in certain quarters, elicit the routine observation that once again, political correctness had gone mad.

Jeremy Clarkson, though, was different. Here was, initially at least, an uncannily sure-footed master of banter. A presenter doesn't hold down a prime-time BBC television career for the best part of a decade and a half without being a fairly unerring judge of exactly how close to the line they can afford to get; Clarkson was simply smarter than his fallen fellows. Tonally, the revamped *Top Gear* was completely and all-encompassingly self-confident, in the way that white, straight, upper-middle-class males often are. It radiated entitlement. During a time of change, of individual and societal identity shift, this certainty was powerful. It resonated strongly with the show's viewers. You're okay, mate, it seemed to tell them. Everyone else is just taking it too seriously, that's all.

Clarkson was a clever pusher of liberal buttons, but he calibrated his public image cunningly. He augmented his thriving TV career with a column in the *Sunday Times* newspaper which manifested a similar tone of bloke-on-his-third-pint-of-Bombardier levity, but he was never as near to the knuckle as professional provocateurs like Richard Littlejohn or Katie Hopkins. This was crucial to his status as the voice of recalcitrant, middle-English manhood; he didn't really mean it. Clarkson was, as the eternally binding banter get-out clause states, only joking.

If Clarkson's philosophy has any degree of consistency, it's probably a form of mild but discernible nihilism – the blasé detachment of a wealthy and well-connected man without a dog in any particular fight. The dutifully politically correct would describe him as a textbook example of privilege. He's been dismissive (but never outright denialist – he's too shrewd for that) of climate change, describing it as 'boring'.[36] He reckoned Donald Trump's victory in the 2016 US presidential election (top geopolitical banter, this) was 'hilarious'.[37] Much 1990s comedy had deconstructed, but *Top Gear* was the comedy of reconstruction and tradition. This was a humour which relied upon the timeless British certainties. Mothers-in-law were always tiresome. Foreigners were either funny or sneaky. Thus, to a certain kind of British gent, Clarkson was deeply reassuring. There was, as implied in the gospel according to Clarkson, a long list of things that you didn't really have to care about.

All this made him incredibly valuable to the BBC. Most obviously, *Top Gear*'s vast worldwide reach made them piles of money. Perhaps more importantly still, the show was a get-out clause. Every time the Beeb was accused of being a haughty sinecure for muesli-munching metropolitan liberals (which was often), *Top Gear* would be invoked as a counter-balance. Jeremy Clarkson's many indiscretions caused the BBC a problem. But that could be managed, as long as he offered the solution to another, bigger issue: the apparently growing number of Brits feeling threatened by the forces of political correctness – and finding them embodied in the national broadcaster. But even Clarkson could only push the BBC so far.

Clarkson's BBC demise might be mischievously characterised as a perfect storm of political correctness and health and safety (at least, as it applied to those working in the presenter's immediate vicinity). If the schism was finally catalysed by his 'fracas' with a member of *Top Gear*'s production team, Clarkson's relationship with the BBC was initially compromised by his arguable tendency to waver on the line separating banter from xenophobia. This reflected a wider, evolving current in British thought: that we'd been too culturally accommodating for too long; that the Empire wasn't really that bad; that those EU bureaucrats needed us more than we needed them. An accompanying complaint of the anti-political correctness lobby was that 'you can't say anything these days'. But people were starting to.

It's hard to imagine that Clarkson himself ever saw much of a political dimension to any of this. Notwithstanding his friendship with David and Samantha Cameron, he has never seemed a particularly political animal (and, it should be remembered, in a moment that surely triggered profound cognitive dissonance across the land, he publicly backed Remain in the EU referendum).[38] But in the context of British politics, Clarkson's banter, like banter in general, was becoming weaponised all the same. The political right has always specialised in obscuring economic issues with cultural ones. Never mind the systemic inequality, went the tabloid narrative, the loony left have banned non-halal meat! Railing against political correctness was, in the early years of the twenty-first century, a crucial component of this strategy.

It was central to the rise of UKIP, a party for whom exiting the European Union (and the grossly underplayed economic upheaval that would inevitably threaten) only ever seemed to be one element of a multi-pronged attack on a new British orthodoxy constructed around the nation's ever-increasing ethnic and sexual diversity. Clarkson's escalating cultural insensitivity took place against a backdrop of UKIP representatives suggesting, among other things, that gay marriage had caused catastrophic flooding in Somerset and that black celebrities should emigrate to black countries.[39] They were part of a cultural climate in which MP Peter Lilley could describe Conservatives as 'that greatest oppressed minority in this country'[40] and receive, in some quarters at least, applause rather than astonished ridicule.

In this context, the BBC's dismissal of Jeremy Clarkson was both inevitable and heavily symbolic. An incident during which Clarkson reacted to being denied a steak supper after a day's filming by punching *Top Gear* producer Oisin Tymon had given them their excuse, but it was clearly the thin end of the wedge – Clarkson had simply pushed his luck too far for too long.[41] Like the *Big Brother* racism scandal, the subsequent furore was a perfect example of Britain as a TV nation; a country in which the machinations surrounding small-screen entertainment can offer illuminating insights into issues of much wider significance. The tank which delivered the petition protesting against Clarkson's sacking was driven by Harry Cole, now a political correspondent at the *Mail* but then one of the men behind the nascent right-wing website Guido Fawkes. The anonymity of The Stig became vaguely menacing in this context – the character transformed into a Spartacus of Middle England. What might happen if they all stood up and proclaimed their identity at once?

This was a coded warning to the BBC – and by extension, to all the people who might be characterised as representing the metropolitan liberal consensus – from the nation's emergent radical traditionalists. 'You won't like us when we're angry', it seemed to threaten. This was about much more than the freedom of Jeremy Clarkson and his friends to destroy motor vehicles and goad foreigners at the licence payers' expense. It was about the last gasp of attitudes and assumptions that might be outmoded but were refusing to go quietly. The Vice website, that epitome of youthful, post-everything insouciance, screamed 'Britain's Dads have gone mad'. But we hadn't seen anything yet. They were only just getting started.

While implacable resistance to notions of political correctness gained considerable traction during this period, it's important to remember that the arguments cut both ways. The PC-averse right has always had its own rigorously policed heterodoxy of trigger points. To test this proposition, express some light-hearted scepticism about the British army, or the wearing of poppies in November, and watch fearless free-speech advocates transform into the most delicate of snowflakes before your very eyes. Apparently, these subjects fall outside the remit of banter, which generally creates a behavioural and conversational zone where debate is shut down rather than opened up.

By implying that something is simply a joke, banter ensures that any subject under discussion becomes trivialised. Still, certain debates need to be had, and humour is often an effective route towards having them. In fact, the century had begun with a potent example of satirical TV comedy which, from a very different perspective, asked all manner of pertinent but uncomfortable questions, challenging viewers to think carefully about both their answers and the roots of their opinions. It also had the effect of highlighting certain incipient fault lines in British society.

Watching the documentary upon which the 2001 *Brass Eye* 'Paedogeddon' special was partly based is an odd and troubling experience. On the one hand, it's impossible not to recognise the wicked accuracy of Chris Morris's spoof – to the initiated, the florid language, sub-B-movie production values and flamboyant presentational grammar of the film all prompt the odd snigger. But any laughter is of the most tentative variety imaginable, because ultimately, the documentary is also a reminder of the hideous nature of the stories underpinning Morris's parody. Before wrestling with the *Brass Eye* special and the circumstances which prompted it, it feels important to remember the basic facts: Channel 4's 1998 *Dispatches* told the story of Sidney Cooke, who along with several other predatory paedophiles was convicted of raping and murdering fourteen-year-old runaway Jason Swift in 1985. There's a lesson here for anyone analysing the medium of factual television: deconstruct and ridicule the delivery mechanism of a story all you like, but never lose sight of the reality of the lived experiences embedded within that story.

In retrospect, *Brass Eye* and Britain's paedophile outcry of 2000 were like two orbiting atoms, destined to fuse and explode. That summer, an example of the kind of media-manipulated mass hysteria that the original run of *Brass Eye* had hypothesised seemed to be enacted for real. First screened on Channel 4 in 1997, *Brass Eye* was a hilarious, gleefully absurd and jaw-droppingly audacious satire which reserved equal scorn for hyperventilating media excess, needy celebrity idiocy and baseless moral panics. Over the course of its six episodes, it prompted an MP to raise a question in the House of Commons about a fictional drug called Cake, saw magician Paul Daniels issue a plea on behalf of a mistreated zoo elephant with its trunk lodged in its own anus, and bemoaned the appalling (and thankfully imaginary) practice of weasel-fighting in London's East End. It was as controversial as it was acclaimed, upsetting everyone from the *Daily Mail* to Channel 4's then chief executive Michael Grade, who admitted he 'developed a serious sense of humour failure with Chris Morris and *Brass Eye*'.[42] Whatever else could be said about *Brass Eye*, it could never be accused of pusillanimity. It prided itself on going where other satires feared to tread.

When the *News of the World* launched its drive to 'name and shame' Britain's paedophiles in June 2000, the sequence of events which followed immediately had the feeling of a Chris Morris spoof, albeit a particularly dark one that might sensibly have been consigned to the cutting-room floor. The newspaper's campaign was prompted by the murder of eight-year-old Sarah Payne by Roy Whiting, a man with previous convictions for sexually assaulting young girls. In response, the *News of the World* resolved to create a comprehensive directory of Britain's paedophiles, arguing that parents had a right to know if danger lurked in their neighbourhood. It published the names, photographs and approximate locations of 100 men, and promised thousands more.[43]

Notwithstanding the horror of the campaign's inciting incident, the tone of the coverage was inflammatory, giving the impression that predators with evil designs on the nation's children lurked on every street corner. However, despite widespread unease, this hue-and-cry was working out rather too well for the paper to easily stop. The *News of the World* had an ambitious new editor in the shape of Rebekah

Wade (later Brooks) – and the campaign was rapidly making her name. After a lengthy period of stagnation, the paper's circulation rose by 95,000 in the weeks following the campaign's inception.

Events snowballed, becoming both ridiculous and dangerous. Vigilante mobs formed. A man in Manchester was beaten up because he was wearing a neck brace similar to one worn by an offender pictured in the newspaper. The Paulsgrove area of Portsmouth became a symbol of the unrest; groups like the Peaceful Protesters of Paulsgrove claimed they had a list of twenty suspected local paedophiles – '15 for definite', according to an interview given to the *Independent* newspaper – despite the fact that, by the reckoning of the Sex Offenders Register, only three such individuals lived in the area. Senior police officers warned that the campaign was becoming actively counter-productive, jeopardising ongoing investigations into potentially prosecutable cases of child sexual abuse. The *News of the World* was accused of 'irresponsible journalism' by Gloucestershire's Chief Constable Tony Butler.[44]

It was in this combustible atmosphere that Chris Morris gathered his intrepid crew and prepared for another assault on the nation's taste boundaries. Unsurprisingly, considerable secrecy surrounded the early stages of the 2001 *Brass Eye* special. It was known within Channel 4 as 'Trombone'; the true nature of the project was revealed on a strictly need-to-know basis. By the time it arrived on television, wider battle lines had already been drawn. The self-styled forces of fearless free-thinking were ranged against the recent displays of ugly mob rule, orchestrated by Britain's endlessly cynical and manipulative press. Except it was never remotely that simple.

Viewed dispassionately and from a distance, the *Brass Eye* special is more of a mixed bag than the uniformly brilliant series which preceded it. For every stroke of excruciating genius, there's an idea that doesn't quite land. It remains uniquely uncomfortable viewing; it milks and manipulates the taboo queasiness of its subject matter expertly, and the belly laughs (of which there are many) are rarely guilt-free. Like any media satire, its success was dependent on audience reaction – those claiming that the show had gone too far had generally failed to understand that, far from being a criticism, going too far was *Brass Eye*'s absolute *raison d'être*. After all, a time-honoured method by which a satirist may explore the limits of free speech is simply to proceed in a particular direction until they are stopped. Chris Morris was prepared – and indeed delighted – to go further than most.

This produced many scenes that retain genuinely transgressive impact. There's a brief but astonishing sequence in which the show's news anchor (played by Morris himself) presents his own prepubescent son to a paedophile imprisoned in a set of stocks. The anchor is clearly expecting the paedophile to confess to feeling aroused, but he's disappointed; the captive simply doesn't find his child attractive. The scene is played beautifully, capturing revulsion, incomprehension and unspoken confusion. It's clear that there is a tiny, bewildered portion of the anchor's brain which is offended by the paedophile's rejection of his son. To dramatise – or even to acknowledge – thoughts like those is to poke around, daringly and illuminatingly, in some very murky waters indeed.

The disquiet is ramped up even further during the climactic, studio-bound song. Centred around the concept of children not being 'ready yet', this is an audacious and deeply disconcerting moment; the deliberately generic familiarity of the song and staging confront the viewer with the inarguable proposition that children are shamelessly sexualised in other media contexts, without that fact eliciting much comment. The 'all grown up' trope, which involves underage female celebrities being presented as sexual objects, will be familiar to any observer of tabloid newspapers. Magnificently, among the flood of red-top opprobrium attracted by the programme, the *Daily Star* somehow managed to place an article decrying *Brass Eye*'s 'Perv Spoof' on the opposite spread to a photo of the then fifteen-year-old singer Charlotte Church under the headline 'She's A Big Girl Now'.[45]

One of the most notable aspects of the fraught aftermath of the *Brass Eye* special's screening was that its content managed to render much of the criticism it attracted almost self-satirising. The *Daily Star* splash was the most obvious example. But that paper was not alone in its ignominy – nor has much changed in the subsequent years. In 2013, for example, the *Daily Mail* described model Heidi Klum's eight-year-old daughter as a 'leggy beauty'.[46] Politicians didn't exactly cover themselves in glory either – the furore was marked by a succession of ministers falling over themselves to condemn the show in the strongest possible terms, before being forced to sheepishly admit that they hadn't actually seen it. Most of them left the impression that if, like the suggestible celebrities featured on *Brass Eye*, they'd been asked to read out a statement claiming that paedophiles were genetically identical to crabs, they'd probably have obliged.

And yet, while the reactions to the show were largely absurd, the binary nature of the divisions the saga revealed feels, with the benefit of hindsight, both prophetic and ominous in terms of the currents building in Britain. The fury of anti-paedophile protesters in 2000 was deceptively complex, and looks even more so from the troubled vantage point of 2020. Underpinning it was a complete disintegration of faith in the authorities, a sense of neglect and abandonment – an instinctive certainty that if they didn't do something about a problem, no one else would. Variations on the phrase 'No one cares about places like this' were common in media reports from the areas affected. The anger was ostensibly directed at semi-mythical paedos, but it also contained a sublimated component of rage related to the suspicion that places like Paulsgrove were exactly where society's outcast and unwanted would be dumped. Class differences were a constant subtext of coverage – there was a march in prosperous Balham in south London, too (which Chris Morris apparently attended for research purposes), but it was under-reported, partly because the objections were couched in less quotably colourful and more reasonably middle-class terms.

How easy it has subsequently proved for unscrupulous, populist figures in both media and politics to tap into such powerful suspicions of betrayal and unfairness. The *News of the World* backed down eventually and stopped naming and shaming. But they'd given a tangible and unnerving demonstration of the kinds of forces they – and media outlets like them – were capable of unleashing. This power could be aimed in multiple directions: against immigrants, against benefits claimants, against politicians, against judges, against entire belief systems. Already brewing – and being stoked by the right-wing press – was a latent resentment towards an apparently uncaring elite, who were keener to poke fun and pass judgement than acknowledge any justifiable concerns that might be at play.

This was a signpost to the emotions that, a decade and a half later, would be unleashed in the EU referendum. It was an early skirmish in the looming culture wars. New Labour, under Tony

Blair, were becoming untethered from their traditional working-class support base. Different battle lines were being drawn – the paedophile outcry set metropolitan hauteur against provincial paranoia. It ranged media assumptions (propagated by newspapers on all points of the political spectrum) against lived experience. In some circles, there was a barely concealed sense of scorn towards the protesters, and considerable hilarity relating to the fact that many of them appeared not to be able to spell the thing they were protesting against. And yet, here was a sign of two parallel Britains developing in not-particularly-blissful ignorance of each other's assumptions and values. A distinct volatility born of mutual incomprehension was becoming evident. From this point on, sparks would be generated by any contact between the two worlds.

Looking back at this building turbulence, how do we assess this provocative landmark of early twenty-first-century TV in its historical context? Despite his anti-authoritarian veneer, was Chris Morris in fact a representative of blithe elitism? Or was he a liberator, attempting to free public discourse from the dead hand of media manipulation? Certainly, Morris succeeded in what he set out to do. He excoriated the hypocrisy, voyeurism and intellectual laziness of the media with devastating, almost surgical brilliance. But he occasionally seemed to forget that the people who were in the media's thrall were, in addition to being their target market, also their victims. At times, Morris's satirical instincts were too unsparing and unforgiving for the subject matter. The comedic beats in the *Brass Eye* special are hit with undeniable precision, and yet there's a brutality to this iteration of the show; a dubious relish in the material which, whatever the intentions, occasionally manifests itself as a lack of compassion.

There's a throwaway joke in which Sidney Cooke is blasted into space by NASA to keep him away from children for ever, only for the rocket scientists to discover too late that an eight-year-old boy has also found himself on board the ship. Does the use, for comedy purposes, of the name of a real paedophile – with real victims who presumably still live with the aftermath of his abuse – cross a line? Does the joke make enough of a point to render that argument moot? Even as you're howling with appalled laughter, there's the sense that Morris's moral rigour and comedic instincts are jostling for primacy, and occasionally deciding to call it a draw.

Even at almost two decades' remove, it's not an easy show to pick the bones out of – and because of its undoubted creative and technical brilliance, and the degree to which it became a cause célèbre among edgelord defenders of the transgressive, it arguably received an easier critical ride than it might have done. Which is to say that, ironically, much like *Top Gear*, it became a symbol, a signifier of cultural identity, a show whose context began to overwhelm its content in terms of what it represented to adherents. Culture wars are, by definition, binary affairs; they don't tend to admit much in the way of nuance.

Yet even allowing for its flaws, the show remains truly exhilarating. In the context of the gradual defanging of satire in subsequent years, the very fact the *Brass Eye* special is a moral minefield that in addition to being hilarious, requires genuinely rigorous contemplation, is part of its enduring appeal. In its best moments, the show trusted its viewers, and asked that viewers trust it back. That trust allowed for an ambiguity that remains a surprisingly rare and fragile thing. It refused to spoon-feed easy answers and accordingly allowed viewers a degree of autonomy; a space for thinking the unthinkable, acknowledging the uncomfortable, questioning the sacrosanct. It demonstrated, and indeed proved, that their instincts were not flawed, that what had been built by the seemingly invincible popular press could be deconstructed if not dismantled, that the public domain was more mutable than it seemed. In some ways, it's the last show of its kind.

In the second half of 2001, the terrorist attacks of 11 September destroyed New York's World Trade Center. They marked the end of something else too. The attacks sounded the death knell of what might be called the long 1990s – the period of relative global geo-political stability heralded by the end of the Cold War in 1989. The scale of the attacks was beyond belief. Their implications seemed too wide and all-encompassing to truly reckon with. The ripple effect of the shock they generated would quickly arrive at the door of television. The licence for a certain strain of righteous, possibly dubious levity had been revoked. Risk-taking, whether gratuitous or genuinely challenging, was off the table for a while. The times were suddenly too serious.

Chris Morris, of course, responded to 9/11 in the only way he knew – by mining it for comedy. In 2002, he and his frequent collaborator Armando Iannucci put together for the *Observer* newspaper *Terror's March Backwards*, an 'Absolute Atrocity Special' in which the funny side of the embryonic 'War on Terror' was somehow located and explored. It was, depending on your point of view, a welcome corrective to the stifling air of solemnity that had suddenly descended upon the cultural discourse – or, as one letter to the newspaper had it, 'one of the most tasteless and offensive pieces of "journalism" that I've ever read'. Morris would go on to write and direct the film *Four Lions*, which further explored this new zeitgeist by tracking the risible yet deadly progress of a group of hapless British jihadis. His instinct for wondering exactly how far he might be allowed to go in a particular direction obviously never left him. But by this point, a new, more cautious era was abroad in British television.

At the time of writing, Morris's final authored small-screen gambit was 2004's *Nathan Barley*, a sitcom written in collaboration with Charlie Brooker. By way of the titular character – an insufferable 'self-facilitating media node' – the show took a satirical sledgehammer to east London's tiny ecosystem of hilariously self-regarding dabblers in film, music, journalism, multimedia and farcical performance art. At the time, *Nathan Barley* seemed oddly dated; the show appeared to be mocking a subculture that had peaked in the late 1990s and been much more acutely ridiculed by cult fanzine *The Shoreditch Twat*. But time has rendered *Nathan Barley* deeply prescient; these absurd urban lollygags have been rebranded as hipsters and walk among us still, cheerfully immune to mockery. In retrospect, *Nathan Barley* embodies a fundamental truth of our times; far from reaching out and engaging with the values of the wider world like *Brass Eye*, it resides in an immaculate echo chamber. The objects of the show's satire are also essentially its target audience. Nathan himself would have adored the *Brass Eye* special. He'd have been jadedly unmoved by Morris's moral message and dismissive of any ethical concerns. But he'd have loved the shock value. As a fictional symbol of the London imagined and loathed by Britain's angry provinces, he couldn't be more perfect.

Unlike adult ball pits and cafés selling hundreds of varieties of kitsch breakfast cereal, echo chambers weren't unique to east London. The internet began to offer up the unimaginably wide dissemination of information, combined paradoxically with closed conversational loops. Meanwhile, 9/11 had proven more than simply a visceral, physical jolt. It had lasting consequences for our collective emotional equilibrium too: it suggested a massing of forces, a gathering of energies; dark, barely considered possibilities swimming into the realms of the conceivable. Most of us, in the febrile aftermath of the attacks, will have had first-hand experience of this jittery new psychological terrain. A few seconds of panicky paranoia on public transport; a sense of creeping vertigo at the perspective-induced juxtaposition of a distant plane with a nearby tall building. The attacks stimulated our imaginations in an entirely negative way. To an extent managed by few other events in modern history, they changed the way we saw the world.

This new reality seemed to demand not just reportage but explanation. And if that wasn't forthcoming, speculation became inevitable. The 1990s obsession with possible alien life forms – as exemplified by *The X-Files* – led to the mining of conspiracy theory for TV drama. But suddenly, even as a patina of this suggestible curiosity remained, such concerns felt frivolous, comprehensively trumped by real-life events. Bigger conspiracies were potentially afoot, with much higher stakes. Accordingly, bigger, bolder theories were required.

The documentaries of Adam Curtis are illuminating psychological companion pieces to this tonal transformation. Curtis began his BBC career as a researcher for jaunty consumer affairs magazine *That's Life*. His work became ever more rarefied and ambitious through the 1990s, touching on themes of covert control, mass manipulation and powerlessness. In the pre-9/11 era, his films and documentaries largely related to our collective experience of neoliberalism and consumerism. *The Mayfair Set* explored asset-stripping vulture capitalists, while *The Century of the Self* examined the role of psychoanalytic theory in public relations and advertising. However, in 2004 he turned his attention to global geopolitics, viewed through the prism of two marginal groups whose ideas went suddenly mainstream. His three-part series *The Power of Nightmares* explored, startlingly, the surprisingly compatible aims of American neoliberals and Islamic fundamentalists. It was remarkably timely, positing an explanation for baffling and alarming events that slipped down with incredible ease for the sizeable subset of viewers who were almost as dismayed by President George W. Bush as they were by Osama Bin Laden.

These, and Curtis's other films, were remarkable, inventive and persuasive. Curtis dug deep into the BBC's vast archive in order to find material suitable for his uncanny juxtapositions and came up with startling bricolage renderings of our recent historical and televisual past. Gently lulling easy-listening music would soundtrack footage showing the bloody, panic-stricken aftermath of a bombing in the Middle East. A global political leader would cough, fix his hair, complain to a nearby aide and personify the puffed-up banality of power. An abrupt jump-cut would catapult the viewer from one train of thought into a different, jarringly dissonant scenario.

The tone of Curtis's films was interesting. They felt simultaneously personal and authoritative. Curtis told stories assembled from fragments of our recent history – but was he an entirely reliable narrator? Indeed, was he a documentary maker at all? Often, his films felt like polemical art installations; intensely satisfying to immerse yourself within, full of visual trickery, emotionally involving, constructing a compelling but unsteady grand theory of everything.

Most of all, they carried an occult quality. They suggested secret knowledge, the joining of dots, revelations which might begin to explain a potentially overwhelming level of geopolitical, cultural and historical complexity. During the first decade of this century, we were collectively confused, our complacency shattered by the triple whammy of 9/11, the Iraq War and the financial crisis. We needed a unifying narrative, even if it was an ambiguous one.

Curtis has always been admirably elusive in terms of his political allegiances. He's frequently assumed to be a figure of the left but his intense scepticism regarding state power and mass control could easily be read as libertarianism too. The battle lines of Britain's culture war seemed binary and in practice, often were. But that didn't mean that the combatants couldn't possess complex motivations and come from perplexing places.

They might have a little more ideology in common than either's adherents would be comfortable acknowledging. But aesthetically, film-maker and all-round provocateur Martin Durkin is the anti-Adam Curtis. Where Curtis will assemble colourful, free-associating mosaics of film, Durkin's documentaries teem with visual clichés.[47] They are blunt instruments. They reduce, manipulate and at times, distort source material in order to make their astonishingly tendentious points. Durkin's journey had taken him from membership of the Revolutionary Communist Party to a position of what might be described as doctrinaire contrarianism. In common with his erstwhile associates at the online magazine Spiked – whose transformation from Marxism to radical libertarianism was now well under way – the very act of offending mainstream liberal sensibilities was an end in itself.

Durkin's television CV reads like an extended prank; an exercise in gradually escalating preposterousness. His 1998 documentary *Storm in a D-Cup*, for example, advocated the health benefits of breast implants. He really struck pay dirt, however, with 2007's *The Great Global Warming Swindle*, which railed against the scientific evidence for anthropogenic global warming and questioned the emerging cultural and political consensus on the subject. The distortions embodied by Durkin's conclusions don't seem worthy of debunking (or even really discussing) here. Durkin wasn't a scientist, let alone a climatologist. He was, as the right-wing journalist and Durkin's fellow traveller in performative scepticism James Delingpole once described himself, 'an interpreter of the interpreters'. Ofcom agreed, refusing to be definitively drawn on the scientific accuracy or otherwise of the documentary. The regulator did, however, have plenty to say about the film's techniques, concluding that it had deceived contributors, made misleading claims and broken rules regarding 'due impartiality on matters of major political and industrial controversy and major matters relating to current public policy'.

That wasn't quite the end of the story, though. *The Great Global Warming Swindle* enjoyed an odd afterlife that has plenty to tell us about Britain's escalating culture wars. In 2007, the Labour government proposed distributing US vice president Al Gore's climate change polemic *An Inconvenient Truth* to British schools. Stewart Dimmock, an HGV driver and school governor from Kent, promptly took the government to court on the grounds that schools are legally required to provide a balanced representation of political issues. On the face of it, this appeared to be a classic David and Goliath story. While making his case, Dimmock's lawyers invoked that now familiar folk devil, the New Labour 'thought police',[48] as if to suggest the common-sense common man was cowering under the jackboot of dubious but rigidly imposed received wisdom. It subsequently emerged that Dimmock's campaign wasn't quite all it seemed – he'd been financially supported by Viscount Christopher Monckton, a global warming sceptic and former scientific adviser to Margaret Thatcher. As an attempt to counteract Gore's film (the content of which was ruled by the judge in the Dimmock case to be broadly correct), Monckton also bankrolled the distribution to schools of DVD copies of *The Great Global Warming Swindle*.

On the face of it, this was simply an odd, eccentric and argu-ably marginal affair. But there were patterns emerging which would have significant consequences. Professional contrarians, formerly of the left but with big, traditionally right-wing money behind them, would become more commonplace and more influential. For example, the Koch Foundation – which is essentially the propa-ganda arm of the unfeasibly wealthy, unfeasibly environmentally destructive private conglomerate Koch Industries – has donated money to the US wing of Spiked. And Spiked have successfully sneaked a representative of their worldview into the world of BBC comedy in the shape of the spoof news reporter Jonathan Pie, whose rants are co-written by Spiked contributor Andrew Doyle. The line between regressive vested interests, ostensibly progressive politics and populist rabble-rousing has become increasingly blurred.[49]

But more widely, the story is telling because the objections to *An Inconvenient Truth* (and to the science surrounding climate change in general) seemed to come from an essentially irrational place; a sensibility in which feelings transcend logic. The objections are cultural. After all, while alternative theories exist, the overwhelming majority of people – climate change sceptics included – would accept the scientific consensus over, for example, the best forms of cancer treatment. Why should climate change be any different?

The answer, surely, was tied up in its wider symbolism. 'Old money' might have been underpinning his campaign, but Stewart Dimmock's blue-collar credentials were significant. As was the case with the *Brass Eye* special, and later with the *Top Gear* controversy, the furore spoke to the gathering notion that somehow, 'normal' people were being dictated to, patronised, told what to think. This was among the foundations of the emerging culture war. It didn't recognise traditional distinctions between left and right; upper class and working class. Instead, it was taking place on a variety of societal battlegrounds, pitching what were perceived as liberal orthodoxies against the forces of tradition and reaction. As former Conservative chancellor Lord Nigel Lawson declared in *The Great Global Warming Swindle*, 'This is the most politically incorrect thing possible: to doubt climate change.' Whether or not taking such a position is logically reasonable was essentially beside the point – in political terms, the symbolism of opposition was all that mattered.

The actual phrase 'political correctness' is worth interrogating. When used pejoratively, it suggests obfuscation, if not outright dishonesty. It hints that a truth is being consciously obscured. It bears the implication that the word 'correctness' rightfully belongs in quotation marks, but that these are absent because, well, politics. Its formulation appears designed to mask something more fundamental that is staring us in the face if only we had the courage to acknowledge it. Something diamond-hard and transformative and therefore unsayable. That somehow the truth it attempts to hide is revelatory but dangerous.

This unspoken truth could be anything; from the idea that the UK is being swamped by immigrants, to the notion that gender equality has gone too far. In many ways, it is all the more powerful for remaining nebulous and amorphous; as *The Great Global Warming Swindle* proved, once an idea is vocalised, it becomes subject to logical interrogation, and risks being challenged and eventually debunked. The right had a number of dry runs in which they attempted to codify, and therefore weaponise, this feeling in a party-political context – most notably when Conservative leader Michael Howard ran for election in 2005. 'It's not racist to talk about immigration', said the billboard. 'Are you thinking what we're thinking?' With the benefit of hindsight, this slogan looks less like a policy promise and more like a genuine question; a testing of the water. In 2005, the nation was still prosperous, tranquil and self-possessed enough to raise a collective eyebrow at this blatant dog-whistle and answer in the negative. Not quite yet, we weren't. But give us ten years and a hefty dose of economic turbulence and we'll get back to you.

Over the following decade, an attritional war bubbled along, always somewhere near the surface of the national conversation. It's long been assumed that education and simple demographic change would largely vanquish overt manifestations of racism from political life. For the time being, this theory hasn't entirely matched events. Research by political scientists Maria Sobolewska and Robert Ford has confirmed educational and demographic change: when Tony Blair took office in 1997, more than 60 per cent of English residents were white and poorly educated, beginning their working lives with fewer than five GCSEs. By 2017, that figure had fallen below 40 per cent, while the proportion of the population who were graduates, members of an ethnic minority or both rose from 17 to 40 per cent. But while demographic change is incremental, economic issues focus minds fast; press upon us with greater urgency. As Britain's economic situation worsened, the discourse sharpened. And of course, change always prompts resistance: there's been a distinct hint of 'dead cat bounce' about Britain's culture war. It exhibits a generational aspect: the suspicion that we're living through the last hurrah of a certain set of attitudes and assumptions about what Britishness might mean.

In common with all disagreements between British people, TV was a regular battleground. The self-reflexive metropolitanism of *Stewart Lee's Comedy Vehicle* versus the radical idiocy of *Mrs Brown's Boys* (a show that could be posited as a safe space for outdated comedy tropes). The ultra-white rural idyll of the determinedly retrogressive *Midsomer Murders* versus the sneakily progressive *Call the Midwife* – whose sentimentality enabled it to become a cunning prime-time delivery system for thoughtful and compassionate storylines involving racism, gender equality and disability. The inclusive, female, liberal historian Mary Beard versus the trenchantly reactionary David Starkey. The inventive, optimistic 2012 Olympic opening ceremony versus the dull, complacent 2012 Olympic closing ceremony. A reckoning was coming.

The cleverest trick the Vote Leave campaign ever pulled was to make the 2016 EU referendum about anything other than the practical implications of leaving the EU. During the course of the campaign, in a quote that in some ways sums up the era, Michael Gove proclaimed that 'People in the country have had enough of experts.'[50] And as if determined to prove himself correct, whatever the reputational cost, Gove later described *Mrs Brown's Boys* as 'pure genius' on Twitter. He knew which side he was on, all right. But, questionable comedy judgement aside, Gove's central point was as politically shrewd as it was morally dubious. It knowingly tapped into the bur-geoning current of British thought that had decided it was better to be on the right side than to be right. Gove was adept at joining the emotional dots. He was appealing to an undercurrent of feeling, to a particular psychological front in the culture war, to a tranche of the country that had discarded traditional political binaries.

The strange, liminal period between the EU referendum and the general election of 2017 was characterised by an unprecedented orgy of liberal hand-wringing. How had this happened? What mysterious forces were abroad? A multitude of well-intentioned television programmes set out to itemise and explore this confusion. Adrian Chiles visited his native West Midlands to explore the moti-vations for the area's decision in BBC One's *Why We Voted to Leave: Britain Speaks*. Artist Grayson Perry's *Divided Britain* (Channel 4) spoke to voters on both sides of the debate, and turned the resulting conversations into art. But neither of these ventures were quite as inadvertently revealing as *Has Political Correctness Gone Mad?*, a documentary made by Trevor Phillips for Channel 4.

On the one hand, Phillips correctly identified that at the heart of the nation's bewilderment was something less than entirely rational. His response, however, seemed on one level to be completely unhelpful and on another, perfectly illuminating of the problem. Is there really a connection between an absurd group of student auto-prudes wanting to ban sombreros from their university bar on the grounds of cultural appropriation, and Tommy Robinson's far-right Pegida UK organisation being prevented from marching through Birmingham city centre? The question Robinson asked at the very start of the film felt ludicrously beside the point in a way that would come to epitomise the whole programme. 'Should people be able, if they're completely peaceful, to come into the city of Birmingham and criticise Islam?' Well, yes. They probably should. But given that, in addition to the rigorous theological debate that has become their stock-in-trade, Robinson's acolytes usually end up throwing bottles around and dishing out abuse, the question is essentially moot. That sometimes they can't is surely nothing to do with political correctness, and everything to do with public order and safety.

Still, perhaps Nigel Farage would be able to clarify matters? After all, is there a public figure who has ridden – and stoked – irritation with political correctness to such definitive effect? At this point, it became clear that Phillips, like so many before him, was making the mistake of assuming good faith on Farage's part; he was pandering rather than interrogating. What else could explain an interviewer letting Farage discuss, disparagingly, 'This group of people inside the M25. The liberal elite. Who want to ban everything.' Farage was, and still is, clearly every bit as willing to treat his opponents as an undifferentiated amorphous group as he suggests his opponents habitually treat the objects of their censure.

Phillips's conversation with writer and activist Caroline Criado-Perez was even more surreal. Criado-Perez was the victim of an almost industrial level of violently sexualised and threatening Twitter trolling as a result of being part of a seemingly innocuous campaign to put Jane Austen's face on banknotes. At one stage, she was told by one Peter Nunn, 'I'm going to rape your ass and put the video all over the internet.' Why, Phillips wondered, did she not simply remove herself from Twitter for a while? So much for free speech. Phillips then spoke to Nunn himself, who hilariously (although Criado-Perez almost certainly wasn't laughing) described the internet as 'a safe space for everyone to have a voice'.

Then, something soul-destroying in its utter, deadening inevitability happened. Nunn described his tweets to Criado-Perez as 'banter'. Of course he did. Because why wouldn't he? Banter, like political correctness, had come a long way. It was, like Charlotte Church in 2001, all grown up. It had become, if this exchange was anything to go by, both the lifelong friend and the mortal enemy of free speech. Nunn's freedom to threaten rape was demanding moral parity with an activist's freedom to campaign for equal representation. 'If you can't threaten to rape a celebrity,' Nunn had tweeted, 'what is the point in having them?'[51] Phillips's failure to adequately interrogate this position confirmed its bitter triumph. Nunn, although one doubts whether anyone connected to the programme realised it, represented some sort of dismal apotheosis of weaponised banter – simultaneously deeply pathetic, feebly self-valorising and terrifyingly central to where we, as a culture, now found ourselves.

In a blog post written on the day after the EU referendum, journalist Tom Ewing suggested that 'One of the things you hear a lot is that talking about racism has stopped us having a "proper conversation" about immigration. But the opposite is also true. Talking about immigration has stopped us having a "proper conversation" about racism.' This line of argument can be extended way beyond its original subject matter. Complaining about the perceived excesses of feminist dogma has stopped us from having a proper conversation about gender inequality. Complaining about 'Health and Safety Nazis' has stopped us from having a proper conversation about the real purpose of regulation. Complaining about 'political correctness' has stopped us from having a proper conversation about systemic hierarchies. Identity politics has always been a strength of the right and a corresponding weakness of the left. It's always likely to be more effective to tell someone a reassuring story about themselves, than to speak uncomfortable truths that threaten existing and deeply held belief systems.

One of the tragedies of the last two decades of British public life is that, at the moment we can least afford it, we've both atomised and lapsed into a sort of collective false-memory syndrome. Our response to complex challenges has been to simplify our solutions. In late 2017, Channel 4 broadcast a documentary called *British Workers Wanted* which explored the potential – and already tangible – impact of Brexit on an employment agency in Bognor Regis. Both of the agency's founders had voted Leave, and both appeared to be standing by their decision, even as the process began to decimate their business – which largely relied on labour from eastern Europe for survival. By the end of the film, one of the pair, Sarah, appeared to be having second thoughts. But her partner, Gaynor, was unyielding. Like many people, she appeared to posit Brexit as a sort of magic bullet; a one-size-fits-all solution to problems ranging from apparently workshy youngsters, to confusing and perhaps unpalatable long-term cultural change.

Take Back Control was such a clever rallying cry because it didn't just mean taking back control of Britain's borders or regulatory powers or sovereignty. It could mean anything anyone wanted it to mean. For a certain breed of Brit, it meant taking back control of vocabulary, of memory, of cultural customs, of comedy, of history and of notions of national superiority. Accordingly, it meant the taking back of power, of agency. What did we actually vote to leave? Yes, a regulatory and trading bloc. But also, the modern world, the endless swirl of evolution, obligation and sometimes unwanted possibility. Brexit, as it was sold, was about certainty – if not in actual outcomes, then certainly in Britain's ability to dictate the terms. But unsurprisingly, Brexit as it has manifested itself, is about anything but.

So, despite what Theresa May might have imagined, Brexit didn't really mean Brexit. In fact, Brexit might well turn out to be the least of it. What Brexit really meant was a tribal flexing of muscles; the settlement of gradually accumulated grievances. As the first – eventually abortive – Brexit Day of 29 March 2019 approached, telling yet transient manifestations of our culture war began to pop up like mushrooms all over our well-fertilised cultural landscape. There was a particularly memorable example on the BBC Two's *Politics Live* on 8 March 2019, as author Will Self and hardline Eurosceptic Tory MP Mark Francois became embroiled in a hilarious spat over Self's seemingly innocuous assertion that 'It's not that you have to be a racist or an anti-Semite to vote for Brexit. It's just that every racist and anti-Semite did.' By this point, the figure of 17.4 million Leave voters had ascended to sacred status within the iconography of Brexit. This was a number that legitimised – almost sanctified – the otherwise directionless political careers of Francois and others like him. And the bloviating Brexiteer wasn't going to have a hoity-toity bien-pensant like Self turning up his nose without a fight.

What followed was an almost perfect demonstration of where we had found ourselves as a country. Francois, either out of obtuseness (entirely possible) or calculation (probably likelier), decided to pretend that Self had called all Leave voters racists – and demanded an apology. With the kind of pained tolerance one might extend to a recalcitrant toddler, Self attempted to explain his point again.

But by now, Francois had made his bed and by God, however uncomfortable it was, he was going to lie in it. Never let it be said that, however much they might gripe about 'political correctness', figures on the British right aren't capable of taking umbrage when they suspect the optics might work favourably for them. Self even acknowledged this with a smirking reference to 'the politics of offence'.

The exchange ended with the pair glaring at each other for several painful, jaw-dropping seconds, seemingly on the verge of taking their disagreement outside. What was truly illuminating was the social media reaction. The clip immediately went viral, and no wonder: it's very funny. But to say that interpretations of the exchange differed is something of an understatement. It wasn't exactly Frost/Nixon, but for all of its triviality, Self/Francois was a sort of Rorschach blot test for 2019 Britain. If you were a Remainer, you saw aggressive ignorance being sardonically called out by a calmer, wiser head. If you were a Leaver, Self's disdain was simply more nauseating metropolitan arrogance. And there we had it: Britain's culture war, writ small.

Adam Curtis's most recent BBC film, *HyperNormalisation*, explored the phenomenon which, in darker moments, seems to epitomise modern public life. Not inappropriately, it appeared in 2016, the year that Britain voted to leave the EU, and America voted to subject itself to four years of populist rhetoric and reality show grandstanding, courtesy of Donald Trump. The central thesis was that politicians, the media, the internet and our economic system have conspired, whether wittingly or otherwise, to create a kaleidoscope of equivalence; a world in which delusion and mendacity are normalised to the extent of constituting a new reality; in which concepts of objective truth have ever less weight. At the heart of the film was a psychotherapy computer programme called ELIZA. The programme was developed in 1966 and eased the troubled minds of its users by simply rephrasing their questions as self-reinforcing answers. Did it work? That depended on what the user was expecting. ELIZA performed a clever confidence trick that, for a limited period at least, gave the impression of control being regained. 'What ELIZA showed', said Curtis, 'was that what made people feel secure was having themselves reflected back to them.'

The footage of the computer in action seemed a startlingly appropriate metaphor for where we'd found ourselves. We all occupy our own bunkers in Britain's ongoing culture war. Nativism, misogyny, homophobia and anti-science climate change denialism are, of course, inexorably losing their respective arguments. What has changed is the decreasing extent to which their proponents are confronted with that fact. While these positions are logical dead ends, they're more easily exploitable than ever, particularly at a time when trust in institutions is low – and pre-existing paradigms of political and economic organisation seem to have run out of ideas. Via the people we allow on to our social media feeds, the news outlets we consume, the television we watch, the YouTube channels we subscribe to and the podcasts we listen to, we effectively curate our own bespoke perceptions of events, often without fully realising it. We risk becoming our own algorithms, critical faculties exponentially atrophying, endlessly confirming our own biases.

This is a particularly perilous development because the challenges we face as a civilisation (ecological crisis, mass migration, automation, population increase) are too large to be addressed without some semblance of global, universal perspective. They demand widespread consensus and collective action. But perhaps that's precisely why we've retreated behind our personalised barricades and become stuck in these adversarial loops at this particular moment in history. Given the daunting nature of our problems, it's little wonder that addressing them feels intimidating. But Britain's culture war is a proxy war. We can't keep fighting it forever.

4

HOW THE BBC BECAME THE STORY

*Newsnight · Panorama · Louis Theroux: Savile
Question Time · The Future State of Welfare · BBC News
W1A · Climate Change – The Facts*

'RACIST, SEXIST AND HOMOPHOBIC? Or a refreshing break from political correctness?' This intriguing question was posed by the Twitter account of BBC Monitoring on 30 October 2018, the day after Jair Bolsonaro was elected president of Brazil. BBC Monitoring went on to offer a link to an article listing a few of Bolsonaro's most notably 'refreshing' points of view. These included his description of congresswoman Maria do Rosario as 'too ugly to rape', his confidence that his son wouldn't fall in love with a black woman because he was 'well educated', and his proclamation that he would 'beat up' any gay couple he saw kissing in the street.

Responding to widespread outrage, BBC Monitoring quickly deleted the tweet. In any case, the Monitoring department is less a broadcast player and more a collator of worldwide mass media. But even so, the mere existence of the tweet was revealing: it hinted at a corporate mindset characterised by deep internal conflict and confusion; a loss of bearings; an inability to identify a definitive moral position and stake a claim to it.

So far, the twenty-first century has been desperately difficult for the BBC. It has fallen out with the government. It has got too close to the government. It has traduced the reputations of the innocent and given a free pass to the guilty. It has, like many British institutions, struggled in the face of change; far too often, it has become the story. Sometimes this has happened through no fault of its own – but frequently the BBC has conspired in its own misfortune.

Consensus and continuity are the BBC's essence, from its funding method to the consent upon which it relies to dominate our mediascape. The BBC represents orthodoxy. Historically, in terms of its survival in as conservative a country as Britain, this has been its greatest strength. But today it feels like a weakness. Orthodoxy is, in itself, a position. It's an implied statement in support of the status quo. It's an implied judgment upon how best to process the past and proceed into the future and it bridles at revolutionary change. But if Britain's prevailing economic, political and cultural orthodoxy has become part of the problem, where does that leave the BBC? What if the BBC is just another on the list of British institutions that is failing to address society's changing imperatives? What if radical change is needed? If consensus is breaking down within Britain, if elites are no longer trusted, if every iteration of 'the establishment' is doubted, then why wouldn't trust break down in terms of our perception of the BBC too?

Ever since its foundation in 1922, the BBC has maintained an unusual position. It is comparable to the NHS in terms of its 'cradle to grave' niche within the British psyche. But the reality of its formulation is much more ambiguous. The first few years of its

THE AGE OF STATIC

existence contained a prophetic parable, with the BBC almost – but not quite – allowing itself to be co-opted for propaganda purposes by the British government during the General Strike of 1926. In his diary, the BBC's founding general manager Lord John Reith recorded the conclusions of a cabinet meeting during the strike: the government needed to be able to say 'that they did not commandeer [the BBC], but they know that they can trust us not to be really impartial'. This position represents an origin story of sorts, and it presages the awkward pas de deux the BBC has danced with the British political establishment ever since.

The BBC operates under a royal charter which comes up for renewal every ten years. While there has rarely been any realistic threat to the renewal of the charter, it does leave the BBC in an odd, compromised place – nominally independent, but simultaneously at the mercy of the government of the day. In terms of criticising the ruling party, it can only go so far. The government ultimately controls the BBC's funding and appoints its governors too. And perhaps more significantly, the government also controls the mood music around the broadcaster. Margaret Thatcher, for example, saw the BBC as a not-entirely-welcome legacy of what she described as the 'authoritarian mood' of the interwar period. In her autobiography, she wrote that the BBC was 'one of a number of areas . . . in which special pleading by powerful interest groups was disguised as high-minded commitment to some greater good'. Thatcher's social conservatism (she was an admirer of Mary Whitehouse, who saw the BBC as a hotbed of socially progressive depravity) dovetailed with her economic liberalism to create a double-whammy of hostility towards the BBC.

Politicians, if they are wise, operate an arms-length policy towards the BBC. But that isn't to say that they can't manipulate its direction, even unconsciously. Thatcher often allowed sympathetic newspapers to do the job of interrogating and, on occasion, intimidating the BBC on her behalf. And, like any other branch of the state, it is subject to the philosophical and logistical currents of the moment. It develops in the image of the era. In the 1990s, for example, the evolution of the BBC mirrored the evolution of the British economy as a whole. John Birt, who became director general in 1992, was appointed to nudge and cajole the Corporation away from what were seen as outdated 'command economy' working practices and towards the imperatives of the market.

In 1993, he initiated a system called Producer Choice. This organisational and commissioning mechanism amounted to an insurgent ideology. Among other things, it demanded the introduction of internal markets in which programme-makers would pitch competitively against one another for commissions, imposed compulsory quotas (set at 25 per cent) of content to be made by external production companies, and led to the casualisation of labour or, if you prefer – as Birt doubtless would – 'a flexible labour market'. Accordingly, this often charming but undeniably ungainly behemoth of paternalistic state broadcasting was gradually forced to walk in lockstep with the neoliberal times. Producer Choice didn't exactly herald increased efficiency, however. It led to intractable internal negotiations, compliance, regulatory oversight and endless auditing and internal monitoring. In short, it created a vast new bureaucracy.

This was the context in which the BBC entered the new century. It was still a broadcaster surrounded by all the expectations (and, of course, privileges) of public service. But it was part of a new paradigm, too; like the NHS, the education system and, indeed, most other iterations of the public sector, both the assumptions and the literal manifestations of private enterprise were becoming forcibly embedded within its culture. External competition was increasingly fierce in terms of both entertainment and news output. And yet, didn't this hubbub of new broadcasting providers – and indeed platforms – reinforce the need for some sort of centralising agency? Might the BBC still retain enough independence to reinvent itself as a relatively fixed point around which a new broadcasting eco-system could grow?

After all, the BBC was still our national broadcaster of record. People trusted it. This trust was destined to become both the BBC's salvation and the root of its problems. Given the perceived political weight of the BBC's judgement, why wouldn't any government intent on a risky and potentially controversial course of action monitor the corporation's response carefully? Ironically, given the Conservative origins of most criticism of the corporation's political position, the most damaging and contested episode in the BBC's recent history pitted it against a Labour government – albeit an unusually right-leaning one. The events themselves are well documented. Andrew Gilligan, a reporter on Radio 4's *Today*, claimed that the government had 'sexed up' – i.e. exaggerated – a Joint Intelligence Committee report on Saddam Hussein's chemical and biological weapons capability. He inferred that Prime Minister Tony Blair had deliberately misled Parliament by claiming that Iraq could deploy weapons of mass destruction within forty-five minutes, in order to better make the case for an impending invasion. The resultant fall-out involved the resignations of the BBC's chairman Gavyn Davies and director general Greg Dyke – and, tragically, the suicide of Gilligan's source, weapons inspector Dr David Kelly.

The initial inquiry into the affair, carried out by Lord Brian Hutton in 2003, exonerated the government and was critical of the broadcaster: 'The allegations reported by Mr Gilligan on the BBC *Today* programme on 29 May 2003 that the Government probably knew that the 45 minutes claim was wrong or questionable before the dossier was published . . . were unfounded.' A further review carried out in 2004 by Lord Butler and focusing more precisely on intelligence surrounding weapons of mass destruction was more ambivalent, saying among other things that intelligence sources 'were seriously flawed' and the grounds for British assessments that Iraq possessed chemical weapons 'no longer exist'. And the Chilcot Inquiry in 2016, which took a further broad overview of Britain's role in the Iraq War, was yet more damning of the government, suggesting multiple flaws in the case for war and finding that 'the judgements about Iraq's capabilities . . . were presented with a certainty that was not justified'.

In *This New Noise*, Charlotte Higgins' fine 2015 history of the BBC, Richard Sambrook, the BBC's director of news in 2003, claimed that 'what Kelly told Gilligan was right. Unfortunately', he continued, 'Gilligan was sloppy in the way he reported it, the *Today* programme was sloppy in the way they handled Gilligan and by the time the row was happening the BBC was at full defensive mode.'

Neither the BBC nor the government can realistically absolve themselves of all blame for the fate of David Kelly. It's possible that no definitive official verdict will ever be reached. What does seem clear, though, is that the affair has had shattering – and still very apparent – consequences for the confidence and courage of BBC news reporting ever since. The risk-taking parameters of BBC News in the twenty-first century remain effectively defined by Iraq and

Gilligan. Sambrook admitted as much to Charlotte Higgins: 'In the end, there is a limit to its independence . . . and I think in the end, that was part of a miscalculation in the Kelly story. We thought we were genuinely independent. And we weren't.'

The BBC, though, is about much more than news. For any child of the television age, the BBC is all our yesterdays. It's a repository for our collective memories; the centrepiece of a thousand half-remembered but retrospectively idealised family nights in front of the box. Many of us can thank the BBC for our cultural education – not simply in terms of the substance of what we have consumed but the knowledge of where it located us, the societal context of the particular things we grew to love. Before the dawning of Channel 4 in 1982, Britain was a three-channel country. Accordingly, the broadcaster's leading ring-masters were hugely significant figures. In 2011, a particularly potent spell was broken in the most awful way imaginable.

The events that followed the death of Jimmy Savile still seem barely believable at almost a decade's remove. But what's really difficult to process isn't the revelation that Savile was a horrifyingly prolific, utterly unapologetic, predatory paedophile. It's that so many people appear to have known this was the case for several decades, and yet somehow that, in the eyes of the law, Savile went to his grave an innocent – and indeed, widely celebrated – man. The aftermath of his death was like snapping out of a lifelong dream. The revelations were so incredibly easy to believe. Of course Jimmy Savile was a sexual predator. He'd never taken any particular care to hide the fact, and even wrote about his taste for coercive sexual opportunism in his 1976 autobiography *Love Is an Uphill Thing*. In one instance, he describes being approached by the police who, aware that he ran club nights, asked him to keep a look out for a young runaway. Savile recalled telling the police that if the girl appeared, he would keep her overnight 'as my reward' before handing her over the next day. The girl did appear at his club and Savile was, in all regards, as good as his word.[52]

Filmmaker Louis Theroux was, along with everyone else, entirely swept up by the weird, hazy force field of immunity surrounding this apparently beloved family entertainer. His initial documentary about Savile, which aired in 2000, was odd, often uneasy viewing in which Theroux raised the vague allegations – which were still persistent but unsubstantiated rumours at this point – about Savile's private life, but seemed content to take his subject at face value. After the full extent of Savile's crimes were posthumously revealed, he returned to the subject with 2016's *Louis Theroux: Savile*, an extended *mea culpa* for both Theroux himself and the BBC. In one extraordinary scene, Theroux meets Sylvia Nichol, a former medical secretary at Stoke Mandeville hospital, the epicentre of Savile's charitable empire. Her life was intertwined with Savile's. Her house was overflowing with memorabilia commemorating his career. She seemingly still struggled to accept the full extent of his crimes.

'I'm a victim,' said Nichol. 'I'm a victim of losing my memories.' It was a shocking moment, and not only because it laid bare the existential horror faced by a blameless woman struggling to come to terms with the knowledge that so many joyful, defining moments of her life were tainted by association with this man. It was also shocking because something similar applied to us all. Jimmy Savile didn't just groom his victims. He didn't just groom the BBC. He groomed an entire culture. The BBC's decades of complicity and pusillanimity were at least partly mirrored by our own. It's become

THE AGE OF STATIC

much more difficult to think of the BBC as 'Auntie' since we learned the painfully unsurprising truth about Jimmy Savile. Like Sylvia Nichol, we all lost at least a few of our memories.

The BBC might, even at this late stage, have been able to limit the damage. But its immediate reaction to Savile's death caused almost as profound a crisis as the aftermath of the Hutton Inquiry. The usual parade of lavish tributes – including some earmarked for prominent spots in the Christmas schedules – were in advanced stages of production. But while one department of the BBC was preparing to eulogise Savile, another was working towards exposing him. Something would have to give. Documentary maker Meirion Jones and reporter Liz MacKean pitched their Jimmy Savile report to *Newsnight* two days after Savile's death was announced, knowing that only now might the corporation be willing to take a risk. It turned out they'd overestimated them.

The labyrinthine tale of how the BBC came to kill, then bury, then be forced to exhume their investigation into the historic crimes of one of their most famous presenters was bleakly illuminating in many different ways. First, it served as a torturous tour around a bureaucratic, corporate dystopia, so utterly suffocated by layers of intra-accountable management that any potential for decisiveness or nimbleness was lost. Second, it indicated cowardice; everyone seemed to be waiting for someone else to decide on what might be acceptable to broadcast. Furthermore, it spoke of complacency: the decision to spike Jones and MacKean's report was surely underpinned by considerable confidence that no one would be held accountable for either the editorial decision or the crimes themselves. Finally, it hints at the risks facing outliers and dissidents inside the BBC. Jones and MacKean were subsequently edged out of the organisation altogether, whereas Peter Rippon, the *Newsnight* editor who refused to run the story, works at the corporation to this day. The Pollard Review, an independent inquiry into the affair, later concluded that Rippon's decision not to air the Savile exposé was 'flawed' but 'done in good faith'. If Rippon was partially exonerated by the review then by definition, the logical conclusion must be that the problems were more systemic, more chronic, more deeply entrenched within the organisation as a whole.[53]

On the face of it, the price of the Savile affair was the loss of another director general (George Entwistle, whose tenure at the top lasted a mere fifty-four days) and a self-exculpatory *Panorama* documentary. On a practical level, the documentary crystallised many of the BBC's more generalised problems: when assessing the BBC, we expect freedom of expression to co-exist alongside strict oversight. We want to see authority held to account, but we don't always recognise that the BBC is in a position of authority itself. The BBC enjoys more soft power than any broadcaster in the world. But it jumps through more hoops, and faces stricter levels of accountability too. These organisational and arguably existential flaws result in constant – sometimes damaging – compromises and evasions.

The *Panorama* documentary was disturbing on a more philosophical level, too. Ultimately, the source of its horror always circles back to matters of trust: both the trust the BBC placed in Jimmy Savile, and the trust we place in the BBC. In the film's plentiful archive footage, Savile is surrounded constantly by children. Savile is a huge star – the extent of his power and his confident exercise of it reduces everyone in his immediate orbit to the status of a suppli-cant. This was a man who made it his business to boast of his friends in high places. And now we knew why. He often spent time with Margaret Thatcher and he was on familiar terms with members of the royal family. To newly opened eyes, the power imbalance was grotesque. His every touch now seemed a violation, not just of the physical boundaries of the children on the screen, but of everyone watching, whether in 1975 or in 2012. What had we been thinking?

If the Savile affair represented a grave but symbolic crisis in our view of the BBC, it took place in the context of events that were grimly, urgently practical. The financial crisis of 2008 marks a brutal severance point in post-millennial British public life. Most of the issues facing the country – growing inequality, regional and generational imbalance, changing attitudes towards immigration and multiculturalism – were bubbling under before the crash. But the relatively calm economic waters made them easier to ignore or mitigate, prevented them from gaining much meaningful traction within our national discourse. The crisis threw these matters into sharper focus. It was becoming harder not to take a side. And neutrality – or, as the BBC would probably prefer, 'balance' – was becoming an ever more contentious concept.

What characterises political discourse in the Britain of 2020? Anger? Bad faith? Bogus arguments being given equivalent weight to empirically logical ones? It was in the harsher, more binary post-crash environment that these unfortunate traits began to establish themselves. As always, the BBC was answerable to everyone who paid their licence fee. But some of the contortions and moral gymnastics implied by that responsibility were becoming harder to manage. The centre of British politics was hollowing out; wilder voices on the fringes were becoming louder. To what extent could or should the BBC accommodate them? And were any beyond the pale? By autumn 2009, it seemed the line in the sand was being redrawn.

Nick Griffin's appearance on BBC One's flagship current affairs free-for-all *Question Time* on 22 October 2009 was hugely controversial. His party, the far-right British National Party, had been going through a period of growth. Several of its members had tweaked their ugly rhetoric, treated themselves to smarter suits, won seats on local councils or in the European Parliament, and were attempting to position themselves as a common-sense, robustly patriotic response to difficult times. The BBC's argument was that the BNP had now achieved a level of electoral success that demanded representation; that to deny them airtime might even breach its charter. They were confident that Griffin would face fierce intellectual opposition on the show and be given little opportunity to set the agenda.

The trouble was, he set the agenda by his mere presence. His appearance on *Question Time* began a process of normalisation of the far right that we're still grappling with today. As opposed to a one-on-one conversation, in which an interviewer can control the nature of questions and follow them up forensically, the *Question Time* format means that by definition, a guest can evade and equivocate, safe in the knowledge that they will get a free hit from time to time; a chance to simply discuss the issues of the day. And this can't help but have a legitimising effect – at one point during the show, Griffin found himself discussing the recent death of singer Stephen Gately, while at other times he managed to move the conversation onto what he doubtless regarded as his home turf – then sat back smugly while guests representing mainstream political parties (Labour's Jack Straw, the Conservatives' Sayeeda Warsi and Liberal Democrat Chris Huhne) squabbled over the minutiae of European law and immigration policy. The overall effect was taken in some quarters to imply that while Griffin himself might be several bridges too far, his relative success was due to his willingness to acknowledge the so-called 'legitimate concerns' that were being ignored by everyone else.

Television reacts to events, but it sets the tone too. It's hard not to look back on this deeply dispiriting hour of debate and recognise multiple harbingers of our deteriorating standards of political discourse over the decade ahead. Using a tactic that was later to be perfected by UKIP's shrewder, more media-savvy leader Nigel Farage, Griffin often managed to obscure economic issues with cultural ones, as his ugly ideas about religious identity and ethnicity took precedence over any discussion of the financial deregulation and systemic inequality that were at the heart of Britain's problems. The dog-whistles were plentiful, with questions from the audience about Labour's 'misguided immigration policies'. And the frequently toxic atmosphere in the studio – which was largely welcomed at the time because of the revulsion that the BNP's policies elicited – generated more heat than light; a taste of the tone that would become the show's default setting, even in situations more ambiguous than this one. In any case, the fury allowed Griffin to play the victim, argue that the reception he received simply proved he was being persecuted by the political and broadcasting establishment for articulating difficult truths that none of us wanted to swallow. *Question Time* lay down with dogs, and we all got fleas.

Sadly, one of the BBC's key takeaways from the Nick Griffin *Question Time* appears to have been the ratings. Eight million people watched the show – more than twice the usual audience. Over the course of the next few years, as British politics in general became more polarised and overheated, *Question Time* became increasingly questionable in terms of its editorial decisions. There followed a series of trends and occurrences which, alone, may have been forgivable, but together, added up to a cumulative impression that standards were on the slide. Nigel Farage has made more than thirty appearances. Even he would surely agree that this is a remarkable degree of representation for a politician who has repeatedly tried and repeatedly failed to become an MP, as leader of a party who have managed to get two MPs elected in their history.

Whenever he appears, his voice is allowed to set the agenda – he dominates every show upon which he appears. Envoys from right-wing and free-market think tanks such as the Institute of Economic Affairs and the Taxpayers' Alliance are frequently invited onto the show, despite a complete lack of transparency about their funding and agendas. It emerged in 2016 that the show's audience producer, Alison Fuller-Pedley, had a history of sharing social media posts from far-right populist group Britain First.[54] But most troubling of all, the show seems to have let concerns about balance detach it from what should surely be a carefully nurtured relationship with facts. Host Fiona Bruce mistakenly interrupted Labour's Diane Abbott in January 2019 to tell her that Labour were behind in the polls. There's been fake equivalency regarding the legal questions surrounding the 2016 EU referendum: in early 2019, Bruce responded to an audience member's assertion that Leave ran a 'dirty campaign' by pointing out that there had been 'questions over both Leave and Remain'. Thus did the presenter of one of the BBC's most high-profile current affairs shows suggest that flawed economic forecasts (Remain) were essentially the same as being fined and investigated by the National Crime Agency (Leave).

Of course, none of this adds up to definitive proof of bias. What it does suggest is a certain carelessness, a declining rigour and most of all, growing confusion over the priorities we have the right to expect from a current affairs show on the nation's flagship TV channel. In 2017, Hilary O'Neill was appointed editor of the show by Mentorn Media, the independent company who produce it. Her mission statement promised 'many adrenaline-packed Thursday nights'. But given the frequent gravity of *Question Time*'s subject matter, flooding the show with adrenaline is surely a misguided ambition. The BBC doesn't merely reflect the tone of the nation's current affairs discourse; it plays a primary role in setting it. Now, more than ever, Britain's primary public service broadcaster needs to take the lead and accept that sacrificing accuracy for sound and fury is no kind of public service at all.

In addition to an ailing economy, the financial crisis also heralded a Conservative-led coalition government which quickly fixed a baleful, beady eye on the BBC. While conflict with Tory prime ministers was nothing new for the BBC, it had rarely faced threats on so many fronts as it did from the government of David Cameron. And, in the wake of the Iraq misadventure, it had rarely faced them in such a weakened and apologetic state.

The years between 2010 and 2014 were bewilderingly schizophrenic. As always, the BBC reflected this confusion – sometimes unavoidably, sometimes effectively, often unconsciously. The period contained much fluttering of national bunting – we were treated to a royal wedding in 2011 which the BBC covered with its customary stolid, curtsying propriety. A more universally uplifting event was the 2012 London Olympic Games, which somehow managed to sneak up on and seduce an ever more cynical and truculent nation. The BBC rose magnificently to the occasion, and for a few golden weeks in late summer, the UK seemed a less fractious and irritable place. Yet all was not well. In the summer of 2011, the country had been convulsed by the most serious outbreaks of urban disorder in three decades. And the consequences of the government's huge public spending cuts were becoming visible all across the public realm.

Cuts were made everywhere. Having a hack at the BBC was always likely to be too good an opportunity to miss, and David Cameron made his intentions clear from early in his premiership. Shortly after taking power, he fired a shot across the Corporation's bows, imposing a six-year licence fee freeze. He described the possibility of further cuts as 'delicious'. Cuts to the Foreign and Commonwealth Office had a knock-on effect on the funding of the BBC World Service.[55]

The ambience surrounding this most ideologically indistinct yet, ultimately, calamitously consequential premiership was always cause for concern. Cameron seemed possessed of a certain moral blankness; his instinctive understanding of the real channels of power seemed to augur badly for the BBC from the start. Even by the standards of recent British prime ministers, Cameron was catastrophically in thrall to money and influence. Generally, in recent British history, this has led politicians to the door of Rupert Murdoch. In his 2012 book *The Fall of the House of Murdoch*, Peter Jukes reports that Murdoch's son James had at least fourteen meetings with Cameron between January 2006 and January 2010. But this was just the beginning: from the day Cameron became prime minister in May 2010, to the screeching halt brought about by the phone-hacking scandal in 2011, more than sixty meetings took place between government ministers and Murdoch representatives. This worrying synthesis peaked when former *News of the World* editor Andy Coulson found his way into the heart of government, becoming Cameron's communications director – before swapping Downing Street for prison thanks to the 2011 scandal.

Murdoch's beef with the BBC has been enduring. As far back as 1985, his paper *The Times* was arguing that 'The BBC should not survive this parliament in its present size, in its present form and with its present terms of reference intact.'[56] They've barely changed their tune since; there's been a continual drip-feed of negative briefing as the Murdoch empire exploits and synthesises its strong presence in both the tabloid and broadsheet markets. A good example is its attitude towards pay at the BBC; the *Sun* has frequently been critical of the wages paid to the Corporation's top stars and in 2015, the *Sunday Times* was delighted to be able to get behind a government Green Paper urging the BBC to 'return to its public service roots' and dispense with the populist likes of talent show *The Voice*. Such a decision would, of course, weaken the case for the licence fee – after all, who wants to pay the same money for a smaller range of demographically appealing programmes?

It's in the context of this threat that we can understand to some extent the BBC's sympathetic reporting of the coalition's austerity programme. Often, these reports were sins of omission; the BBC regularly used government and City sources to present the case for cuts without giving equal weight to the many dissenting voices within mainstream economics who argued that a fiscal squeeze could choke Britain's recovery. Sometimes the reporting was more specific; John Humphrys, for example, presented *The Future State of Welfare* on BBC Two in 2011. The documentary enthusiastically underwrote the 'skivers versus strivers' narrative promoted by the government, and duly received the ultimate journalistic Mark of

Cain when it was endorsed as 'thoughtful and intelligent' by Tory cabinet minister Iain Duncan Smith. The programme was later found by the BBC Trust to have breached impartiality guidelines.[57]

Achieving balance is difficult enough when you start off from a position of stability. When you're already wobbly, indecisive and scared of your own shadow, it's more or less impossible. Sadly for the BBC, in terms of national turmoil, we hadn't seen anything yet. Balance was to become the most contested issue in news broadcasting and, as always, the BBC would be the baseline; the context in which all such issues were judged. The BBC's coverage of the most important issue facing humanity deserves to be seen as more than a dry run for what was to follow. And yet it's been a red flag for the best part of two decades, warning that occupying a unique position at the heart of the national narrative can distort perspective.

The BBC's climate change coverage had been a bone of contention for years. Here was a phenomenon accepted by the overwhelming majority of the world's climatologists. By the start of the century, there wasn't much of a conversation to be had about the reality of man-made climate change. The only real debate revolved around what should be done. And yet as recently as 2018, a sequence of events took place that encapsulated the BBC's equivocation.

That April, Ofcom announced that the BBC had breached broadcasting regulations as a result of a radio interview the previous year with climate change sceptic Lord Lawson. An Ofcom spokesperson said, 'statements made about the science of climate change were not challenged sufficiently during this interview, which meant the programme was not duly accurate.' A few months later, Fran Unsworth, the BBC's director of news and current affairs, made a very welcome admission of error, not just over the Lawson incident but over the BBC's climate change coverage in general. In a note sent to staff but obtained by the website Carbon Brief, Unsworth wrote the following encouragingly decisive words: 'Man-made climate change exists: If the science proves it, we should report it. To achieve impartiality, you do not need to include outright deniers of climate change in BBC coverage, in the same way you would not have someone denying that Manchester United won 2–0 last Saturday. The referee has spoken.'

How long could this new era of enlightenment last? About a month, as it turned out. By October, *Newsnight* had extended an invitation to climate change denier Myron Ebell to contribute to a debate on a UN report warning of catastrophe if carbon emissions were not radically curbed. The show's excuse was that Ebell represented the views of some members of the current US government. But Ebell had never served in the US government – he was a marginal figure occupying a marginal position in the debate.

Among the unique challenges of the twenty-first century to date is that, thanks to the proliferation of alternative news sources, the very notion of objectivity is being contested. By 2014, marginal voices were taking centre stage all over British politics, with new stories to tell. Things weren't about to get any easier for the BBC. The Scottish independence referendum was the next big challenge. The referendum was uniquely awkward for everyone involved in either fighting it or covering it in the media. It pitted the establishment against an insurgent political movement with nothing less than the future of the United Kingdom at stake. But there was no external 'enemy'. The combatants on both sides were us: friends and family, taxpayers, TV licence holders. Once again, the BBC, as an organisation of consensus, of orthodoxy and of the status quo, struggled to understand and reflect the breadth and depth of the currents at play. Here, the problem was not one of particularly overt bias; it was more a question of framing. The Scottish National Party leader Alex Salmond got closest to the heart of it, saying: 'if the BBC were covering, in my estimation, any referendum, in any democracy, anywhere in the world, they would cover it impeccably, in a balanced fashion. What they don't understand is they're players in this.' Salmond said this in an interview on the BBC, naturally; to a problematic but probably unavoidable extent, the Beeb often finds itself simultaneously groundsman, player and referee.

Once again, the BBC had become part of the story. What it demonstrated in the Scottish independence referendum was the problem it had with fairly representing any political or social movement that didn't rely upon or even recognise official channels. A regular complaint was that the BBC focused too much on the official campaigns at the expense of semi-official movements. This was a big problem in terms of balance: it disproportionately affected the Yes campaign, which was, almost by definition, more of a grassroots, outlying, anti-status quo proposition. In political terms, the BBC, arguably like the UK itself around the turn of the century, has a narrow Overton Window. Coined by American scientist Joseph P. Overton, the Overton Window is a means of illustrating the range of ideas considered potentially electorally viable in a nation's political discourse at any given time. Around the turn of the century, the UK's consensus was centrist, neoliberal and unionist. The nation's Overton Window has widened markedly in recent years, accommodating everything from militant euroscepticism to Corbynism. The BBC, perhaps unhealthily accustomed to the middle ground, hasn't found the capacity to deal with these shifts. It understands the mechanics of formal politics: the press release, the two-party structure, the 'first past the post' electoral system now seen by growing numbers as inadequate, the theatrical but often alienating cut and thrust of parliamentary democracy. As various expressions of populism and direct democracy seem to loom, the BBC's struggles represent a lack of nimbleness but perhaps more importantly, a failure of imagination.

There was a certain high-handedness to the aftermath of the referendum; certainly on the part of the Unionist establishment – who had won the battle but may yet lose the war – but also on the part of the BBC, who had been their probably unwitting accomplices in counter-insurgency. As a result, the issue of Scottish independence doesn't feel settled. In fact, everything about it reeks of unfinished business, a suspicion of wounds that might not quickly heal. Its conclusion was accompanied by a sense of splintering, if not yet from the union then from any real faith in its centralising institutions – which, sadly, very much included the BBC. With that in mind, the last thing the corporation needed immediately afterwards was another contentious referendum. Which goes to show that, while it has brought much of its trouble upon itself, in recent years fate hasn't always been kind to the BBC.

The BBC's modus operandi for covering general elections is relatively simple. Equal representation for the two main parties is carefully policed. Manifestos are dissected and questioned. Policy positions are interrogated. The minutiae of BBC election coverage has been contested throughout the Corporation's existence. But formulas exist – first for planning and producing coverage, and second, for monitoring and critiquing it. The EU referendum of 2016 – and its furious aftermath – dragged the nation in general, and the BBC in particular, so far outside the comfort zone of normal political discourse that it's tempting to wonder if there's any way back.

Brexit isn't about traditional political left/right binaries. Instead, it activates deep-rooted cultural schisms to do with identity, race, region and class. It creates unlikely alliances while pitting lifelong allies against each other. It also creates a range of incompatibilities even within the ranks of the supporters of particular outcomes. For example, how can any version of Brexit possibly hope to satisfy both a neoliberal advocate of the free market in the Home Counties, and a trawler operator in Hull? Literal impartiality in terms of left versus right politics might be hard to achieve, but it's at least possible to quantify and understand the parameters of the discussion, and to explain roughly what's at stake. But how could any broadcaster give equal weight to the nebulous, wildly varied, often seemingly irrational multiplicity of views (and motivations) that underpinned the arguments surrounding the EU referendum?

Corralling the voices around Brexit was like herding cats. Some views were expert. Some were ill-informed. Some were hysterical. Some were pragmatic to a fault. Some were xenophobic. Some were actively mendacious. Some were sentimental. Some were self-righteous. Some were deeply calculating. Some people were arguing with their heads. Others were arguing with their hearts. But all were loudly demanding of representation and ready to cry foul at the slightest opportunity. And the BBC, as our great, shared cultural and political clearing house, was where that representation needed to be seen to take place. Because everyone who – however reluctantly – pays their licence fee is a stakeholder, and has a dog in the fight.

There is a partial answer to this challenging situation. And it's to attempt to deal in objective, verifiable truth. But now, even to talk about such a concept is to risk appearing gauche. More than ever before, everyone has their own version of truth and their own self-reinforcing matrix of information sources. The arguments surrounding Brexit involved, by definition, attempts to predict future outcomes. This gave us Leave voters' beloved 'Project Fear', a phrase which has had to do a frankly unreasonable amount of heavy lifting in the years since the vote. The chancellor of the exchequer, George Osborne, threatened that economic mayhem would follow a Leave victory. A 'punishment budget' was mooted. Aside from some volatility in the financial markets, this chaos did not immediately come to pass, and its absence has subsequently been used relentlessly as a stick to beat anti-Brexit prophets of doom.

But what of the Leave campaign? Any suggestion of an equivalence of falsehoods, of the inaccuracies of the two campaigns balancing each other out, is logically unsustainable. For example, Leave's suggestion that Turkey was about to join the EU was instantly and demonstrably false – full members have a veto on new arrivals, so any British government operating inside the organisation could have chosen to block them. And yet the assertion was barely challenged. The now-notorious 'Brexit Bus' which claimed that the £350 million per week that Britain apparently sent to the EU could be spent on the NHS, was even more risible, with every Treasury projection calculating that the economy would be negatively affected by Brexit. And yet, several years on from the referendum, the 'Brexit Dividend' is still being trotted out.

The root of the problems is plain. The arguments are coming from – and aimed towards – different and incompatible places. The

EU referendum, and its aftermath, was a battle between reason and emotion. One of the BBC's recurring mistakes has been to allow Leave advocates to colonise the emotional territory and bypass evidence while simultaneously failing to explore emotional arguments for remaining in the EU. From a practical point of view, this is understandable. After all, trying to find a wide range of economists who are willing to make the case for Brexit is not unlike trying to find mainstream, peer-reviewed scientists willing to make the case against man-made global warming. The main argument among economists concerns not the likelihood of damage, but the possible extent of it. But if the economic case for Leave didn't stand up to scrutiny, the BBC should have been more willing to interrogate it robustly, and eventually report their findings.

Instead, too much BBC coverage has compared apples with oranges. Thus, a frequent sight on BBC news programmes has been an emotion-driven vox pop (typically a Leave voter arguing that no-deal Brexit will be fine because Britain got through the Blitz) ranged against an economist discussing the dry practicalities of trade regulations, tariffs and border control. But these are not equivalent perspectives. There's a place for both, but like should be pitted against like. This approach to news resembles balancing a tearful outburst from someone mourning the loss of a loved one with a few words from the undertaker who will be handling the funeral. One is an exclusively emotional response, the other entirely practical.

Neither of these positions has much to say to the other, but many viewers inevitably find the former easier to identify with than the latter. Accordingly, a new received wisdom is enshrined. In an attempt to be seen to represent northern and provincial working-class Leave voters – whose collective verdict on Westminster politics has acquired almost sacred status in the years since the referendum – the broadcast media in general and the BBC in particular has unwittingly created an ugly new stereotype: that of the querulous, vaguely threatening, intractable, evidence-averse, hardship-fetishising Brexit belligerent. Whether it emerged from simple liberal guilt or something more sinister, this has helped precisely no one, least of all the demographic grouping under discussion.

Once the referendum was concluded, the BBC decided to quarantine it and move on. 'The duty we broadcasters had to "broadly balance" the views of two sides is at an end,' wrote *Today* presenter Nick Robinson on his BBC blog in April 2017. 'Why? Because there are no longer two sides.' The result was decided, went the logic, so discussion must proceed to the terms of withdrawal. But actually, nothing was settled. To start with, there was no sign of a credible, coherent withdrawal plan from the winners. None of the main political architects of Brexit seemed to want to touch the toxic aftermath, leaving Theresa May – who had campaigned for Remain, albeit with a suspicious lack of zeal – to pick up the slack. But equally significantly, there appeared to be serious questions surrounding the ethical and financial conduct of the Leave campaign. To any news-gathering organisation actively seeking to report, interrogate and uncover stories, there was much fertile ground for public interest investigation.

This was a political moment that exposed the limitations of BBC News to a painful degree. As Richard Sambrook conceded after the Iraq affair, the BBC was less independent than it thought. By now, this lesson had been fully absorbed and had become enshrined in institutional muscle memory. It appeared self-reinforcing. The BBC could reflect what it interpreted as the consensus of British opinion as filtered through official channels, but that was about it. It no longer seemed to have the appetite or the wherewithal to follow evidence wherever it might lead and set a different agenda.

In 2018 it became clear that Vote Leave, the official campaign for leaving the EU (fronted by senior cabinet ministers Boris Johnson and Michael Gove), had broken the law by overspending. This much has been established; the electoral commission found against them and a mooted appeal was dropped. The result of the inquiry was leaked to the BBC, and political editor Laura Kuenssberg's report arrived – at an undeniably convenient moment for the accused – on 4 July, the day after the England football team had won a World Cup knockout game on penalties, and the nation's attention was elsewhere. Kuenssberg's report allowed Vote Leave's former chief executive Matthew Elliott to subtly undermine the revelation in an accompanying interview and claim that the commission had 'listened to one side of the story'. It failed to offer a counterpoint.

In a sit-down interview with Elliott, Kuenssberg prefaced one question by suggesting that Vote Leave 'might be innocent in theory but it sounds like you were guilty in practice'. Coming before the official publication of the report, this feels like a question designed with pre-emptive damage limitation in mind, providing exactly the sort of ambiguous framing that Vote Leave might have hoped to establish. That morning, Michael Gove appeared on the *Today* programme and airily congratulated the BBC on a 'great scoop'. As Peter Geoghegan pointed out in an article on the Open Democracy website, Vote Leave appeared to 'have given the BBC a "scoop" that looks more like crafty PR . . . than a genuine revelation.'[58]

Whether knowingly or not, it's often felt that the BBC has been influenced by Leave advocates, from the beginning of 2016 right up to the present. For example, in April 2019, a Channel 4 News story shone a harsh light on the newsroom atmosphere during the campaign. Channel 4 obtained evidence that, via Facebook advertising, Leave.EU had targeted the votes of far-right groups including the English Defence League, the National Front and the BNP. The BBC had received a tip-off about this targeted campaign in early 2016 but decided not to run a story after a fierce counter-attack from Leave.EU's Arron Banks and Andy Wigmore, who claimed bias and threatened legal action.

What happened next is both alarming and illuminating. The pair appealed to the BBC's then head of political programmes, Robbie Gibb. Banks, in his referendum memoir *The Bad Boys of Brexit*, recalls: 'I woke up to news that the Beeb is planning to run a smear story about our Facebook pages. Robbie Gibb is being quite helpful and says he's trying to hose it down.' The BBC have subsequently claimed that the story was dropped because they were unable to definitively establish the facts and that in any case, Gibb wasn't responsible for the decision. Gibb, who later became Theresa May's head of communications, was accused by former Tory MP Nick Boles in 2019 of being 'a hard Brexiter who wants to destroy the PM's search for a cross-party compromise'.[59]

The ease with which figures like Gibb move between broadcasting and political roles is one of the keys to understanding the BBC's timidity and confusion in this period. It failed to handle the outsider insurgency represented by the Scottish independence referendum. But Brexit was an insurgency of a different kind, and much easier for the BBC to rationalise. Its arguments fed into existing biases and emerged from familiar quarters. Boris Johnson, Nigel Farage and Jacob Rees-Mogg are personifications of the kind of arrogant British exceptionalism that occasionally dwindles, but never truly dies – and it's very hard to escape the impression that the higher echelons of BBC News harboured similar insider mavericks.

Accordingly, the suggestion that Brexit represented a revolt against elites was always absurd but always allowed to stand. These 'rebels' may have enlisted swathes of the working class to their dubious cause, but they still represented money, connections, vested interests and ancient, entrenched power structures. Advocates of Brexit were speaking the BBC's language, and had an inside track to an extent of which Scottish independence campaigners could never dream. Ironically, their ascendency surely ensures that the Scottish issue will return.

Eventually, Brexit as represented on the BBC became white noise; endless sound and fury signifying both nothing and everything. Instead of forensic analysis, we've entered the era of the pundit. After all, as has often been the case with climate change, experts are problematic in terms of maintaining the BBC's current interpretation of broadcasting balance. Even if all the evidence tends to be heading towards the same conclusion, the impression of multiple, equally valid perspectives must be maintained. Thus, everything becomes furiously contested but highly subjective. In April 2019, for example, Toby Young and Mariana Mazzucato crossed swords on BBC One's *Politics Live*. Viewers were treated to the unedifying spectacle of Mazzucato, a celebrated economics professor whose work makes a pioneering contribution to the analysis of the relationship between state and private enterprise, being shouted down by Young, who by his own admission relied upon a phone call from his father to obtain his Oxford University place. Young, it transpired, hadn't read Mazzucato's most recent book, which was under discussion during the segment. But he had, he sneered, 'read the press release'. It's hard to think of a more perfect illustration of the entitlement of Britain's complacent elite, or of the way in which false balance and a contempt for expertise militates against constructive, informed discussion of important issues.

This kind of exchange might fit the post-truth era very neatly, but it's surely the antithesis of the BBC's mission statement. Viewed from a wider perspective, it means that BBC news programming in 2020 is too often pure spectacle without substance. Marches, petitions, furiously aggressive interviews that feel like performative verbal punishment beatings rather than true attempts to cast light on events. Arguably, the prevailing atmosphere fits very well into the 'adrenaline-packed' agenda promised for *Question Time* in 2017. But whether you identify as Leave or Remain, the BBC owes us more than cheap thrills. In the years immediately after the referendum, the nation felt like a cartoon character zooming off a cliff: it was running frantically, but on fresh air. The trouble with relying on adrenaline for sustenance is that adrenaline is finite. Eventually, there has to be a crash.

This book, like all books, comes from a particular political and cultural perspective. It's easy enough to find correspondingly furious complaints from right-leaning, pro-Brexit commentators alleging anti-Brexit bias at the BBC during this period. Indeed, the last two decades have been a practical demonstration of the sheer impossibility of the corporation's position in turbulent times. That might be an argument for cutting it some slack – but it doesn't mean the BBC can afford to be complacent about the very real threats it now faces. At many times during its lifespan, the Beeb has seemed embattled; threatened; compromised. The ominous difference is that it's fighting on multiple fronts now. It hasn't pacified its perennial enemies on the political right, because they're essentially implacable – they oppose the BBC on ideological grounds and in any case, their reaction to being given a little of what they want is to demand more. Sucking up to bullies never works: it simply indicates weakness which can then be exploited more regularly.

But in appearing to do so, the BBC has managed to open up a whole new front of conflict among natural allies on the progressive left. And it's not hard to locate the causes of their disquiet. For example, on 29 September 2019, while covering the Tory party conference – and at the end of a week during which prime minister Boris Johnson had been found guilty of illegally proroguing Parliament and accused of improper use of funds during his time as London mayor – the BBC website offered up an array of headlines that might have come straight from Conservative Central Office. A tweeted photo of three ministers on stage hailed 'Three Brexit champions'. The site's headlines were an uncritically presented roll call of governmental policy pledges and attack lines. 'Government plans billions for hospital projects'. 'Johnson: I've been the model of restraint'. 'Government of national unity "a Remoaner coup"'. It's hard to see this kind of assimilation and framing of an embattled government's platform as anything other than hopelessly, dangerously compliant. It's certainly hard to regard it as having much to do with public service broadcasting.

Accordingly, within the demographic groups normally sympathetic to the BBC, it's now easy to find people who are convinced of its entrenched hostility towards Jeremy Corbyn, people angry at its equivocations over climate change, Remain voters furious about its Brexit coverage. And none of these positions is completely without justification. At the end of this extraordinary period in our national life, we'll need to take stock, honestly discuss what went wrong, and think about how we can move forward. The BBC will host many of these discussions. But unavoidably, it will be part of the story too.

No one does a *mea culpa* quite like the BBC. After all, it's had plenty of practice. Since the Corporation was consistently becoming the story, why not steer into the skid? John Morton's comedy *W1A*, which began in 2014, must have appeared a manoeuvre of considerable audacity when it was commissioned. This was the BBC holding its hands up; satirising itself, but also attempting to cock a snook at its critics by parading its own self-awareness and therefore, pre-empting their criticism.

W1A was a spin-off from Morton's gently acid sitcom *Twenty Twelve*, which followed, in the now commonplace spoof documentary style, a fictionalised Olympic deliverance team as they attempted to organise events around the summer Games. It was well received, and with good reason; it punctured the absurd grandiosity of the build-up to the Olympics, speaking instead to a keenly felt but tentatively voiced undertow of national anxiety as the Games approached. Might Britain screw this up? Very possibly – after all, we'd been screwing lots of things up recently. If so, the show suggested, the screw-up would be quirkily and distinctly British in flavour, and we'd all find a way of laughing at ourselves afterwards. In fact, the resonance of the show's wittily comforting vision must have convinced everyone involved that the idea and format were too good to waste. With the Olympics safely delivered, the show – and its main character, Hugh Bonneville's Ian Fletcher – managed a transition to a more permanent corner of national life.

The problem was, the Olympics were almost certainly a once-in-a-lifetime deal. There was a finishing line, a moment at which judgement could be passed. The games would succeed or fail but either way, they would end. The BBC – the subject of *WIA* – was a more ambiguous subject. Contested as it was, is and presumably will always be, we are all to a greater or lesser extent invested in its ongoing operation. What seemed reassuring in *Twenty Twelve* was therefore somewhat disconcerting in *WIA* – if much of it prompted uneasy self-recognition in real-life BBC employees, then surely that was a bad thing? The muddle-through Britishness of *Twenty Twelve* reflected a need for reassurance in the face of a unique national challenge. In *WIA*, it curdled into something less admirable. Operating without an endpoint, the charmingly ridiculous seemed simply smug and complacent. It might be argued that only a brave organisation would hold its own feet to the fire in such a sustained way. But in satirical terms, *WIA* was more a shrug than a scream. It felt like the most calculated kind of risk-taking imaginable; an organisation offering itself up for ridicule in the hope of receiving a gentle ribbing, rather than the kicking it arguably deserved.

'You're at the centre of something genuinely important,' says Ian Fletcher as he begins his new job as the BBC's Head of Values in the show's opening scene. 'And the really exciting thing is to think that part of my job is going to be to establish where that centre is, and exactly what it's in the middle of.' Straight away, this was the BBC in the twenty-first century laid bare. It's a bellow of existential confusion, expressed in a mixture of barely comprehensible managerial gobbledygook and British understatement. There was a nostalgia underpinning the show – the opening credits toyed with signifiers of the corporation's past, and all the crazily banal and pointless meetings throughout the series take place in rooms named after former stars ('meanwhile, back up in Frankie Howerd . . .'). How has it come to this, the show seemed to wonder. How did the broadcaster that gave the world David Attenborough and Victoria Wood and *Monty Python's Flying Circus* find itself cowering under the jackboot of this motley collection of digital strategists and ideation architects and trending analysts? When did the posh, gormless interns and drifting, over-promoted nonentities and overbearing, oversensitive compliance officers grab the reins?

But *W1A* never seemed to wonder how anyone inside the organisation might take the reins back and refit the BBC with real vigour, courage and agency. In fact, the middlebrow tone, the middlebrow performances and the middle-aged kidults with their folding Bromptons and their hi-vis cycling gear looked and felt worryingly like the result of stasis; as if the self-styled British liberal broadcasting elite was making carefully calibrated jokes about itself in a spirit of self-loathing self-defence. The actual compliance meetings surrounding *W1A* might have been where the really biting satire was – we'll never know. This wasn't the output of a particularly healthy broadcaster, but it was inadvertently revealing of the identity crisis at the heart of the BBC in the twenty-first century. It was stuck, and it knew it.

But while it might be struggling to understand its place in the face of revolutionary change, the BBC, as an idea, remains unambiguously worth saving. Much of the criticism it faces (and certainly the criticism in this chapter) comes from a place of love, not hate. It originates in the fact that the Corporation is cherished by so many of us and, like the NHS, stands – albeit sometimes unsteadily – for values which despite feeling out of step with much of modern British life, we seem collectively determined to try and maintain. The BBC still churns out hours and hours of fine, distinctive television and nurtures talent, both in front of and behind the camera, on a unique scale. Imagining Britain's media-scape in its absence isn't comfortable – BBC haters on all sides of the political spectrum might be advised to ponder the USA for an example of a country in which news providers have no codified or enforced structure of wider accountability. But it does need to take the many bitter lessons of the last two decades seriously and think very carefully about how it proceeds.

In early 2019, a plan was mooted to hand over one day's worth of Brexit coverage to a group made up of 'carefully selected' members of the public who would work closely with broadcasting professionals at the BBC. From an internal perspective, it probably seemed a worthwhile democratising initiative and a demonstration of humility. But like *W1A*, it looks from the outside to be more an admission of weakness on the part of an organisation which then responds to that admission by passing the buck. The implication of the scheme seemed to be that rather than confronting failures of journalism, it would simply create a babel of balanced but uninformed voices. The result, almost inevitably, would be less expertise, not more.

There is a different way. The new ease surrounding alternative news channels, citizen journalism and user-generated content is one of the biggest challenges the BBC faces. But might this represent an opportunity too? Not in the sense that the BBC should bend over backwards to incorporate these voices but in fact, the absolute opposite. Carole Cadwalladr has written about the 'circular knowledge economy'[60] in which verifiable facts come a distant second to the relentless, dizzying churn of content; media becomes an amoral, hyper-marketised, lightly regulated free-for-all and social media is a news source in itself. In this new arena, algorithms actively direct consumers towards sensation and self-reinforcement, and hard-headed accuracy often falls by the wayside. In September 2019, Channel 4's chief executive Alex Mahon gave an interesting if chastening speech at the Royal Television Society in which she pondered a challenging future for television. 'The global telly of the future', she warned, 'will not be – and isn't being – designed to reflect Britain back to itself, to bring the nation together at particular moments, to inform and educate a particular society or to care about promoting any kind of social cohesion'. This future might sound worrying, but it contains the germ of an opportunity too. A centralised, universally accountable organisation like the BBC, independent of commercial funding, could become a circuit breaker in an age of information overload, performing a more important public service than ever. The BBC has drifted along on similar currents to the rest of British society through the century to date. But it remains in a position to help us steer in a different direction.

One of Facebook's founding principles was famously to 'move fast and break things'. This could easily act as a mission statement for most of the arch-disruptors of the social media age. Could the BBC's destiny be to act as a bulwark; an institution that, try as they might, the sprawling, exponentially multiplying and diversifying tech giants can't quite break? It's not impossible. But first, the BBC needs to address the various issues of trust it faces. Trust means facts, their dogged pursuit and verification and their unvarnished presentation. Pointing out the facts is sometimes inconvenient and unpopular. The establishment of trust is sometimes anything but adrenaline-packed. But as a news organisation, the BBC will live or die by its approach to these virtues. It's become a trite truism to speak despairingly of 'alternative facts' and 'the post-truth era' as if these phenomena are now set in stone. But the BBC has the resources and the profile to challenge this apparent fait accompli – and its survival might depend upon it finding the strength to do so.

It will need to seriously consider radical ideas. For example, doing away with live political interviews and only airing them once statements made in them have been fully interrogated. Imagine if an interview with any prominent politician or media figure were to be broadcast an hour after it was conducted, accompanied by annotated, fact-checked corrections? There'd be considerable anger. But the standard of discourse would surely improve as a result. Imagine if the BBC elected to do away with its rolling news channel altogether, recognising that the sheer amount of time needing to be filled made unsatisfactory interviews with agenda-driven pundits operating in bad faith almost inevitable.

Imagine a renaissance of reporting from the nation's regions, whereby the BBC meaningfully engaged with communities and came back from encounters with the wider British public with more than simply vox pops. Britain's current discord hasn't sprung from nowhere, and the BBC should be investing time and resources in exploring its root causes. It's not impossible to imagine a new era of reconnection, sobriety, rigour and unashamed expertise. As we've seen, speaking truth to power might sometimes be a tricky political decision for a publicly funded, government-regulated broadcaster. But sometimes, short-term expediency must be ignored: ultimately, this is an editorial and eventually, a moral decision too.

In terms of entertainment programming, the BBC has adapted to technological change in frequently effective ways. The iPlayer, with its flexible range of unique content, interactivity and space for niche voices, is a success story. The BBC is working in collaboration with international broadcasters and production companies to produce programming of admirable scope and ambition. Its news brief needn't be commercially expansive because the news operation is where the BBC's public service imperative is most keenly felt. It's where our trust – or otherwise – in the organisation is developed or squandered.

It's hard not to look wistfully at some of the journalistic talent the BBC has lost in recent years. Since 2000, Paul Mason, Robert Peston, Michael Crick and James O'Brien have all had spells at the corporation before finding more comfortable homes elsewhere. Their respective reasons for departure are varied and unique. But the quartet share a certain prickly distinctiveness; a disdain for convention; an urge to question rather than accept. Space for such voices needs to be maintained. The BBC needs to be much more wary of the revolving door between party politics and its own higher management echelons. It's a door through which both Labour and Conservative figures have passed, and it's obviously unrealistic to expect senior figures in either politics or broadcasting to be entirely devoid of political allegiances. But the line between broadcaster and political operative has begun to look dangerously porous.

The British broadcasting model is unique, and that fact is both cheering and worrying – the BBC is an outlier, and things don't always end well for them. Brexit continues to be a brutal national audit. It has eviscerated Britain and left its institutional guts spilling out for all to see. It has shone a viciously harsh, almost surgical spotlight upon everything from our political system to the foundations of our economy. It would have been strange if broadcasting had escaped its shattering pressure. It threatens destruction in many areas, but it's also helping to illuminate problems that have been developing, only vaguely detected, for years.

So it is with the BBC. This period of unprecedented turbulence will be analysed exhaustively. Hard questions will be asked. But if the right answers materialise, it's not impossible that renewal could follow. For better or worse, the BBC will be part of the story for many years to come. Our collective relationship with it will probably always be complicated. In fact, it's quite possible that Brexit is in the process of testing the BBC to destruction. But maybe the result of this test will be regained strength and purpose. In April 2019, the BBC broadcast an hour-long documentary called *Climate Change – The Facts*. Even the title was striking – it felt stark and bold but also promising in the prevailing atmosphere of equivocation. What followed felt refreshingly, bluntly effective. The film acknowledged the existence of climate change denialism, but much in the way that a programme about race relations might acknowledge the existence of white supremacists – from a distance, as an irrelevant absurdity, a self-evident dead end. Instead, the documentary was replete with experts; climatologists and scientists laying out the facts, simply and persuasively. Better still, it didn't hesitate to apportion blame; towards the fossil fuel lobby and even towards the president of the United States of America. And finally, tentatively but decisively, it ventured a few potential solutions.

It was a signpost towards a potential solution for the BBC too. *Climate Change – The Facts* is precisely the kind of programme the BBC should be looking to make if it truly desires to recover lost trust. That it felt so incongruous and unfamiliar is both a sign of how far the BBC has fallen and, viewed more optimistically, an indication that change might be in the air.

And yet even now, there's a sense of the BBC taking two steps forward followed by one step back. In autumn 2019, another entirely avoidable controversy engulfed the corporation and offered an insight into where the organisation now found itself. Back in July, following a discussion about Donald Trump's suggestion that four non-white Democrat congresswomen should 'go back' to the 'places from which they came', BBC *Breakfast*'s Naga Munchetty and Dan Walker were exploring the meaning of his words. 'Every time I've been told, as a woman of colour, to go back where I came from,' said Munchetty, 'it's been embedded in racism.' She went on to clarify that 'I'm not accusing anyone of anything.' But she did continue that Trump's words made her 'furious'.

After a complaint from a single viewer, Munchetty was found by the BBC's Executive Complaints Unit to have breached impartiality guidelines. (Walker, although also being included in the complaint, mysteriously escaped censure.) In justifying this decision, the BBC tangled themselves in the mother of all semantic knots, seeming to claim that while Trump's words were racist, Trump himself was not. After several excruciating days of outrage, half-apologies and embarrassing attempts at justification, director general Tony Hall was forced to step in. He overturned the decision, telling staff that Munchetty's words were not 'sufficient to merit a partial uphold' of the complaint.

But, as was the case when BBC Monitoring tweeted Jair Bolsonaro's 'refreshing' opinions, the damage was done. And just as in that incident, a misguided notion of 'balance' seemed to underpin the error. Speaking about the controversy on BBC Two's *Newsnight*, comedian Nish Kumar said, 'Racism is like gravity. There's a position that is correct and a position that is incorrect.' In the aftermath of the

Munchetty incident, Hall was forced to confirm that 'racism is racism and the BBC is not impartial on the topic'. That such a clarification even felt necessary surely meant that once again, the BBC had found itself in a terrible, compromised place, seemingly struggling to locate a fixed moral point and unambiguously claim the territory.

There's a distinct sense that what the BBC means to us has changed since the turn of the century. There is anxiety, suspicion and anger where, broadly speaking, there used to be respect. Everything is questioned and too often, the organisation seems paralysed in the face of these challenges. There's now a sense of genuine jeopardy, which often seems to induce relativism, weakness and timidity. There's often a suspicion that the BBC doesn't quite understand the extent of its own power – either for good or for ill. It could, if it chose, set agendas. Instead, it too often seems to react to them. Perhaps the best we can hope for is that before long, this existential threat will concentrate minds and help the BBC regain its lost balance.

5

A VERY BRITISH
IDENTITY CRISIS

The Great British Bake Off · Downton Abbey
Southcliffe · This Is England '90 · The League of Gentlemen
Detectorists · Brexit: The Uncivil War

THE FIRST NOTABLE USE on television of the prefix *A Very British . . .* came in a surprisingly subversive context. In 1988, *A Very British Coup* – a Channel 4 drama serial adapted from Labour MP Chris Mullin's novel of the same name – imagined a left-wing Labour leader elected prime minister, but gradually and bloodlessly brought to heel by the faceless forces of reaction. The formulation meant something real in this setting: it spoke of the velvet glove concealing the iron fist of British statecraft. It implied that Britain's innate suspicion of genuine radicalism extended to both revolution and counter-revolution. Power would be given – and taken away – by insinuation, but the status quo would always prevail. Even so, the establishment would never be so crude, so overt, so downright un-British, as to forcibly overthrow a democratic decision. Instead, the main protagonists would be nudged, as gently as possible, in the direction of some sort of fait accompli.

By the mid-2000s, the trope, and its close relative in nominative wishful thinking, *The Great British . . .* had started to fulfil a subtly different, but not altogether unrelated brief. It now expressed a subliminal but very insistent soft power. It expressed a facet of British (and specifically English) identity, both real and imagined. If there had been a certain pointed irony in the way the title *A Very British Coup* evoked an almost aggressive strain of British politesse, its intentions had evolved by the time the phrase truly established itself on television. Now it manifested exceptionalism, but from a pacified, fond, uncritical perspective. All countries have some sort of unifying national myth. But does any nation guard, nurture and project its own self-image as relentlessly as Britain?

Suddenly it seemed there was nothing that couldn't be designated and celebrated as being Very British. Hotels? Airlines? Problems? Murders? Sex Shops? Why not? The more the merrier. The label persists to this day, and has started to look like a slightly maniacal exercise in mass branding. The definitive patina of Britishness must be willed into being everywhere. We must mark our own unique cultural territory, like a wolf spraying scent around its hunting ground. It has begun, as persistent over-emphasis generally does, to smack of insecurity. Particularly as this profusion has coincided with an era during which we have had plenty to be insecure about.

If the prefix *A Very British . . .* appealed to exceptionalism, to the idea that any emotion, institution or phenomena could be designated a role as a facet of a unique national character, *The Great British . . .* spoke to unity and continuity. *The Great British . . .* suggests a longstanding tradition, something we've come to rely upon, set our watches by. As very often in matters of national identity, the notion was something of a phantom – so many of Britain's identity problems stem from its veneration of a past that never really existed. But that didn't necessarily matter. Perhaps such an identity could be wished into being? After all, that's how myths are generally made: for the most part, they're simply seductive stories which resonate widely because they've been skilfully told at the right time. So it was with *The Great British Bake Off*. The programme launched in 2010, shortly after David Cameron became prime minister and began to institute his programme of austerity. Quickly, *Bake Off* proved to be a particular show for a particular time, enshrining a specific view of Britain.

The show was a finely balanced ecosystem of signifiers, right down to the bunting-strewn, tent-bound setting which gave it the look of a village fete attended by the Famous Five. Indeed, if Timmy the dog had wandered into shot, it wouldn't have felt hugely surprising. *Bake Off* was twee but earthy; earnest but far from unaware of its own absurdity. The judges embodied yin and yang too, with Mary Berry's prim, matronly twinkle offset by Paul Hollywood's Scouse bearishness. The original presenters, Sue Perkins and Mel Giedroyc, were amiably silly public-school head girls. The fact that *Bake Off* was on the BBC was an intrinsic element of its appeal. This was the national broadcaster telling us what we were like – at a time when we weren't quite sure. And we liked what we heard. We were gently funny; culturally and racially inclusive; modest but extremely capable. When, in apparent defiance of all notions of propriety and good taste, the show moved from BBC One to Channel 4, there was, briefly, a Very British Kerfuffle at the prospect of the intrusion of commercials into this Very British Idyll. Is there honey still for tea? Yes, but there will be regular advertisements for Amazon Echo, too.

In the wider culture, *Bake Off* wasn't alone in its attempt to weave a narrative of reassurance and continuity. In 2008, the global financial crisis had shaken belief in the hierarchical economic system that, for a couple of decades, we'd been assured was the only game in town. Everything seemed up for grabs. But revolutionary and fundamental change? Steady on, old chap. It was around the time that the full, miserable implications of the financial crisis became clear that a Very British meme became ubiquitous. Posters bearing the stirring injunction to 'Keep Calm And Carry On', printed during the Second World War, hadn't been widely distributed at the time. But after an old poster was discovered at a bookshop in Northumberland in 2000, their spread became viral.

Both the message and the underlying sensibility were perfectly calibrated to connect the imperilled past with the uncertain present. Writing in the *Guardian*, Owen Hatherley summed up the aesthetic, describing it as 'austerity nostalgia'.[61] The design was pleasingly retro; the origin story – an understated but determined rallying cry from a wartime government under duress – equally satisfying. But the semantics now seemed very different. In its original incarnation, the poster had been a response to an external threat posed by an expansionist genocidal dictator. In contrast, its post-2008 revival seemed a passive-aggressive and simplistic endorsement of the status quo which was essentially to blame for the problems the nation faced; an inward- and backward-looking response to a crisis created by a financial elite who were, at that moment, enjoying a bailout which would suck the nation's public services dry. The posters – and indeed, the whole aesthetic – made kitsch capital out of the iconography of the paternalistic state. Meanwhile, back in the real world, that state was in the process of eviscerating itself in order to restore almost the exact system that had caused the crisis in the first place.

By definition, the posters accepted the inevitability of approaching hardship. But they also implied that anyone who wanted to tear up the script and start work on a new one might be suspiciously lacking in British spunk and stoicism. However, there was the problem of what 'Carry On' actually meant in this new context. Carry on borrowing and spending? Carry on accepting the authority which was at that moment engaged in kettling students with the temerity to demonstrate against funding cuts and tuition fees that had the potential to jeopardise their future? Britain's survival and ultimate victory in the Second World War is, justifiably, a potent national totem. There's no reason why people shouldn't be proud of that chapter in our country's history. But however much some of us might wish it were possible, the tropes of one era can't always be neatly transposed onto the problems of another. When the idealised past begins to jostle the problematic present out of the way, national myths can become actively harmful.

Myth-making involves codification. But by definition, a myth-maker moulds abstract ideas rather than communicating objective truths. In a 2001 BBC Proms Lecture, titled 'Deep and True? Reflections on the Cultural Life of the English Countryside', academic Patrick Wright discussed what, on a certain powerful but intangible level – and in what might be called mythical terms – the English countryside has come to mean:

> This is an appropriate time to reflect on the cultural dimension
> of the countryside. Not so much the way we farm it, but the

way we have imagined it as something closely connected to our
sense of identity, both locally and in a more national sense. The
countryside, then, as a repository of values that neither farmers
nor scientific conservationists may immediately recognise as
belonging on their turf: ideas like innocence, beauty, peace,
tradition, nature and, of course, nationhood too.

To that list we might add continuity. From economics to culture
to changing demography, most of the objective truths surrounding
Britishness – or, perhaps more pertinently, Englishness – around this
time were perplexing and disconcerting to traditionalists. Which was
all the more reason to idealise the imaginary certainties of the past
and, if possible, set them in amber. Television was crucial to this.
Witness the picture-postcard whimsy of a fictional TV village like
Cranford: a 2007 BBC One drama so cloyingly twee it appeared, at
times, almost to be parody. This was a place where George Orwell's
'Old maids bicycling to holy communion through the morning
mist' truly came to life in the popular imagination. Or Midsomer,
the quaint (and yet oddly crime-bedevilled) village which was the
setting for the hugely popular ITV drama *Midsomer Murders*.

In 2011, the latter show's producer Brian True-May landed himself
in trouble thanks to a series of ill-advised remarks during an interview with the *Radio Times*. 'We just don't have ethnic minorities
involved,' he said. 'Because it wouldn't be the English village with
them. It just wouldn't work.'[62] Inflammatory as it might have been,
this statement did have some basis in verifiable fact – Britain's most
recent census (also in 2011) found that 45 per cent of the country's
non-white population resided in London, with the vast majority
of the remainder living in other major cities. But True-May wasn't

quite finished. He went on to describe Midsomer as 'the last bastion of Englishness'. This was divisive, defensive, almost martial language (a bastion is, after all, a fortification) that seemed to suggest a 'native' culture under siege from alien insurgents. True-May was suspended and then reinstated by the show's production company All3Media but stepped down as producer around a year later. But what now seems remarkable about the affair was that he made these remarks in the first place – and seemed genuinely surprised at the offence they caused. This was Deep English myth-making internalised; an illustration of a cognitive process so ingrained that its expression was almost unconscious.

Most period dramas have more to tell us about the era in which they are made than the era in which they are set. And so it was in September 2010, when ITV introduced the period's definitive example of the form, ushering us back to a world in which newspapers were always ironed and kedgeree was served for breakfast.

Ostensibly, *Downton Abbey* was about the aristocratic Crawley family and their large coterie of domestic staff, all of whom lived in a sprawling, beautiful country pile in pre-First World War Yorkshire. But really, the lead character was the English class system, whose resilience to a wide variety of potentially serious trauma injuries rivals that of the Terminator. 'The aristocracy has not survived by its intransigence,' stated the Dowager Countess of Grantham, Violet Crawley (played by Dame Maggie Smith) in season two. And rarely was a truer sentence ever spoken on British television.

Downton Abbey was a stunning propaganda exercise. The English class system morphs and shapeshifts according to the times. Unfailingly, it finds ways to justify its existence to enough people at any given moment; to present itself as part of the solution, not part of the problem. It certainly Keeps Calm and Carries On. The national obsession with *Downton Abbey* was never entirely earnest or straightforward. As with the enduring popularity of the royal family, there often seemed an ironic component to it. There's a certain camp absurdity to these totems of very genteel class war, which has been heightened by their self-conscious absorption into the world of celebrity. Often, we're partly laughing at ourselves for hating, loving and, eventually, tolerating them. The grip might attach itself to a different part of our brains, but it certainly doesn't weaken.

Downton Abbey was the creation of Julian Fellowes, a Conservative peer and a lifetime member of the House of Lords. The show didn't thrive on conflict; in fact, it did precisely the opposite. 'Not even the subtext [but] the supertext of Downton', Fellowes told the *Wall Street Journal* in February 2013, 'is that it is possible for us all to get on, that we don't have to be ranged in class warfare permanently.' A benign enough sentiment – except for what it left unspoken. The implication is that the essential hierarchies underpinning class difference would, of course, remain intact in perpetuity. To that end, Fellowes conjured a drama full of shrewdly constructed and easily decoded ciphers. There was Hugh Bonneville's patrician but well-intentioned Earl Grantham. His three unmarried adult daughters; variously haughty, flighty and mildly frumpy. A potential male heir to the estate whose good character compensated for his regrettable lack of pure noble breeding. And a range of variously saintly and cartoonishly villainous below-stairs functionaries headed by Jim Carter's butler Carson. Carter's sheer screen presence – and in particular, his voice – was key to the show. It's a magnificently seductive and sonorous rumble, the kind of gloriously emphatic brogue you could happily listen to all day. Carter/Carson was the guarantor of the house's probity; he kindly but diligently policed the line between its two worlds, making sure everything remained in its right place. He was the personification of a linguistic and behavioural code that can't easily be explained, only obeyed, learned and internalised.

Essentially, everyone involved was simply a delivery mechanism in human form for a series of hilariously unambiguous moral messages. Bad deeds were punished. Good deeds were rewarded. It was perfectly calibrated heritage porn, recognising that British TV viewers have often sought refuge in the nearest country house during troubled times. In 1981, with riots tearing the nation's inner cities apart and Margaret Thatcher's brutal programme of monetarism emptying factories and filling job centres, many found solace in a serialised adaptation of Evelyn Waugh's *Brideshead Revisited*. But Downton felt different somehow. Its lack of heft and nuance was striking. This country house was a new build; *Downton Abbey* wasn't an acknowledged literary classic. It didn't explore paradoxes or ask difficult questions. Unlike, say, a Jane Austen or a George Eliot adaptation, it didn't carry the distracting weight of time-earned artistic merit, of a place in the canon to anchor it. It was as light as a feather and as comfortable as a pillow. It was a simulacrum, not just of the idealised rural community of the early twentieth century but of the costume drama itself. It was pure signifier; style over content to a degree that would seem audacious to the most daring post-modernist.

In the wake of the New Labour decade, which was at least gesturally egalitarian, noblesse oblige was making a comeback. In his 2011 book *The Reactionary Mind*, American political theorist Corey Robin described modern Conservatism's mission as being 'to make privilege popular'. *Downton Abbey* represented its entertainment wing in action. Before becoming prime minister (a position he achieved a few months before *Downton Abbey*'s premiere), David Cameron – a man who once had the remarkable nerve to describe himself and his wife as 'middle class' despite being related to the royal family – suggested he was aiming to lead the country 'because I think I'd be good at it'. This was pure officer class entitlement; the idea that a person can simply drift towards the highest elected office in the land, not through any particular sense of mission but because the role was vaguely adjacent to an already existent set of personal expectations.

Cameron was a very *Downton Abbey* sort of politician, and a very Capitalist Realist one too. He was once said to have 'risen without trace' through the Conservative Party. And in terms of personal profile, there was nothing much to attach to him. He was a former PR man, and therefore adept in the arts of image creation and crisis management. In the wake of the Blair era, during which the Labour PM's public image was carefully managed by his Director of Communications Peter Mandelson, these seemed like key attributes for any modern politician. To many in his party, Cameron simply seemed the right sort and that was about it – he was a *tabula rasa* upon which almost any version of modern Conservatism could be written. He did his best to appear almost entirely post-ideological; while his determined shrinking of the British state was very much of a piece with vigorously right-wing doctrine, he managed to give the impression that his policies were essentially a fait accompli. There was no alternative. It had fallen to him – and by extension, the Conservative Party and the British upper class as a whole – to fix the mess we'd got ourselves into. To his supporters at least, he was a symbol of continuity, and of that most British archetype: the safe pair of hands.

Cameron's social liberalism – his willingness to meet the modern world halfway – was central to his branding. Like *Downton Abbey*, he represented the timeless ability of the English aristocracy to bend but not break, to move far enough but no further and to do whatever it took to maintain the status quo. As this process was taking place in British politics, it was being dramatised in the show too. There was often a strangely staccato quality to *Downton Abbey*'s narrative structure, a sense of cosmetic friction – a problem would arise, seem briefly intractable and then resolve itself, often within the course of a single episode. These incidents (some stolen silver, an illicit night of passion) were like stones causing ripples in a pond: simply a moment of turbulence before the previous shape and structure restored itself.

This is mirrored in the show's attitude towards larger events (the sinking of the *Titanic*; the First World War). The structure is rocked by them, but soon absorbs the blows and, in fact, incorporates the energy they imparted. During the Great War, Downton Abbey is opened up to recuperating soldiers. Initially, there's chaos and disruption; everything seems up for grabs. But eventually the turbulence both begins to diminish, and even becomes positively beneficial. It adds to the myth; the narrative that the show, the family and the system that sustains them have established. While at first it might have been imagined that nothing could ever be the same again, before long calm has returned. The potential for change has been neutralised by incorporation. This is why British people love period dramas, particularly during difficult times. They tell us that we can rely on our history: that we've been stuck here before and found a way out. That things are, more or less, as they should be. That the past isn't really another country after all. 'I hanker for a simpler world,' says Violet Crawley, setting out a manifesto in episode one of the series. 'Is that a crime?' It seemed that she and her fellow characters were speaking for many of us. If reality looked complex and troubling, perhaps comfort could be found in myths.

Central to this maintenance of mythical British identity is war. In early 2019, Conservative MP Daniel Kawczynski tweeted that Britain had received nothing from the American post-war European reconstruction initiative, the Marshall Plan. Within a few minutes, dozens of Twitter users had ascertained that Britain actually received more aid than any other country (something that, in fairness, Kawczynski himself might have been well advised to do before sending his tweet) and very vigorously set him straight. And yet, oddly, Kawczynski was right – if not in quite the way he imagined. In fact, Britain hadn't been given any help to recover from the Second World War. Imagine a psychic Marshall Plan, in which humility and self-awareness are the currency. Many other European countries, most notably (and necessarily) Germany, undertook such a cognitive audit after the war. Britain did not, thanks to its assumption of the righteousness of its victory. There is a German word, *Mahnmal*, which roughly translates as a monument to national tragedy and shame. The English language contains no such word. Britain has faced no such reckoning with itself, has engaged in no comparable mental reconstruction. Its myths are unchallenged, and it goes its own sweet way.

These myths solidify with the passing of time. For example, Remembrance Sunday used to be a day of unimpeachable national dignity; a calm, solemn reflection upon another generation's sacrifice.

But there is a slightly coercive hysteria surrounding the wearing of poppies now. Could it be that poppies, like the conflicts they commemorate, have become more and more politicised, the further the wars in question drift into the past? After all, each year, fewer veterans are left to demystify what actually happened in, for example, the First World War. Because there are fewer direct witnesses to this history, it can be tweaked, simplified and repurposed. In the UK, the defeat of fascism led to socialism, to the creation of the NHS, to attempts to universalise education and opportunity. But that's never the thrust of Poppy Day commemorations. In fact, sympathies now seem to flow in quite the opposite direction. What was once a barely remarked upon personal choice is now policed vigorously. In 2001, BBC World actually asked a guest, journalist Robert Fox, to remove his poppy on the grounds that the symbol wasn't recognised overseas. In 2020, it's rare to see anyone on British television during November without one.

Television celebrating Britain's military identity has proliferated in recent years. For example, over the course of a few far-from-untypical months in 2011, BBC channels offered up *The Spitfire: Britain's Flying Past*, *Young Soldiers*, *Sandhurst*, *Regimental Stories*, *The Bomb Squad*, *Our War*, *Entertaining the Troops* and *Harry's Arctic Heroes*. We've scrolled through seemingly endless minor variations on the theme of fearsome military training: from the BBC's *Special Forces – Ultimate Hell Week* to Channel 4's strikingly similar *SAS: Who Dares Wins*. We've even seen Z-list celebrities subjected to these brutally cathartic rites of passage – characters essentially constructed by one branch of reality TV being summarily deconstructed by another. Hardly any of this military fetishism is critical or even analytical – indeed, for it to be so would defy the point.

This is television about the creation and maintenance of national character. Its upper lip could hardly be stiffer. It's hard to escape the conclusion that poking around inside these value systems might uncover some uncomfortable truths.

What happens when television does pluck up the courage to enter the void at the heart of this frenzied, khaki-clad boosterism? The two decades since the turn of the century have produced few more prescient – or gloomy – television dramas than Channel 4's 2013 *Southcliffe*. When it came to exploring the murky depths of Britain's id, *Southcliffe*'s creator Tony Grisoni had form; in 2009, his adaptation of the first part of David Peace's *Red Riding* quartet summoned up the ghosts of 1970s Yorkshire to harrowing effect. This was a world in which claustrophobia reigned; power had corrupted everyone in its proximity; the police were no better than the criminals; and life was lived in a cancerous fug of cigarette smoke and casual violence. It reeked of small-town brutality, bad faith, bad sex and dead ends wherever you looked. 'This is the North,' went the ominous refrain from the bent coppers at the heart of the story, 'where we do what we want.' It was a narrative of closed loops, exploring isolation and the dysfunction that can result.

Southcliffe transposed that process to a different but strikingly congruent southern English milieu. The series began with a spree shooting in the fictional market town of the title. The actions of the shooter, Stephen Morton (portrayed by Sean Harris with an intimacy that was terrifying in the circumstances), spoke of an identity crisis writ catastrophically large. Morton's fatigues and unsparing severity suggested military training – and, possibly, traumatic experience – curdled into nihilistic blankness. He was known locally as 'The Commander' and presented himself as a former Special Forces soldier. He turned out to be simply a fantasist; an inadequate man drawn towards people who had lived the experiences he could only imagine. But you can't pick a new identity in a small town; reality will always catch up with you. This was a drama about enclosure, about never being able to escape the truth about yourself.

After suffering brutal humiliation at the hands of a couple of soldiers he befriends, Morton snaps. As the series begins, we see him looking after his disabled mother, cooking breakfast, and then taking to the early morning streets and shooting whoever he encounters. And yet, somehow, Morton's breakdown, and the carnage that ensued, wasn't the most horrific thing about *Southcliffe*. The way the serial unfolded, the prolonged, stunned aftermath of Morton's murders, encapsulated a much wider, deeper study of English neurosis. The ambience of small-town England is evoked to nightmarish effect. The visual grammar of *Southcliffe* suggested an anxiety dream. It was dingy, almost perpetually twilit. Cameras lingered uncomfortably and deliberately long on scenes of quotidian mundanity. A car parked on a muddy road outside a country pub. A deserted town square. A railway bridge recurred in the narrative, offering two different kinds of potential escape (one of which a character eventually takes). The landscape was endless but dull; flat and scrubby. Cookie-cutter suburban houses squatted under dank, grey skies. In the context of the mundane modernity of this setting, the army represented the only reflected glamour in town.

One masterstroke was Grisoni's use of Radio 4's *Shipping Forecast* at the bleakest moment; as the shooting began. Somehow this simple, unadorned weather report on Britain's coastal waters is embedded in the country's consciousness. There's something deeply melancholy about it; it evokes insomnia and the murky hinterland between sleep and wakefulness. It speaks of the empty early hours and also of our sense of scope, of borders, of Britain as an island, hemmed in by storms, self-absorbed and isolated. It can, at certain moments, feel like it's arrived from the subconscious, as if it's living within us all. It's a sad and beautiful abstract poem hymning our country's maritime past, our national sense of being and loss, our collective nostalgia.

Southcliffe's setting was a town full of nostalgics. It's a condition common to much of provincial England; after all, this is a country that has a lot of past to reckon with. The town of Southcliffe, it was clear, set considerable stall on honouring its veterans. But what does our military identity really mean now? The veneration of 'Our Boys' abroad has increased in direct proportion to the pointlessness and moral ambiguity of Britain's military entanglements. Since the beginning of the twenty-first century, via Iraq and Afghanistan, the ethics of Britain's conflicts have become ever harder to unpick and unpack. That isn't, of course, the fault of the soldiers themselves. But *Southcliffe* dramatised what can happen to British warrior identity when it runs out of meaningful places to go. It becomes simply a feeling, in and of itself – and questionable at best in the context of the modern world.

In his 2014 film *'71*, Yann Demange tells the story of a young British soldier lost in a hostile sector of Belfast at the height of the Troubles. The key to the film is the soldier's almost mute cluelessness; his lack of heroism and agency. He is a victim. He is scared and confused, at the mercy of the forces menacing him from all sides. He doesn't know why he's there. In fact, he doesn't even know whether he's Catholic or Protestant, a state of affairs almost literally unbelievable to the people he encounters. At one point, seriously injured by a bomb, he's sheltered by a Catholic man and his daughter. The man offers an unsparing verdict on the British army and their role in his city. 'Posh cunts telling thick cunts to kill poor cunts,' he says. 'That's the army for you. They don't care about you. You're just a piece of meat to them.' *Southcliffe* addressed the lengths we go to in order to soothe the cognitive dissonance created by the gap between the pageantry and valorisation of military life and the harsh realpolitik of what lies beneath. It dramatises what can happen when these obfuscations become unsustainable and the identity they engender becomes poisonous. There are huge gaping holes in the logic underpinning Britain's military fetishism. It often feels like an attempt to perpetuate myths about our place in the world that simply no longer make sense.

In *Southcliffe*, it takes the shootings to turn the spotlight onto this contested territory. Rory Kinnear's David Whitehead has escaped. He's left for London and become a successful news reporter. As a former local boy, he finds himself sent back to the town to cover the aftermath of the killings. It's an acute study in grief, but it's something more existentially resonant on a national scale too. What emerges is a prophetically discordant meeting of two different Englands; a snapshot of a polarised country that has lost the ability to comprehend and manage its own myths and internal divisions. Suddenly, Whitehead clearly understands misgivings he's had all his life. No one will talk because they've got nothing to say. This identity is guarded so jealously precisely because of its fragility. It isn't sturdy enough to bear any significant weight. It's a mirage. And in this absence of candour, the identity has become something ominous – a baleful ghost, one that lingers and haunts rather than nurtures or sustains. Infuriated at the town's emotional inarticulacy and closing of ranks, and dealing with submerged trauma of his own, Whitehead goes rogue. 'How come "good folk" didn't put two and two together?' he rails at a pub full of furious, bitter locals. 'Perhaps because "good folk" don't really give a shit. You asked for it. I'd have pulled the trigger myself.'

This was one of the era's most convincing depictions of the divide that would, three years later, be politically quantified by the result of the EU referendum. Two incompatible viewpoints meeting, both with grievances, both with certain justifications, neither quite sure who they are or what they're for. The two sides refuse to listen to each other, perhaps because neither is quite sure it can handle what the other is going to say. It's emotional austerity.

Of course, austerity – emotional or economic – is nothing new to huge swathes of twenty-first century Britain. 2015 was an ominous year, and a decisive one in recent history. Bookended by terrorist atrocities in Paris, and with a pivotal election at its heart, it seemed to represent a destination of sorts. This was where we had been heading. The election result, which saw the Conservatives handed a majority despite five years of devastating spending cuts in coalition with the Liberal Democrats, seemed as much as anything to represent a failure of imagination on behalf of both politicians and the people they represented. The electorate didn't express massive enthusiasm for the Cameron project. They simply seemed resigned to this new reality, to this continual winnowing away of the public realm and the indefinable sense of solidarity that went with it. However, the Conservative triumph also guaranteed 2016's EU referendum – which, as we were to discover, represented a generational and destructive challenge to this sense of stasis.

That September, Shane Meadows' drama *This Is England '90* arrived on Channel 4. It was the fourth and – at the time of writing – final instalment of a story that had begun in the early 1980s with a film following the fortunes of a group of friends as they attempted to negotiate their formative years in provincial, working-class England. It offered perspectives that were becoming rare in twenty-first century television. These were relatable, recognisable characters. They had drunken knee-tremblers in pub toilets. They gobbed on their chips so they wouldn't have to share them. They haggled over hilariously tiny lumps of hash. These were stories of identities; as they formed, as they were challenged and as they settled. Identities that reacted to the economics, politics and culture of the era. *This Is England* had begun, in its initial, cinematic incarnation, with the Falklands War, a conflict which cost isolated and unhappy pre-teen Shaun (Thomas Turgoose) his dad, and rescued Margaret Thatcher from the doldrums during her troubled first term as prime minister.

The opening credits of the final series are a highly evocative snap-shot of a year when, briefly, everything was in flux. The Poll Tax riots raged, and eventually Thatcher was deposed. There were new free-doms in the world's darker corners. There was a new kind of music and a new drug to go with it. *This Is England* always recognised the personal in the universal. Throughout its run, the series proved adept at capturing the putative attempts at identity formation encouraged by pop culture. There's a charmingly homemade quality to, for example, the provincial B-boy look adopted by Andrew Ellis's character Gadget in *This Is England '86*. It felt acutely reflective of an era before the internet became supercharged, spoon-feeding new developments in music, film and foreign-made high street fashion to successive generations. Back in 1986, to dress in a certain way took considerable effort, and to do so was to take a risk and make a statement. There is an understated but tangible sense of tribal rivalry running through the series; mods, skinheads, ravers, metallers, indie kids, goths, crusties and baggies all have their moments.

In the series (but arguably in a wider sense too), these transient but resonant pop cultural moments culminate in a field, on half a pill, standing at the doorway to a rave. This was Britain's last great youthquake, the last nationwide, tabloid-bothering line in the sand. What was the rave movement if not an attempt to merge – to engage with a lost collective identity? Briefly, it seemed to threaten the codified false barriers of both pop discourse and land owner- ship. That it so often happened in England's various leafy idylls added extra potency. It was youth culture at its purest and most utopian; an attempt to reclaim a slice of our birthright and to celebrate it with almost pagan intensity.

There's a wonderful, almost painterly shot of Kelly (Chanel Cresswell) and Gadget, the morning after the night before, gazing at the British countryside, at dawn, in early summer. What gives the shot – and rave in general – real piquancy was the proximity the scene often created between beauty and real danger. At times, it was akin to having one foot in heaven and another in hell. It felt like our last moment of true collective wildness; the unleashing of a certain latent power. The opening credits of the episode capture this giddy catharsis. People are gurning, sweating, losing their minds. These weren't prescribed entertainments, they were Temporary Autonomous Zones in which new rules were established; moments of radiant, benign lawlessness.

Like no pop cultural moment since, rave crossed boundaries of class, race and even generation. Shaun meets a much older woman at the rave – and they simply have a chat. Shaun talks about his dad and cries, unburdening himself to a friendly stranger. It's a lovely moment with a real ring of truth to it. Initially, ecstasy culture opened people up, blurred identity in an entirely positive way. It made people realise the amount of baggage they were carrying and understand that letting some of it go wouldn't hurt. It felt evolutionary, even rubbing off on Britain's football culture, that pernicious hotbed of toxic nationalism and morbid identity dysfunction. It was a moment of collective exhalation, a release from ego, a sigh of relief. Collectively, it was as close as we've come in recent years to discarding old notions of identity and establishing something new.

Pop feels more stratified and codified now. It doesn't interact with the wider culture as seriously as it once did. The concept of 'selling out' retained some currency back in 1990 – mainly because youth culture still regarded itself as an agent of potential subversion. Changes to the benefits system have made it harder for young working-class people to survive on a wing and a prayer for long enough to make music. Furthermore, because of the technology via which we now consume our music, we're led down reality tunnels, into echo chambers, towards algorithmic choices. *This Is England* often traded in nostalgia about our recent pop cultural past. It often filters back as sadness. It's tinged with melancholy, as the memory of lost euphoria often is, like a wasted opportunity. The promises of the era didn't actually go anywhere – other than back indoors.

Still, at least Thatcher was gone. It was fitting that the show climaxed in the year of her defenestration. Because Thatcher always hovered like a hidden, unseen character in *This Is England*. She'd been present throughout the series: in the death of Shaun's father, and in the privations she wrought on working-class England, which were a permanent backdrop to the drama as it progressed through the decade. But 2015 was a year in which a bitter truth about Thatcher became clear: she'd never stopped being prime minister. Really, 1990 – as volatile as it had seemed at the time – simply heralded the post-Thatcher Thatcher era. The 2015 election completed the loop and confirmed it. The era that began in 1990 ended in 2015.

The meaning and nature of community has changed. Our sense of identity is less collective. The ways in which we relate to our surroundings, our working lives and our respective places in the world have shifted. This is the process dramatised in *This Is England*. Crucially, it isn't explored in blunt political terms but as an ambient, background hum, a context in which foregrounded events play out. The narrative arc of Stephen Graham's Combo is central to this. We first meet him as a ferocious but brittle National Front-aligned skinhead who, in the original film, returns from prison to disrupt the mischievous but cheerful little gang helmed by Woody (Joe Gilgun). The gang have adopted Shaun; offered him respite from bullies and a sense of comradeship. But despite being mixed race himself, Combo enforces a different, bleaker notion of identity, centred around racism and violence. At the conclusion of the film he brutally beats the gang's only black member, Milky (Andrew Shim), almost to death. If *This Is England* is about anything, it's about belonging; to family, to friends, to lovers, to class, to region and, if all else fails, to country. Eventually, Combo's youthful, rage-fuelled identity crisis culminates in him being denied a second chance at belonging to anything.

Milky, it becomes clear, doesn't really belong either. At least, not by the end of the series. His racial identity is explored with great subtlety. He's entirely assimilated. He's Woody's best mate, despite having had an affair with Woody's soulmate Lol (Vicky McClure). In many ways, he's the heart and soul of the group. And in the end, it still isn't quite enough. His race is always there, even in his nickname. And when Combo returns, so does the othering of Milky. Because racism depersonalises, it can't ever be quite forgiven by its individual victims. After all, if someone has reduced a whole race of people to an undifferentiated mass then what right does one member of that group have to forgive them? It's one of the most unsparing explorations of racism ever seen on British television, all the more so for how much of it goes unspoken. Milky is the blameless original victim of Combo's fury and, as it turns out, the final one too. An almost fatal racist attack he suffered in his youth has been lurking in the background of the entire series. Eventually, as Milky seals Combo's fate, the revenge in which he's complicit leads to his alienation from his other white friends.

As both a physical and narrative presence, Combo is like dynamite. Meadows deploys him sparingly but devastatingly. His final scene is the dark heart of the series; the moment when his neuroses and the wider, more universal identity loss that has contributed to them dovetail. As he's dragged away – reformed but unforgiven, and presumably heading to his death at the hands of former far right henchmen – it feels like the end of not one but several brokendown, dead-end ideologies and value systems. Most obviously, there's Combo's journey through the grimmest iterations of identity politics. But there's wider resonance too, connected to the area depicted in the show, its sense of purpose and its relationship with the real world. Shortly after the 2015 election, the writer and anthropologist David Graeber told the *Guardian*: 'the historical defeat of the working classes has now become the UK's export product'.[63]

This defeat is what makes Britain investible: it's a safe place to put money. The nature of the defeat has more to do with lost political agency than decreasing financial heft. Thanks to the decline of industry and the trade union movement and the centralising, metropolitan nature of politics, working-class Britain has been divided and conquered. It's about a loss of identity: what happens to places and people who no longer understand quite who they are, what they are for and how they can take back control of their lives?

Combo's final scene was filmed at the old ice factory in Grimsby. As represented in *This Is England '90*, it's a post-industrial, almost post-apocalyptic hellhole. But the building was once central to the town's fishing industry – which in turn, was central to the town's economy and identity. It ceased operations, with perfect poetic symmetry, in 1990. In a 2018 investigation into the town's economic prospects, the *Guardian* described the ice factory as

> a marvel of engineering when it opened. However . . . it has now become a looming example of the trouble with heritage. The structure has its own dedicated trust that campaigns for its future, and the machinery inside is Grade-I listed, but that hasn't stopped a layer of rust, algae and pigeon excrement from covering its once-cherished interior.[64]

The building has become a living metaphor. This was England. Our past is everywhere, from *Downton Abbey* to the Grimsby ice factory, bullying us with its alternately gussied-up and broken-down glory. Our past is a film set but reality continues to edge into the picture. We now use physical symbols of that past to commemorate and memorialise identities we used to have but have subsequently lost. More recent history it may be, but *This Is England '90* isn't any less a period drama than *Downton Abbey*. And it isn't only country house fables that illuminate the era in which they're made.

There are, of course, multiple, submerged versions of Britain's past. Much as the past is habitually tidied up, its lack of neatness is sometimes its greatest attraction. Often, it can support an optimistic, even revolutionary narrative, hinting at a nation comfortable with a greater degree of flux and turmoil than is usually acknowledged in modern myth-making. Dotted around Britain's small-screen history are surprisingly numerous uncanny diversions: psychedelic mushrooms sprouting on an otherwise obsessively tended lawn; programmes that remind us of our singular, underlying oddness. It's an oddness we should be happier to embrace.

Amid the grotesquerie of BBC Two's *The League of Gentlemen*, with its exploding pets, homicidal clerical workers and general small-town barbarism, it's easy to forget the sheer strangeness of the ambience it conjured. This was a Britain that, in glorious isolation, made its own rules. And yet a big part of the show's appeal was the familiarity: not literal of course, but certainly atmospheric. Who hasn't felt momentarily unnerved by encountering a world simultaneously full of recognisable archetypes yet seemingly operating according to its own inexplicable internal logic? Who hasn't pondered the weirdness lurking behind the closed doors of small towns? *The League of Gentlemen* imagined lifting up the rock and then dramatised what might be scurrying around underneath. The show appeared to be a freaky singularity when it arrived on our screens in 1999, but it was actually a harbinger; the comedy wing of a spasmodic but eventually insistent wave of television celebrating darkly eccentric Britishness.

Cultural archaeology has been a feature of the post-2000 era. There's been a flurry of documentaries, piecing together our past in fragmentary, non-linear ways, aiming to locate emotional truth rather than construct literal narrative. Paul Wright's spellbinding 2017 *Arcadia* used startling editing to shape footage from the BFI's vast archive into an expressionist collage interrogating our relationship with the land. It invoked an irrepressible British mystic tradition; a line running from ancient rural folk ritual through to rave. It explored a constant push and pull between elemental and rationalised forces; the battle to maintain wildness and reverence for nature in the face of the flattening effects of industry, urbanisation and consumerism.

Urban Britain's folk history also got its dues. In 2013, Martin Kelly and the band Saint Etienne created *How We Used to Live*. Depicting a journey through post-war London, a wilder, grubbier, emptier and more romantic place than anything its current inhabitants might recognise, the film captured the city during a liminal period: vibrant and self-confident but poised between two eras. The state paternalism of the post-1945 settlement was still freshly minted – this was a city and a nation yet to succumb to the blandishments and coercions of Thatcherism.

Meanwhile, Jarvis Cocker and Martin Wallace's *The Big Melt: How Steel Made Us Hard* presented remarkable footage of Sheffield's heavy metal heyday. Although a documentary, it lent the industry an occult quality; the vats of white-hot metal bubbled like witches' cauldrons, suggesting their realm contained truths that, from our current vantage point, we can never fully comprehend. The lineage of working-class potency was strong; to work in steel production was to engage in routine risk-taking. This stuff was properly dangerous, and therefore, it's implied, properly character-building too. These films were celebrating identities hewn from life's most tangible and essential foundations, but are presented with a hint of reproach in their twenty-first century context; as reminders of previously sturdy facets of Britain in abeyance and decline.

The period has also seen renewed recognition for two unruly off-spring of 1970s television, both of which hurled themselves into deep history, returning with something untimely, but also oddly timeless. Jeremy Burnham and Trevor Ray's 1977 ITV series *Children of the Stones* was the subject of a radio documentary by comedian Stewart Lee. Surely the most complex and unsettling serial ever aimed at children, it mapped the adventures of an astrophysics professor and his son after they move into a village with a megalithic stone circle at its heart. Alan Clarke's BBC drama *Penda's Fen* was more remarkable still; it finally caught its moment in 2016, achieving a DVD release and a proper level of appreciation, having presumably loitered, semi-submerged, in the subconscious of everyone who encountered it back in 1974. On one level, it worked as a coming-out and coming of age story. But it was also an audacious, hallucinogenic journey through class politics, folk ritual, ecological awareness and paganism.

But why now? Was there a reason why these murkily expansive visions and lost utopias suddenly seemed so fascinating in the twenty-first century? After all, it wasn't only happening in TV: films like Ben Wheatley's 2013 Civil War freak-out *A Field in England* explored similar terrain, and there was a resurgence of interest in traditional roots music with the likes of Lisa Knapp and Alasdair Roberts reviving and refitting ancient texts. Rob Young's dazzling 2011 book *Electric Eden* located a sense of continuity that connected Britain's folk history with its resurgent present. The implicit connection between rave culture and folk ritual was explored by techno producer James Holden on his 2017 album *The Animal Spirits*. There was a double level of nostalgia at work: certainly a sense that we were living in more cautious and constrained times (*Children of the Stones* must surely have blown the minds of the vast majority of the 70s kids who encountered it; any modern equivalent would almost certainly be subjected to destructive levels of interference). But they also spoke to a gathering confusion about national identity in general. Who were we? Were we industrial pioneers or city slickers? Deracinated suburbanites or rural mystics? Did our deep, wide history constrain us or liberate us? Were we destroying our past? And were any of these visions compatible with each other? These works were largely telling us who we were not, rather than who we were. But still, we clearly longed for our own version of their earthy atavism.

Sky Atlantic offered a slicker, yet somehow madder, version of ancient British history in 2018. Its big-budget epic *Britannia* told the story of the Romans' arrival in Britain in AD 43, touting straight roads and assumptions of cultural superiority only to be confronted by stinking, babbling seers and warrior queens who threatened to pluck out their eyes and eat them. It was an entertaining misfire, and yet it did complete an unlikely circle. Could Mackenzie Crook be the era's unlikely TV avatar of British identity? In *Britannia*, he appears as terrifyingly enigmatic head druid Veran. He's the embodiment of ancient Britannia unchained: savage, semi-feral, frequently disappearing into trances and returning with unearthly insights dragged from the ether. Veran was the best thing about *Britannia* and certainly a long way from Gareth Keenan, Crook's infuriating yet strangely sympathetic admin-monkey in *The Office*.

Keenan was the epitome of dismal, impotent, twenty-first century white-collar servitude: working in a paper merchant's in Slough, pretending he was in the army, indulging in joyless banter and complaining about people stealing his stapler.

And yet Crook somehow located a midpoint between these two extremes. In fact, he was responsible for the most charming, subtle and uplifting small-screen expression of British identity in recent memory. During an interview with the *New Statesman* around the time of the final series of his understated but gently rapturous BBC4 comedy *Detectorists*, Crook was asked if he believed in ghosts. 'I love the idea of them,' he replied. 'Voices from the past, calling to us.'[65] In *Detectorists*, Crook's Andy Stone spent his life dreaming of finding something that *Britannia*'s Veran had tossed away.

Detectorists crept up on viewers gradually. A series that seemed at first to be gently comic eventually turned out to be truly profound. Since 2000, much TV comedy has traded in snark at best and outright cruelty at worst. Ironically, this trend probably first hit mainstream paydirt thanks to *The Office*. In this context, if people like Andy and his comrade in metal detecting, Lance (Toby Jones) are ever seen on television at all, they're likely to be the butt of the joke. Eccentrics if they're lucky, but sometimes just losers. In terms of both performance and writing, it takes real skill, grace and lightness of touch to imbue such characters with this kind of modest yet discernable heroism.

Detectorists mines bathos as unerringly as Lance mines discarded ring pulls and scaffolding brackets. The pair work in unsatisfying jobs and live in small, boxy estate houses (Andy dreams, touchingly, of owning a shed). They frequently baffle and infuriate their nearest and dearest. And yet Andy and Lance are content. They're surprisingly self-aware. They deal, as best they can, with their emotions. They're self-deprecating and have a good handle on their own capacity for absurdity. They know who they are (and who they are not) and are fine with it. And they understand why they do what they do. There's the generally illusory hope of finding something valuable. There's the chance to sit under a tree with your best mate and eat Scotch eggs while discussing last night's *University Challenge*. But most of all, there's time travel.

'Metal detecting is time travel,' explains Lance in the final episode. 'We unearth the scattered memories, mine the stories, fill in the personalities.' This mini-manifesto, delivered entirely without pretension or pomposity, but rather as a statement of self-evident fact, is the moment the whole series has been building towards. There's a startling sequence early in season three where Lance digs up an old falconer's whistle and Andy dusts it off and gives it a blow. In doing so, he summons eternity – and just as he and Andy were about to head to the pub, too. 'Magpie', a song by folk sisters The Unthanks, plays. The field warps, the trees billow in the wind, snow falls, and a pagan ritual takes place. The soil is churned; seeds are sown and harvested. The life of the land, its past, present and future, opens up in all its confounding glory. This grandeur is all around us if, like Lance and Andy, we're willing to use our imaginations. They understand that life is only as mundane as you allow it to be. Something bigger, more dazzling and infinite is always closer at hand than we realise. It's lurking in your peripheral vision if you'll let yourself see it. This is the real treasure the pair are seeking – and they find it every time they venture out together. Lance and Andy never seem bitter or thwarted or denied, because their Gold Dance is still in front of them; theirs for the taking.

Detectorists is the absolute polar opposite of most recent expressions of British identity. In every sense, it's about hidden depths. It's antithetical to pomp and circumstance; to puffery and bullshit; to empty bombast. To a casual observer, *Detectorists* could appear modest, but it contains multitudes. It's inclusive and generous in spirit; Andy and Lance long for more people to see the value of what they can see. They live firmly in the present – albeit sometimes reluctantly. They simply understand that the past is closer and more accessible than we think. And it's entirely devoid of gratuitous conflict or confrontation: Andy and Lance are powered by love – for the land, for nature, for their families and for each other. *Detectorists* crystallises our recent tendency towards cultural archaeology and answers many of the questions it poses. It's about an urge to escape, downwards into buried history and backwards into the past, in the hope of finding something that might sustain us in the context of the present.

In celebrating the British folk tradition, the show has surely become a part of it. *Detectorists* deserves to be seen as belonging to a lineage which also includes the songs of Nick Drake and the poetry of William Blake. In fact, it's Blake's 'heaven in a wild flower' rendered in the form of a sitcom. It doesn't ask anyone to buy into idealised or imaginary virtues. It simply appreciates and celebrates – deeply, movingly and profoundly – the virtues we already have.

As British public life has grown more fractious and toxic, there have been signs of a longing for symbols of community and functionality. *Detectorists* was a prime example of this – one possible reason for the devotion it generated was its sense of quiet, stoical tolerance. Danny Boyle's 2012 Olympics opening ceremony also touched this particular nerve, appealing to our better natures by reminding us that Britain could, if it chose, tap into sources of national identity that were politically and culturally unifying rather than divisive. There's also been a flood of factual programming celebrating versions of communally based identity that we all share. Channel 4's shows *One Born Every Minute* and *24 Hours in A&E* venture into public hospitals and emerge with alternately heartbreaking and uplifting stories of loss, compassion, redemption and heroism. They are, essentially, television about the social contract. The wonder of the NHS is that it gives us all a stake in the outcomes it achieves, and some semblance of pride in the process. These shows document what that means in practice.

Accordingly, they act as social glue. They show us where our tax money goes and defy us not to feel proud of it. We watch them and are reminded of our own experiences: the time we broke our arm in a drunken accident, the day our first child was born, the night our dad died. They're universalising, and yet they foreground the individuals within this huge, noble project. They imply something positive about our relationships with each other. In our moments of most extreme need, we still have each other's backs. As easy as it is to be cynical about the relentless emotional button-pushing – not to mention the laziness of the commissioning processes involved – these are remarkably benign offerings in the context of prime-time entertainment. Like the *Educating . . .* reality strand, which is set in various state schools across the country and celebrates the efforts of both teachers and children as they struggle with the knotty business of offering and receiving a decent education, these shows are celebrations of kindness, community and people doing their best for others in trying circumstances. Their popularity hints at a profound yearning for a more modest but uplifting national story.

This chapter has explored national identity via myths and their relationship with reality. Sometimes, as we've seen, the fictions and the truths have become catastrophically intertwined. They've been used to confuse rather than illuminate. This process culminated in both the form and the substance of Channel 4's 2019 *Brexit: The Uncivil War*. During the early stages, Dominic Cummings (Benedict Cumberbatch) is plotting Vote Leave's campaign strategy. He's looking for an animating theme, a still, central, consensual point around which his mendacious narrative can be constructed. Eventually, he writes the letters 'NHS' at the centre of his white-board. Paradoxically – and tragically – it was precisely because the NHS pushes our buttons to such an extent that its preservation could be misleadingly weaponised in the service of a right-wing coup.

Brexit: The Uncivil War was a controversial gambit. Was it really a good idea to turn such sensitive recent events into a TV comedy-drama, when they were still unresolved, still pregnant with the potential to cause national tragedy? And how could such a show possibly hope to reflect the questions related to electoral malpractice – questions that remain contested to this day – without overtly taking sides? In terms of the latter issue, the drama solved the problem by ignoring it altogether, apart from a box-ticking caption just before the end credits. In terms of the former, well, probably not. The tone was always going to be impossible to get right and predictably, writer James Graham struggled. Still, he struggled in a way that, at least in terms of illustrating British television's response to crisis, was illuminating. In its own flawed way, *Brexit: The Uncivil War* told us plenty about how we came to be where we are.

There's hardly anything that British television writers can't reduce to the status of jolly japery. Not even a referendum which has divided the country, undermined its political system and threatens to impoverish it for many years. Those lovable rascals Nigel Farage and Arron Banks were written and played as blustering, faintly comical blowhards. Which, of course, they are – though, crucially, that's not all they are. But for Graham to fully acknowledge the cynicism at the heart of their campaign would have taken the drama into the kind of dark waters that would have jarred with the rest of the action. Meanwhile, the fact that Cummings, the ruthless strategist at the heart of Vote Leave, was portrayed by national-treasure-in-waiting Benedict Cumberbatch was problematic in itself. Cumberbatch lent him a degree of vulnerability and vision which seemed frankly ill-deserved. Happier memories of Cumberbatch's nuanced and eventually heartbreaking portrayal of actual British hero Alan Turing hovered over the part, endowing Cummings with a legitimacy that he arguably doesn't deserve. Indeed, the political meltdown of autumn 2019 brought Cummings – who by now was prime minister Boris Johnson's provocative sidekick in constitutional mayhem – uncomfortably into the light, revealing exactly the kind of character Cumberbatch was endowing with such vision and insight.

Still, a drama without a sympathetic lead is a tough sell. So, in the interests of narrative convenience, Cummings was tentatively humanised. It's a tougher sell still if there aren't any laughs. Accordingly, Brexit became The Great British Mishap: A Very British Constitutional Crisis. In January 2019, at around the time the drama was broadcast, *The Times* greeted one of Theresa May's many humiliations at the hands of her restless party with the headline 'A Very British Coup'. It was hard not to wonder if there was any situation, however grave or chaotic, that couldn't be subjected to Britain's tendency towards cloying, twee exceptionalism. Even the drama re-enacting the farce as it continued to unfold wasn't immune.

If its portrayal of the main players was flawed, *Brexit: The Uncivil War* did a more illuminating job of exploring the ground war. 'Britain makes a sound,' says Cummings, early in the piece. 'It groans. It's been groaning for some time.' There's a narrative of thwarted heroism and lost grandeur around the impulse towards Brexit; a sense that a generation wanted their own war. For that reason, predictions of economic chaos tend to wash over true Brexit believers. There's sometimes a sense that the possibility is regarded, in theory at least, as being a price worth paying. But for what? The television discussed in this chapter has, to a considerable extent, been about identity loss. From the idealised, prettified vision of *Downton Abbey* to the suffocating air of decline surrounding *Southcliffe* and *This Is England*, it's explored ways in which television has documented and dramatised a certain loss of agency, mighty Britannia brought low.

Brexit enabled the construction of a weird Frankenstein's monster of ersatz Britishness, built from idealised wartime stoicism, born-to-rule upper-class entitlement and sturdy working-class fortitude. Brexit suddenly made Britain matter again. And even if it mattered only as a vivid symbol of dysfunction, populism and barely suppressed nativism, that seems to count for something. During *Brexit: The Uncivil War*, there's a striking moment in a focus group convened by the official Remain campaign. The group is demographically mixed: urban and provincial, black and white, young and old. A middle-aged woman feels besieged by a couple of the Remain-inclined participants and snaps. 'I'm sick of feeling like I'm nothing.' This was Leave psychology in excelsis; Leave as an emotional reaction. It wasn't necessarily rational – in fact, it was all the more heartfelt for being half-formed.

Cummings has a lightbulb moment while pondering Vote Leave's original campaign slogan 'Take Control'. He realises that there's a key word missing from the sentence. That word is 'Back'. Brexit is its own stunted, illusory version of time travel. Unlike *Detectorists*, it doesn't seek gold or indeed, any physical traces of the past at all. It seeks something more nebulous. It seeks a feeling – possibly one that never existed. It's striking how often 'the spirit of the Blitz' and 'the spirit of Dunkirk' are invoked by adherents. It's nostalgia for a past that is considered only as a set of signifiers – the war, empire, economic and industrial pre-eminence. When Britain really was Britain. When it didn't apologise for itself but did whatever it pleased. For the purposes of the people fighting this battle, the enemy of this ideal turned out to be the European Union. But really, its identity, as Cummings realised, was irrelevant. 'Europe just becomes a symbol,' he explained. 'A cipher for every bad thing that's happened.'

Britain is in thrall to its history, but only selectively. The scorched-earth economics of the Thatcher years disconnected us from each other, did serious damage to our collective histories; our notions of community and continuity. But they did allow certain idealised facets of identity to remain intact; facets that pacified, that nurtured passivity and disdained subversion. Thatcherism decimated British industry, but it left residual traces of its identity for Thatcherites like Nigel Farage to reanimate as pure grievance when the need arose. We struggle with a sort of temporal parochialism – because of our almost blind faith in the iconography of recent British history, we find it impossible to believe it might let us down. We still hang on to the idea that chaos or fascism or economic collapse 'couldn't happen here'.

But, ironically and counter-intuitively, it now seems entirely possible that this faith in continuity might itself create flux, destructive change and an overturning of many of the timeless homilies idealised in our national tropes. Thanks to our longing for things we perceive ourselves to have lost, discontinuity may well win the day. Our yearning for self-assertion could result in deeper humiliation – after all, what was Theresa May's rejected Withdrawal Agreement, if not a formal expression of the new balance of power between a powerful trading bloc and a former member who has stormed off in a sulk? That's why Brexit true believers loathed it – it was a manifestation of what happens when dreams come face to face with reality. In this context, the tone of *Brexit: The Uncivil War* seemed absurd – it felt like a self-fulfilling prophecy, managing to treat a deeply serious situation with the complacent, jocular levity that had partly caused the situation to arise in the first place.

Brexit is a cautionary tale. It's what happens to a country that allows myth to override reality. When it won't deal with the present and instead takes refuge in the past. When it prefers easy solutions presented by chancers to complex ones suggested by experts. Part of the fictionalised Dominic Cummings' strategy was to tap into 'little wells, pockets of resentment', irritations that had lain semi-dormant for years waiting for expression. His Remain counterpart Craig Oliver (Rory Kinnear) also acknowledged as much. 'Their campaign began twenty years ago, maybe more. The slow drip of hate and fear.' Craig Oliver, however, was David Cameron's director of communications before the referendum. And this hints at a problem. On screen as in reality, his side didn't have any answers either. In fact, not altogether unfairly, they were presented as part of the problem. Brexit was the wrong answer to the right question. However misguided, Brexit was an insurgency. An insurgency orchestrated by charlatans, but still powered by deeply felt grievance at the existing order of things.

This is the problem faced by the country and so, inevitably, by those wishing to represent it in art, in literature and on television. Our familiar signifiers of identity have ceased to feel like answers and started to feel like millstones; they aren't helping us to understand ourselves any more. Truisms have become clichés. National identities aren't fixed – in fact, in a healthy society, they're in a state of constant, evolutionary flux. There have been some promising signs. The dead-end, *Downton Abbey*, Deep England aesthetic was effectively exploited by David Cameron but it probably culminated – and curdled for good – in Theresa May's boundlessly peculiar 2017 general election campaign. What were May's now-legendary anecdote about running through a wheat field as a child, or her discussion of 'boy jobs and girl jobs', if not a cynical branding exercise, calibrated to appeal to notions of twee, olde Englishness, casting May as the apple-cheeked golden child of some imagined prelapsarian idyll? It was cultural and political kitsch; an attempt to drag us back to a past that only exists on commemorative plates displayed on pensioners' mantelpieces. And, happily, it tanked. New iterations of Britishness are available, and they are emerging in outline. But the old ones need to move aside first. Maybe it's time to throw out the bunting, knock down the country house, turn the post-industrial wreckage into affordable housing and start to live in the present.

EPILOGUE

CRADLE TO GRAVE

63 Up · Gogglebox · Doctor Who · Killing Eve
Years and Years

EVERY NOW AND THEN, you meet someone who will tell you, often with a certain performative relish, that they don't watch television. To which the only reasonable response is surely: why ever not? Dismissing television as a medium on the basis of its worst offerings is a bizarrely absolutist and self-defeating position to take, like insisting that music as an art form is fatally compromised by the existence of advertising jingles. It's also out of date. Television has grown exponentially in heft since 2000. In addition to what it tells us about the times in which we live, television at its best can be as sublime and elevating as any other artistic activity – there's a good argument to be made, for example, that David Simon and Ed Burns' Baltimore municipal saga *The Wire* is the most complex, emotionally involving and perfectly realised artistic statement of the twenty-first century to date. Like any other art form, television is as substantial and as meaningful as its creators are willing to try and make it. Some television has reached levels of immersive intricacy more readily associated with cinema or literature. But great television can also work thanks to its heartfelt and earnest simplicity; it can be nurturing and sustaining.

In June 2019, the latest instalment of Michael Apted's astonishing *Up* documentary series premiered on ITV. Apted's project, to follow fourteen children through their lives from the age of seven, began in 1964. They were born at the height of the post-war baby boom – and also at the dawn of the TV age. Apted has since had a successful career as a movie director, and *Up* has transferred from ITV to BBC and then back again. It has lost participants over the years and regained them too. In the best way possible, *Up* feels like a relic of an older kind of television: it is mainly just people sitting and talking. It's the ultimate in reality TV, but there is no competitive or eliminative element. No one's idiosyncrasies are being mined for laughs or scandal or taken out of context for the creation of potentially shareable viral content. The programme makers know better than that. Instead Apted has formed a lifelong relationship with these people based on trust. And, therefore, so have we.

Through the simple expedient of asking gently probing questions and letting participants answer them in their own way, the show sheds light on character, mortality, mental illness, the class system, gender inequality and much more besides. More than that, though, it demonstrates the often unsung heroism underpinning many apparently ordinary lives – and illuminates the inescapable fact that everyone, however apparently average, has a story to tell. 'I wake up every morning,' said Neil Hughes, a participant who has suffered more slings and arrows than most, 'and I really don't know what's going to happen.' This ambiguous statement gets to the heart of the show, because it gets to the heart of life; no situation is ever as predictable or intractable as it seems.

To watch *63 Up* was to engage in a form of national group therapy. Black and white footage of East End scamp Tony Walker running through his school playground in 1964 was intercut with film of him jogging through a wood in Essex in his later years. Although more than half a century had passed, this was palpably the same person; the same coiled gait, the same earnest sense of purpose and absorption. There's something about *Up* that boils its participants down to their essence. And in doing so, it can't help but have a similar effect on viewers. How much time do we really spend thinking about the span of our lives, what they have meant, where they still might go? *Up* forces us to take stock; to reckon with the passing of time. It is true public service broadcasting, stimulating meaningful contemplation, prompting self-recognition, exploring sadness and loss, but balancing those emotions with sources of encouragement and redemption. It's interactive entertainment in the truest possible sense, and one of television's crowning glories. It's helpful, too, in the context of our current national confusion, offering a through line back to a shared past; a sense of resilience in the face of change.

It probably didn't feel like it at the start, but – like the work of that other totem of British television's exploratory baby steps, David Attenborough – *Up* has become a symbol of the medium's potential and possibilities. 'Give me the child until he is seven,' says the Jesuit motto underpinning the series, 'and I will give you the man.' This doesn't speak only to the evolution of *Up*'s participants. It feels relevant to the development of television as a whole. The *Up* series was, at its inception, the beginning of a wave of high-minded, self-consciously serious and genuinely ambitious epics of factual TV. The scope of the medium was also being explored by the likes of the BBC's *Man Alive* documentary strand, Kenneth Clark's art history *Civilisation* and Jacob Bronowski's celebrated survey of human thought, *The Ascent of Man*.

It's something of a received wisdom to compare modern television unfavourably with these canonical offerings. But it's also unfair. There is, of course, more bad television around now – because there is simply more television. And yet all is not lost. Over the past two decades, there's been much talk of declining human attention spans as a result of mobile technology. The science on the subject is hotly debated and inconclusive, but in any case, it's quite possible to argue that television has bucked any such trend. In 2008, the creator of *The Wire*, David Simon, was interviewed by Lauren Laverne on BBC Two's *The Culture Show*. Laverne asked him if the narratives of his shows were too complex and ambitious to attract casual viewers. 'Fuck the casual viewer,' he replied. 'Seriously, who wants a casual viewer? If you're a writer, do you want a casual viewer? I don't want those people.' Whether this was unspeakably arrogant or admirably blunt, there was an undeniable truth underpinning Simon's statement. Modern television viewers will commit to seriousness, to the pleasures of the slow burn. They enjoy being trusted and are willing to submit to delayed gratification.

Although they originated on high-end American pay-per-view channel HBO, the success of 2000s epics like *The Wire* and *The Sopranos* had a knock-on effect. They created a new space for genuinely ambitious television storytelling – so when free-to-air British television challenges viewers, the challenge is frequently accepted. Witness the success of Jed Mercurio's labyrinthine police corruption

THE AGE OF STATIC

procedural *Line of Duty* – or the same writer's *Bodyguard*, which only displeased viewers when it started to lean too far towards the action-packed conventions of the thriller. There remains a clear and enduring pleasure in the communal viewing experience; as anyone who has been in an office the morning after the climactic episode of a Jed Mercurio drama will attest, Simon's disdain for casual viewers has led not to elitist snobbery, but to the normalisation of narrative complexity.

The remarkable success of Channel 4's *Gogglebox* – a show in which viewers watch other viewers watching television – suggests that we continue to take pleasure in even an ersatz shared watching experience. As much as they seem to belong to different worlds, the *Up* series has underpinned the formation of the sort of collective viewing culture that culminates in a show like *Gogglebox*. *Up* represented part of a national tradition at its moment of formation; *Gogglebox* is a celebration and an affirmation of it. Do we risk losing this kind of shared small-screen experience?

Over the past twenty years, there's been a sense that television has, at times, been a symptom of systemic polarisation, as well as a communal hearth around which we can gather. Its attempts to adapt to technological change and embrace of the dogma of choice has often had the paradoxical effect of limiting what was universally available. As has been the case in other public services, so-called progress has led to rationing and scarcity. Televised sport is a perfect example. Boxing, which as recently as the late 1990s used to fill pubs with cheerfully antagonistic fight fans, is now largely relegated to a pay-per-view backwater. World title fights are now often mythical, mysterious happenings; largely unseen by the masses, reported on next day's news through the ironically arcane medium of still photographs, taking place in the small hours of the morning at the behest of broadcasters in America. In football, free-to-air coverage of Europe's most prestigious club tournament, the Champions League, was first reduced to an hour of highlights per week, and eventually dragged behind a paywall in its entirety. And cricket, a sport whose playing hours and duration makes pub-bound consumption both unwise and impractical, disappeared from free-to-air television in 2006 after a series between England and Australia the previous summer that had enthralled and united the nation.

What has followed has the appearance of a test case demonstrating the risks inherent in monetising your existing audience, rather than nurturing your product: if you don't bring the next generation on board, you risk sacrificing long-term sustainability in the interests of short-term profit. Notwithstanding England's 2019 World Cup triumph, the final of which eventually found its way on to Channel 4, a sense of cricket's slow dwindling for want of exposure is ever more apparent – tumbling participation numbers and an increasing lack of recognition of the English game's big names are becoming chronic problems. The game's rulers are beginning to find out that a sport as rarefied as Test cricket can't hope to thrive – or even maintain a foothold in the nation's consciousness – if potential converts from across all areas of society can no longer stumble across it in the great, dull expanse of summer daytime TV schedules. With alarming speed, cricket is becoming the sole preserve of public schoolboys and well-to-do over-forties. And, as 'Crown Jewel' sporting events continue to disappear from free-to-air television, the centrality of the terrestrial channels becomes further weakened. Free-to-air television needs sport, and sport needs free-to-air television. Indeed, that same summer, the Women's Football

World Cup benefited hugely from exposure on the BBC, with 11.7 million people watching England's semi-final against the USA.

The television fate of cricket might seem a niche concern. But it's not without wider resonance. Wherever you look, previously communal events have been privatised. Could something similar happen to TV drama? In the early years of the century, BBC Four developed a reputation for acquiring interesting drama and comedy imports. Utilising the freedom that came from being a small channel with a brief to explore the marginal, it took a punt on an American drama about the machinations of drunken, womanising advertising executives in 1960s New York. *Mad Men* established an audience and a reputation on the channel, before satellite broadcaster Sky swooped in with their comparatively tiny audience share but extremely deep pockets. A similar fate befell offbeat musical comedy *Flight of the Conchords*. A pattern emerged. BBC Four would test the water, before Sky (who have subsequently cut out the middleman by simply buying up HBO) stepped in with the big bucks.

Apart from the occasional subtitled detective series, BBC Four's drama output has withered since its late-2000s heyday. It now concentrates on historical and music documentaries and the occasional sitcom. Sky's ability to effectively use BBC Four as a talent scout was short-lived – soon Netflix arrived on the scene offering more refined but more circumscribed choice still. The digital footprint of Netflix is vast, but the shows nudged in the direction of individual viewers are digitally tailored. Your choices are making your next choices for you. But how healthy is it to only ever be exposed to what previous viewing habits suggest you will enjoy? The notion of television as a communal clearing house is being replaced by confirmation; a refined, ever-narrowing targeting. As will be the case with the stark class and generational divides evident today, the effects of changes like these will become clearer over time. But the sense is growing that, as a society, we are increasingly fragmented – and therefore struggling to understand each other.

In 2006, the BBC cancelled *Top of The Pops*. Anachronistic as the show might have become in the context of a music industry undergoing technological transformation, it did still provide a valuable function: it was where we all came to agree or disagree about pop culture. Can there be anyone of a certain age who doesn't have a seminal musical moment – a sense of doors opening and horizons expanding – connected to the show? Whether it was David Bowie, Kate Bush or Nirvana, what defined *TOTP*'s importance was that viewers were ambushed, on a weekly basis, by the thrillingly unfamiliar. The show offered glimpses of possibility; routes into different worlds. And crucially, you, the viewer, weren't choosing. These transformative visions were being bestowed upon you, but the most important factor was the awkwardness of the juxtapositions within the show. In conversation with journalist James O'Brien on his Amazon Prime show *Full Disclosure*, actor Steve Coogan talked about the 'cultural balanced diet' presented by the BBC during his formative years. Constructive tension was created; you weren't just being shown what you liked, you were being confronted with what other people valued too. Even if you decided to define yourself against that consensus, it was still a form of self-definition based on an awareness of the breadth and nature of the alternatives. That isn't how popular culture works now. Algorithms do much of the heavy lifting these days – but, by definition, algorithms aren't going to drag you out of your comfort zone.

If there's a single psychological phenomenon that describes the last few years of British political life, it's mutual incomprehension.

Politically, culturally and socially, we are all settled in our bespoke comfort zones now, and extracting us may not be easy, or even possible. It's in this context that the battle for public service television will be fought. There's an argument that the very concept of public service television is anachronistic, redolent of post-war paternalism, the elite taking it upon itself to impose a particular vision upon the masses. As we've seen, the BBC's independence is a constantly contested and debatable topic. The 2019 decision to scrap universally available free TV licences for the over-75s feels like the latest step in a gradual but systematic process of undermining. Eventually, it may be that the concept of public service broadcasting will run out of people willing to defend it.

According to Ofcom figures published in 2018, 16–34-year-olds consume less than half as much BBC output as the national average. The BBC needs to curate its next generation of supporters, but the young often don't seem to be a priority to the Beeb – youth channel BBC Three became an exclusively online concern in 2016, and aside from the comprehensive annual Glastonbury Festival coverage – which, in 2019, gave some long-overdue BBC airtime to the likes of Stormzy and Billie Eilish – there is almost no music, or indeed, youth cultural representation at all, on BBC television now. It's as if the BBC has accepted defeat in certain demographic areas; surrendered the ground to insurgent platforms like YouTube and Netflix. Ofcom also reported that as of early 2018 there were more subscribers to Netflix, Amazon and Now TV than to 'pay TV' services from Sky, Virgin Media, BT and TalkTalk. These customers are still, of course, dwarfed in number by the holders of TV licences. But that hardly seems like grounds for complacency – between 2013 and 2017, 3.5 million UK residents cancelled their TV licences.

There are two ways of looking at the licence fee. On the one hand, it's inarguably a regressive tax. Everyone is charged the same, regardless of their ability to pay and regardless of how well served they feel by the Corporation's output. A more idealistic and perhaps rose-tinted version of the story is that the licence fee is a contract; an agreement between the nation's broadcaster and its public. When judged across the whole of its output – from the radio to the website to the iPlayer to the local services – the BBC remains remarkably good value. But that's mainly thanks to the creatives working miracles on tight budgets, and hardly at all due to the endless layers of management.

The Netflix model of television is still in its infancy, and its ability to endure is far from guaranteed. The company has grown prodigiously in terms of reach. And yet it's still oddly amorphous and lacking in identity. In terms of quality, its hit rate is low: often, its strategy seems to involve churning out as many programmes as possible – in formats ranging from drama to comedy to reality – and seeing what sticks. Huge chunks of Netflix's bandwidth remain the province of old films, material from American broadcast channels and content acquired from the BBC and Channel 4. But this looks set to change: the BBC and ITV have amalgamated chunks of their archive on a streaming platform called BritBox, while Disney and NBC/Universal will shortly take control of their output via their own streaming services. For now, at least, despite all the money spent and the big names lured towards the small screen from the world of cinema, a version of Netflix comprised only of Netflix originals wouldn't be much of a prospect. That it remains impossible to assess Netflix via the industry standard method of ratings is telling too – the company's caginess about exactly how many people consume which elements of their output prompts suspicions that its strategy might not be built to last.

Even if Netflix represents a transitional phase rather than television's next great leap forward, the chances are that smaller, less comprehensive platforms using similar technology will be. So, in this new world, what will be the purpose of 'traditional' television? Can it hope to survive? Well, yes. In the face of such intense competition, it's remarkable how much centrality broadcast television retains. It is striking too, how much difference it can make, even today, to our perceptions of particular issues. Television still, somehow, matters. The nation continues to engage with it like no other medium. Which means that it remains a battleground.

As we've seen, 2016 proved to be a pivotal year in recent world history. Britain voted to leave the European Union, and America elected a reality TV host as president. Trump's ascent seemed to mark a line in the sand; a moment for picking sides. The backlash was swift. Much of it centred around television, and in the process reinforced the latent power retained by the medium. In summer 2017 Channel 4 screened the astonishing first season of *The Handmaid's Tale*. Clearly, this Margaret Atwood adaptation depicting a patriarchal dystopia had been in the pipeline long before Trump's ascent to the White House – but it did feel both horribly prescient and uncannily timely, the opening cultural salvo in the resistance. And, being screened on a free-to-air channel in the UK, it reached wide and deep, prompting serious reflection on the nature and roots of misogyny. It became a heightened fictional counterpoint to the real-life challenges to equality that were becoming apparent across the Atlantic.

At around the same time as *The Handmaid's Tale* premiered, the BBC published a report detailing the wages received by their highest-paid presenters and performers. This was public service broadcasting less as agent of change than as publicly accountable cautionary tale. According to a review of salaries, it turned out men were being paid, on average, 9.3 per cent more than women, and that nearly 500 employees of the BBC were being paid less than colleagues in comparable roles simply because of their gender. When it came to the highest-paid on-air stars, it was necessary to scroll down to number eight in the list before you encountered a woman. It seems only fair to note that the average gender pay gap across the UK workforce at the time of the furore was more than 18 per cent. In that context, the BBC could regard itself as existing within the realms of respectability. And yet due to the nature of its funding, the BBC seemed uniquely culpable: it was telling that it had taken a scandal at the BBC for this issue to come to the fore. The Corporation retains remarkable symbolic power, even when it's being (rightfully) criticised – because we all have a stake. The BBC is obliged to justify itself to us and it is held to high standards. That in itself is valuable and worth preserving.

The culture war that had been building for a couple of decades was raging fiercely by summer 2017. So, with television yet again at its heart, it was a good moment for political correctness to once more take leave of its senses. In a turn of events that seemed entirely appropriate for the year, the BBC dropped yet another bombshell. There are few more potent avatars of Britain's status as a TV nation than *Doctor Who*. The Time Lord owns a place in the hearts of multiple generations and possesses global as well as intergalactic reach. The unveiling of a new Doctor is a national event. The casting of

Jodie Whittaker in the part was, therefore, a potent moment if only because of the reaction the decision engendered. Katie Hopkins, for example, was moved to take a break from her divisive day job to tweet, 'Doctor Who is now a woman. She plans to go on maternity leave in six months and return part-time during office hours only.' Television had, at exactly the right moment, managed to annoy exactly the right people.

Despite current indications to the contrary, Britain's underlying character is changing. The grim irony of the vote to leave the European Union (and the reactionary attitudes it has emboldened in regard to race, nationality and gender) is that the generation keenest on Brexit are almost certainly the final cohort of Brits who would be in favour of such a course of action. New stories are emerging, embodying different identities and with a different emphasis at their heart. If Jodie Whittaker is the new Doctor, then perhaps Jodie Comer is the next 007. *Killing Eve*, which was adapted by Phoebe Waller-Bridge from a series of novels by Luke Jennings and appeared on the BBC in 2018, was a very fresh kind of drama constructed out of familiar parts. Ostensibly, it was a spy thriller – but the conspiracy at its heart was the least interesting thing about it. In fact, its plotting was almost a snarky snigger at the many gratuitously labyrinthine and portentous espionage dramas to have passed through prime time since 9/11. Its gender subtext, which was the real point of it, felt both new and strikingly subversive.

The Bechdel Test originated in Alison Bechdel's 1985 comic strip *Dykes to Watch Out For*. Two female characters stipulate that they will only go and see a film if it satisfies the following criteria: the film must have at least two women in it; the women must talk to each other; and they must talk about something besides a man.

While being gleefully and joyfully entertaining throughout, *Killing Eve* was Bechdel television in excelsis. In the context of any other espionage thriller ever made, it was a fabulous category error; a scoop of ice cream on a cheese board. Instead of the po-faced faux gravitas usually associated with the genre, *Killing Eve* was giddy, knowing, whip-smart and hilarious. It ran on emotion – or, perhaps more appropriately, since Comer's character Villanelle was a psychopath – on instincts, on submission to urges. It was about female autonomy and freedom from consequences.

Crucially, there was nothing strident or explicitly political about the show, no sense of gender beefs being pursued; the show simply wasn't about the male characters. The two leads – the assassin Villanelle, and her MI5/6 pursuer Eve Polastri (Sandra Oh) – were only interested in each other, for reasons they couldn't quite explain. They didn't really have to. The heart of the show was always to be found in Eve and Villanelle's interactions, even if they took place at a distance. Villanelle steals Eve's suitcase and tries various items of her clothing on for size. Villanelle picks out a wardrobe of beautiful designer clothes for Eve and then, spookily, delivers them to her. But as initially alarming as this was, there was no real sense of threat. The clothes didn't represent a gratuitous flaunting of wealth or an expensive but ostentatious gift. They represented metamorphosis. Villanelle, whose first words to Eve are a well-judged piece of advice about how to style her hair ('wear it down'), is an adult child dressing a doll, a woman playing with a fascinating stranger's identity. It quickly became clear that the two women were flirting with each other, via the unusual medium of an international murder investigation.

Throughout the first season, the grim serial-killer TV trope of murdering, often sadistically, female characters – and therefore using them as dramatic sacrifices – was beautifully inverted. It was largely the men who copped it in *Killing Eve*, often in amusingly inventive ways. On one occasion, Villanelle sneaks into a fetish club, poses as an employee, and slaughters a businessman with an oxygen pump. It was hilariously gruesome, and one of the more brilliant subversions of the male gaze ever depicted on film. The men in *Killing Eve* – even the nice ones like Eve's long-suffering husband Niko and her MI5 colleague Bill – weren't in control. In fact, they were essentially props. In season two, Eve has a one-night stand with gormless, sexy, posh underling Hugo and then casts him aside, treating him much as Roger Moore-era James Bond might have treated one of his stunning but vacuous debutantes. As the show's by now established traditions dictated, poor Hugo ended up in a puddle of his own blood in a hotel corridor. *Killing Eve* was gloriously and correctly unapologetic about all this – it just wasn't about him.

In *63 Up*, Michael Apted was taken to task, entirely reasonably, by participant Jackie Bassett. 'I thought you treated us, as women, totally differently,' she said. 'And I didn't like it.' With the benefit of hindsight, this proposition is inarguable – in early instalments of *Up*, the female participants are mainly asked about husbands, children, domestic circumstances. To discuss this issue isn't necessarily to criticise Michael Apted – the show's attitude towards gender balance simply mirrors that of the era in which it was spawned. The ratio of male to female participants is in itself revealing: ten men are tracked by the show and only four women. In 1964, it was clearly assumed that women's lives were likely to follow more predictable paths than those of men. These attitudes have lingered stubbornly around society, and *63 Up* is the first iteration of the show in which they've been seriously discussed. Across the historical span of this noble project, this blockage has begun to shift, and the shift has been acknowledged in *Up*, just as it is being explored and dramatised in other areas of the medium. Television shadows life, and life shadows television.

When he first conceived his 2019 near-future drama *Years and Years*, Russell T. Davies can't possibly have imagined the circumstances in which its concluding episode would be screened. And if any dramatist had written it thus, they'd have risked accusations of contrivance. As a drama exploring the effects – both on society and on a single family – of the rise of populism, the advent of climate change, the transformative effects of technology, the inexorable sprawl of the gig economy and the anxiety of increasing financial instability, *Years and Years* was an ambitious affair. As such fictions always do, it risked stretching the bounds of credibility. Things won't get this bad, surely?

And yet the finale followed hot on the heels of a debate in the Conservative leadership election. But not just any old debate – this was the kind of debate that should have prompted serious introspection from anyone who cared about the future of Britain as a vaguely functional democratic state. A cabal of middle-aged men were competing for the opportunity to take the helm of the Conservatives, just in time to attempt to steer the party (note: not the country) through the most serious national crisis since the Second World War. But this was a party whose rank and file had gone radically rogue. This was becoming an era of mainstreamed and exponentially multiplying extremity. YouGov polling published in the week of the debate suggested that a majority of Tory members (54 per cent) would be willing to countenance the destruction of their own party in the name of facilitating Brexit. Over half were prepared to see Brexit lead to the break-up of the United Kingdom. We were dealing with a political kamikaze mission – albeit one in which the rest of the nation was strapped, terrified but paralysed, into the passenger seat.

So who were the runners and riders? Who were the men offering to grapple with this feverish chaos? There was Boris Johnson, of course, the closest Britain had to a reality TV politician in the vein of Donald Trump: a man with a history of dishonesty, incompetence, opportunism and buffoonery; a man who compared Muslim women wearing burkas to 'letterboxes' in 2018. There was Dominic Raab, who was threatening to effectively suspend parliamentary democracy if that was what it took to get Brexit over the line, and who had just refused to withdraw his description of feminists as 'obnoxious bigots'.[66] Jeremy Hunt, who that week had sided with Trump against London's Muslim mayor Sadiq Khan after Trump retweeted Katie Hopkins' description of Khan's London as 'Londonistan'. And Michael Gove: consistent at least in his disdain for experts, he'd recently denied that hate crime had risen since the EU referendum and defied the police's judgement in doing so.[67] Not in the contest, but doubtless smirking somewhere just out of shot, was Jacob Rees-Mogg, who had a few days earlier used the word 'snowflakes' to describe people who objected to Johnson's various provocations.[68] If these men had anything in common, it was their increasing disregard for both the facts about the situation facing the country, and the normal standards of British political discourse. And yet, it was also worryingly difficult to sense any cohesive opposition.

After what was surely among the most dispiriting hours of political television in British history, there can't have been many viewers prepared to swear on their hastily stockpiled no-deal Brexit emergency supplies that the themes explored in *Years and Years* were particularly far-fetched. Suddenly, this was genuinely alarming. 'Beware those men, the jokers and the tricksters and the clowns,' says Muriel Deacon (Anne Reid) in *Years and Years*. 'They will laugh us into hell.' And so – just a handful of years into our imagined future – unfolded a tale of cancelled BBC charters and faked political gaffes; of hidden internment camps for foreigners and forcibly gated communities for working-class locals; of bloviating populists and willing lackeys. Could it happen? Suddenly it was very hard to rule anything out with absolute confidence.

The visual and sonic grammar of television is constantly evolving; for example, the angry, urgent livery of the 'Breaking News' banner has become a part of many dramatists' visual armoury since 9/11. In the opening episode of *Years and Years*, a nuclear attack on Britain is narrowly averted. But the warning siren is sounded, an evocative enough piece of aural imagery in itself. Now, it felt like a call-back. Chillingly, it was hard not to revisit the memory of the apocalyptic drama *Threads*, which screened on BBC Two back in 1984, and remains arguably the most relentlessly horrifying 112 minutes of television ever made. Subsequently and happily, the sound of the nuclear alarm lost much of its potency as the Cold War ended and the immediate threat passed. But now we were back in that dimly familiar landscape of jittery paranoia – the siren in *Years and Years* was grimly potent in a way that it hadn't been in decades. Much of *Years and Years* was scattergun and unsatisfactory, replete with wild imaginings and logical flaws. But what it did manage to do, with almost uncanny brilliance, was speak to our collective subconscious; to how many of us were feeling at that terrible, pregnant moment. It gave form and shape to our fears; showed us one possible direction of travel; suggested what might happen, how easily and how fast.

Elements of the series will no doubt seem ridiculous in five years' time. After all, *Years and Years* was, by definition, speculative. And nothing dates more quickly than misconceived futurology. But the show will still carry an emotional charge, evoke a traumatic collective psychological moment. Fictions like *1984* and *Brave New World* are no less potent for never having come true – in fact, they still resonate as warnings and as prophecies. Winston Smith's eventual acceptance in *1984* that two plus two equals five feels terrifyingly appropriate to the post-truth era. Similarly, *Years and Years* will represent a prescient, immediate and resonant response to the national confusion of summer 2019. Television, as a popular art form which comes to you, which looms out of the screen in the corner of your living room, in which we all have a stake, is uniquely well placed to capture and conjure with these moments. It's sometimes our best chance of making sense of them.

In 1996, *Our Friends in the North* marked the dawning of the 'post-historical' era. It explored, wisely and affectingly, the political and cultural signposts of Britain's recent past. On the face of it, the show didn't have much to say about the future. And yet, in retrospect, it's possible to draw a line between *Our Friends in the North* and *Years and Years*. *Our Friends . . .* marked the end of the era in which class defined British political divides. In the years before the show, the only issue for the majority of working-class people was what kind of Labour Party they would be voting for. And in the years following it, the only real electoral question seemed to be which party would manage neoliberal capitalism most efficiently.

By also telling a bigger story through the travails of a group of ordinary individuals, *Years and Years* represented the working through of that process, and the final rejection of the stasis it implied. It suggested that something more volatile had replaced our traditional binaries and explored the prospect that we might be straws in the wind, vulnerable to all manner of emotional and psychological manipulation. As Rory Kinnear's Stephen Lyons puts it in *Years and Years*: 'We were born in a pause.' But that pause has ended. History has begun again, with a vengeance. This wasn't a particularly cheerful vision of the future. But it did pose many timely questions about where we might be going, and attempted to answer them with more humanity, sensitivity and honesty than the politicians on our screens an hour earlier. That in itself is valuable: it represents television continuing to do what it always has.

Television is incredibly versatile. It is both poacher and gamekeeper. It's politics and comedy. It's sport and art. It's music and love and war and history. And, as it showed in June 2019, it's also fact, fiction, and the increasingly porous line separating the two. In the space of two memorable, terrifying hours, it managed to show us the real-life chaos on the political front line – before serving up a drama set in a possible future lurching out of that chaos. It's rare, of course, for such perfect synchronicity to arise. But when it does, it proves that the medium still animates and illuminates the life of our nation like no other art form.

POSTSCRIPT

VIRAL CONTENT

BBC Parliament · The Crown · The Windsors
BBC News · Panorama · Hospital · Gogglebox · Newsnight
Our Finest Hours

ON 31 DECEMBER 2019, just eighteen days after Boris Johnson's emphatic election victory seemed to have drawn a line under many of Britain's most contentious contemporary political issues, the World Health Organisation's China office was informed of a cluster of cases of a novel coronavirus. Later to be named Covid-19, the virus was thought to have originated in a wet market in the city of Wuhan. But it was proving worryingly mobile. The comparatively tranquil new era apparently promised by the election result was being undermined even as we began to come to terms with its implications.

The previous few months had represented the tumultuous climax to a furious half-decade in British public life. The BBC's Parliament channel, previously the dry, forbidding headteacher's office of the TV schedules, suddenly gained millions of viewers as the nation's political skip fire blazed out of control. During the week of Johnson's failed prorogation of Parliament, the channel racked up

2.6 million viewers. Of course, these unheard-of viewing figures were in part just a reflection of deeply unusual times. But BBC Parliament's success also felt like an amplification of television's status as a societal battleground. There was an aesthetic dimension to our sudden obsession with parliamentary wranglings. Viewers were able to place the House of Commons in various contexts they recognised. The arcane rituals and air of faded grandeur gave proceedings the feel of a period drama. There were squirm-inducing interrogation scenes worthy of *Line of Duty*. There were echoes of the vivid authenticity of the best reality TV in the raw, intense veracity of the dialogue. People started treating Britain's new political reality like a particularly binge-worthy Netflix series, joking that the latest season felt a little hyperbolic and far-fetched. And so it did. But even so, you couldn't take your eyes off it.

The subsequent election was an ugly, rancorous affair. Predictably, mainstream broadcasters in general and the BBC in particular found themselves pulled in every conceivable direction; once again they struggled to locate a fixed moral position and hold firm to it. And once again, they found official narratives easier to accept than to challenge and left themselves open to accusations of client journalism in the process. The context in which the broadcasters were operating was, of course, impossibly difficult. The Conservatives rebranded one of their official Twitter accounts as a fact-checking site during a leaders' debate. Footage of Labour's Keir Starmer, then the party's Brexit spokesman, was unfavourably manipulated – and the manipulation was shamefully defended by Conservative Party chairman James Cleverly. Fact-checking non-profit organisation First Draft suggested that 88 per cent of the Tories' most heavily promoted Facebook adverts contained factual inaccuracies.

Broadcasting's response to this blizzard of bad-faith electioneering was, at best, infuriatingly naive. Allegations of bias in the media (and particularly the BBC) peppered the campaign but they now came from all sides. Mainstream media outlets had made enemies on all points of the political spectrum. With hindsight, the media's main crime was weakness: rather than outright bias, there was evidence of naivety and a failure of courage. They allowed themselves to be manipulated, particularly by the well-funded, streetwise and unscrupulous Conservative operation headed by Boris Johnson's chief adviser Dominic Cummings. Unsourced stories from anonymous insiders were repeatedly and helpfully reported – there was a particularly disgraceful episode during which the political editors of both ITV (Robert Peston) and the BBC (Laura Kuenssberg) tweeted of an assault by a Labour activist on a Conservative adviser. The story turned out to be false – but by the time this was ascertained, the two journalists had spread it far and wide.

Television hadn't had a good election. But even as the BBC looked to have frozen, paralysed by the increasingly threatening language of the now all-powerful Conservative government, events were moving fast. The period between the election and Britain entering its anti-pandemic lockdown on 23 March now feels like a temporal ghost limb; still tangible but amputated from any particular context. But even though it was effectively a blueprint for an era that is now doomed never to be born, it still contained a couple of hugely consequential developments. The national conversation continued, with television at its heart.

In the period between 2016 and 2019 we'd bought our tickets. In early 2020, it was time for the show to begin. Just as the EU referendum had been fought and won on a simple three-word slogan ('Take Back Control'), so was the 2019 election ('Get Brexit Done'). The parliamentary vote was a formality. On 31 January (the day after an emergency committee of the World Health Organisation declared the coronavirus outbreak to be a public health emergency of international concern), Britain officially left the European Union. At first, very few of the television presenters paid to guide us through the pomp and circumstance surrounding this momentous event could come up with much in the way of insight. As almost every news anchor found themselves obliged to say, we were 'about to begin a new chapter in our national history'. But we all knew that. The revelations were in the gaps, the omissions, the evasions.

In the days leading up to Brexit Day, the BBC had repeated Laura Kuenssberg's documentary *The Brexit Storm Continues*. This was a peculiar affair; immaculately sourced, courtesy of Kuenssberg's bulging contact book, but strangely airtight, as if the extreme insider access it offered precluded any kind of wider perspective. Dramatic and yet oddly unrevealing, it felt like political theatre, pure and simple – the cut and thrust of Parliament divorced from all context. This was reactive rather than proactive journalism; like much of the BBC's output around Brexit, it hammered viewers with the notion of an event's importance without ever really explaining why it mattered so much in practical terms or where it might be going next. Still, in its own way, this did confirm an unsettling truth. Brexit was always a nebulous, symbolic gesture rather than a practical aspiration. As such, it quickly became an article of faith for its adherents. But with its enactment, something has changed. Now, Brexit is simply policy; a Conservative manifesto pledge. Up to a point, its poison has been drained: like any other manifesto pledge, its wisdom is now open to scrutiny.

Here, it was possible to detect a few shifts in the national broadcasting blockage that reflected our polarised and unyielding national dialogue on the issue. Up to this point, most journalists conducting televised Brexit-related interviews with members of the public had seemed content to simply find people who wanted Brexit, ask them if they still wanted Brexit and cut back to the studio. This, suddenly, was slightly different. Some journalists, even on the BBC, were beginning to ask people why they wanted Brexit and even, in a few cases, attempt further critical dialogue beyond that point. The results weren't pretty. In fact, from the frighteningly low level of understanding many of the answers revealed to the creation of the ugly hashtag #thick which Remain supporters soon had trending on Twitter, they reflected poorly on everyone involved. But maybe this was a start – after all, the first step to recovery is accepting you have a problem.

All the same, Brexit Day certainly didn't feel like a moment of national renewal or triumph. It was too raw an experience for the defeated and too ungraciously celebrated by the victors. The phrase 'it's time for the nation to come together again' did an unseemly amount of heavy lifting on the day itself. The problem was, every time news producers cut to Parliament Square, the prospect of Britannia United seemed more absurd. There were EU-baiting songs. There were banners imploring the government to 'Lock Up The Traitors'. Nigel Farage was bellowing at his disciples, who were bellowing back. Even among the people who were getting exactly what they wanted, there was still every appearance of furious anger. If this was the atmosphere at the Leave campaign's moment of greatest triumph, it is troubling to imagine how any bumps in the Brexit road might be received.

The post-election, pre-pandemic micro-era was characterised by a sense of endings. There was Britain's membership of the EU. Jeremy Corbyn's leadership of the Labour Party. But something even more fundamental to national identity was up for grabs too. Just before Christmas, Netflix launched season three of its lavish, earnest royal drama *The Crown*. The timing was piquant; Prince Andrew had just blundered though an extraordinarily damaging interview with *Newsnight*'s Emily Maitlis during which his description of the nature of his relationship with recently deceased multi-millionaire paedophile Jeffrey Epstein elicited widespread scorn. Then, as 2020 dawned, the news broke that Prince Harry and his wife Meghan Markle had decided to withdraw from royal duties and move abroad.

In terms of its content, *The Crown* is unusual. Most serious TV drama dealing with the royal family has mined Britain's deep past. Shows like ITV's *Victoria* and BBC/Showtime's *The Tudors* have observed what seems to be an unspoken rule stating that you can't milk royal secrets for scurrilous entertainment until a century or more has passed. These are origin stories, while *The Crown* engages with the events of our lifetimes. And much of its potency comes from the knowledge that the era it dramatises is almost over.

The Crown is about self-sacrifice. It resonates because it shows the Queen as a young, vibrant woman. A woman whose sense of duty came to override her personal happiness. Throughout, we sense her unease and her resolution. Her story dovetails with rose-tinted memories of that idealised post-war period in British life: Britain, still central to the global narrative, still just about in possession of an empire but tired, poor and putting itself back together after a painful victory. It's the beginning of an ending as British influence over world events continued to decline. But superficially, it looks like a fresh start. And that's what Queen Elizabeth II has presided over. Managed decline. The Queen is a comfort blanket to multiple generations of Brits and *The Crown* validates their shared past. Accordingly, it's a warning too; post-Princess Diana, self-sacrifice hasn't looked like such a brilliant deal. And the Queen is ninety-four years old.

It seems very possible that before long, we will start to wonder what our royal family is really for. *The Crown* is creative with the historical facts when it suits the show's emotional narrative – for example, there's no real evidence that the Queen took Winston Churchill to task over his handling of the London smog of 1952. We relish *The Crown*'s suggestion that she might have done because it tells us an optimistic story about how Britain works. And yet royalty's status as a constitutional check and balance was undermined by the political chaos of autumn 2019, during which Prime Minister Boris Johnson misled the monarch in an attempt to bypass Parliament and was rewarded with a thumping electoral majority. In political terms, the institution of royalty is entirely decorative.

Which brings us back to the family's disappearing future. Harry and Meghan's break for freedom represents the end point of many of the trajectories explored by *The Crown*. Harry himself isn't all that important. He's sixth in line to the throne. In our national fable, he's narrative colour – a character actor at best. But to many, his and Meghan's decision represents the antithesis of the doggedly dutiful Queen represented in *The Crown*. In dramatic terms, they represent a potential continuity break at an inopportune moment for both the institution and the nation as a whole.

Below the Queen, what we want from the royal family has changed. From the 1980s onwards, the family began to drift from the shadowy world of hereditary privilege towards the harshly lit realm of celebrity. Ironically, this process was probably sent into overdrive by Princess Diana, a trending hashtag in a tiara and therefore a woman ahead of her time. For all the genuflecting respectfulness of the dramas, other small-screen representations of the family have become less reverent, more knowing and ironic. Channel 4's comedy *The Windsors*, for example, takes great delight in treating the family (and particularly its younger members) as essentially one step up from reality TV stars. They are gormless stooges; much like Jade Goody, they're famous for being famous. Tellingly, the Queen herself is never seen in *The Windsors*. Her presence would be a category error: correctly, the show's writers have understood her to occupy a different reality altogether.

The story of the royal family over the last forty years has been of their transition from enigmatic appendage of British statecraft to flat-out celebrity. In some ways, this has worked well for them, helping them maintain their grip on our collective imagination. But celebrity consumes as well as creates. We haven't quite admitted this to ourselves yet and while the Queen still presides over us, we'll be able to postpone the reckoning and trace a line between Britain in its modern iteration and the country of the early seasons of *The Crown*. But the clock is ticking. Writing in the *Observer* in early 2020, Will Hutton described Harry and Meghan as 'canaries in the mine, foretelling the end of royalism'. In *The Crown*, the young Windsors strike an uneasy balance between duty and happiness. The next generations – of royals and commoners alike – might wonder about the purpose of their sacrifice.

The Crown is a drama about identity and duty. It's also a drama about the gap between fantasy and reality. Elizabeth II is the idealised figurehead of an idealised Britain. If the show explores the human drama behind the façade, it's predominantly in the service of maintaining the larger fiction. *The Crown* feels like a perfect representation of Britain in the early months of 2020. With the Windsor family, with Brexit Day and with Boris Johnson, England was dreaming. Optimistic fantasies about exceptionalism and unique national attributes were colonising our discourse; clogging it like bindweed. But along with the rest of the world, Britain was about to receive the harshest of wake-up calls.

There are, of course, many perspectives from which the 2020 Covid-19 outbreak can and will be analysed. It's a scientific event. A geopolitical one. A sociological one. But television, particularly in Britain, has been at the heart of the story in many ways. It's how most of us have experienced the pandemic. And it's how we've coped with it too. As ever, for better or worse, it's shown us who we are.

One of the main small-screen narrative strands of the Covid-19 outbreak began with the Conservative election victory. For three months, it seemed that after years of baleful intent towards the BBC, the party might just have arrived in a position where it could make good on its many implicit threats to dismantle it. A prominent Downing Street source spoke of the government's intention to 'whack' the Beeb. Former culture secretary Nicky Morgan made a typically specious comparison between the BBC and defunct video rental chain Blockbuster and spoke longingly about the possibility of a Netflix-style voluntary subscription funding model being introduced.

In early February, Morgan launched a public consultation on whether the non-payment of the TV licence fee should remain a criminal offence. The suggestion that failure to pay might be decriminalised was in effect a dog whistle to the culture warriors who now constituted the party's electoral base. It was cowardly and passive-aggressive but by design profoundly harmful: an attempt to de-fund by a nod and a wink; a tacit promise to look the other way. Its implications for the BBC's finances were potentially massive – an estimated £200 million a year would be hacked from a budget already painfully stretched by the assumption of liability for providing free licences for over-75s. (These free licences would have to be abolished by July.)

Knives were being sharpened and cuts mooted: the cost to the corporation's output hardly needed spelling out. According to an anonymous BBC editor speaking to the 'slow news' outlet Tortoise, 'I was pretty sure we were buggered – as close as it gets to oblivion.'

Has the Covid-19 outbreak saved the BBC? It's clearly too early to say – the Conservative majority remains hefty and it's unlikely that the government's malign intentions will have gone away. But the terrain on which this national conversation will take place has been utterly transformed. Part of the problem the BBC has recently faced is that the very idea of public service television had started to feel quaint and anachronistic. Who were the public now and what were they being served? What if it wasn't what they wanted? In recent years, 'service' has become a concept connected to retail and, significantly in the context of broadcasting, to consumer choice. But it used to be a concept connected to community and duty. Since lockdown began, the idea has recovered something of its old meaning. It feels important again. Would market forces offer virtual gallery tours and musical performances? Would Netflix launch universally available educational programming initiatives to help children keep up with their studies? Would Amazon Prime dig into a vast archive of sport, drama and arts content to help entertain a quarantined population?

The BBC did all this and more. It responded to the moment in a way that other broadcasters simply couldn't, and the public responded in turn. During the course of lockdown, 94 per cent of the UK's adult population used BBC services.[69] And during this period, the BBC did something less tangible too: it functioned as a reassuring ambient presence. At the height of the crisis, the BBC repeatedly ran an ident in which various trusted and familiar faces took turns to reassure us that normality would return and that in the meantime, they had our back. It was twee, it was slightly cheesy, it was emotionally manipulative; but it was oddly comforting too.

Suddenly, the foundational values of Lord Reith felt pertinent again. This really was a moment for education, information and entertainment. And, for once, the BBC moved speedily and intuitively to provide these lockdown emergency services. Now, it needs to maintain its new nimbleness and focus. The aftermath of the Covid-19 crisis is likely to be at least as disturbing as the crisis itself. The BBC must continue to make the running. By getting out into the country and exploring our lives as they change, it can truly serve, reporting the nation and speaking for it too.

And yet there remains a tension at the heart of the BBC, and the pandemic has amplified it. Is the BBC's job to report government policy or to interrogate it? Can a balance be found between the two positions? And does this balance change during a crisis of generational significance? In early May, an anonymous senior journalist attempted to explain their position during the crisis to *The Economist*: 'The BBC does have a responsibility to provide what the nation needs . . . it doesn't need a great bust up about what's gone wrong in the recent past. The bosses are keen that we come out of this with the sense that we looked after the interests of the nation, not just our journalistic values.' This statement seems to imply that 'what the nation needs' might clash with 'journalistic values'. But this is surely a false choice. The quote suggests the potential for a worrying and conscious acquiescence to government narratives. It's a deeply questionable position when government mistakes have the potential to cost lives. What if 'a great bust up' was necessary to prevent corrupt governance or a catastrophic policy error? During April and May, the nation came closer than it would have liked to seeing these questions answered in real time.

The uneasy consensus that characterised the early stages of the pandemic was never likely to hold. Failings in the government's handling of the crisis became ever more manifest and as the UK's death toll approached and then surpassed those of other European countries, tensions emerged and 'journalistic values' began to chafe against pressure to accept government lines. The first notable shots were fired by Emily Maitlis who, in early April, introduced *Newsnight* with an attack on the 'trite and misleading' language used by ministers discussing Boris Johnson's recovery from Covid-19. 'You do not survive the illness through fortitude and strength of character,' she said, 'no matter what the Prime Minister's colleagues might tell us. This is a myth which needs debunking.' She went on to explore the statistical links between poverty and vulnerability to the virus. It was a stirring moment and a sign that the BBC's better journalists were becoming impatient with the crisis being used as a pretext for the force-feeding of pre-cooked, pre-packaged narratives.

Soon television, in its blanket coverage of the pandemic, was unavoidably homing in on the specifics of the UK government's strategic and even moral failures. A startling *Panorama* documentary

– subtitled and indeed, definitively answering the question, 'Has the Government Failed the NHS?' – explored the dangerous shortage of personal protective equipment (PPE) available to medical staff and, perhaps most shamefully of all, exposed the breathtakingly cynical government decision to downgrade the seriousness of the pandemic in response to that shortage. In January, Covid-19 had been designated a high consequence infectious disease (HCID) and according to health and safety rules, the government was legally obliged to provide all staff dealing with such a disease with respirator masks, full-face visors and gowns. As the virus began to spread, the government downgraded the designation – formally, Covid-19 is now of lower consequence than the likes of earlier coronaviruses such as SARS or MERS. According to presenter Richard Bilton, 'it seems clear that the rules have been changed because of the shortages.'

Inevitably, this was the cue for the two sides in Britain's culture wars to prime their guns once again. The government and the right-wing press quickly seized on the fact that a number of the medics interviewed had connections to the Labour Party. Handily, rubbishing the context of the criticism prevented them from having to seriously address the issues raised in the film. It also suggested that however much goodwill the pandemic might have garnered for the BBC, the Conservative Party still had the corporation in its sights.

In the light of this hostility, the BBC is understandably delighted to be associated with the NHS – given the esteem in which the health service is held, any subliminal connection the public can be encouraged to make between the two national institutions works very nicely for the broadcaster. This can, however, lead to a delicate balancing act. The BBC's two-part 'Coronavirus Special' edition of their *Hospital* documentary strand was, in many ways, an immaculate piece of public service broadcasting. It certainly would have met our senior BBC journalist's criteria of providing 'what the nation needs' while avoiding 'bust ups'.

This was a lovingly assembled and in places, incredibly moving hymn to the health service. It was full of crushing, devastating personal details that humanised the horrendous numbers – desperately ill 88-year-old patient Peter attempting to video-call his family, the lingering shot of piles of patients' belongings in a store room, the staff's emotional applause in the hospital corridors as elderly former nurse Nancy was wheeled out after her recovery. But it outright refused to address anything politically contentious. PPE shortages were a non-issue. Levels of preparedness were unmentioned. Instead, the documentaries chimed perfectly with the UK's weekly, doorstep-bound rounds of applause for key workers – bursts of communal goodwill that began as a stirringly spontaneous outpouring and eventually became a little grating and prescribed.

As a nation, we rightly celebrate and honour NHS staff for their selflessness, expertise and compassion. But collectively, we don't seem quite able to join the dots and begin to understand why so many of them have died fighting Covid-19, or why government co-option of the weekly applause feels so opportunistic, jarring and unseemly. Despite the various fundraising initiatives endorsed by the BBC during the pandemic, the NHS isn't a charity. Nor is it a branch of the military. As one nurse bleakly put it in the *Panorama* film, 'Calling us heroes just makes it okay when we die.'

Throughout the pandemic, Britain has been quite unable to resist its taste for a wartime narrative. So the imposition of this trope onto careworkers was probably inevitable. However, it reached its zenith in BBC One's series *Our Finest Hours*. If the Churchillian title wasn't a broad enough hint of the buttons being pushed here, perhaps the title sequence, in which scenes of everyday heroism from the pandemic were intercut with images of the Blitz, would be. 'Now, as we did in World War Two,' boomed the voiceover, 'we're uniting in a common endeavour . . . once again, we can be proud to be British.' Without wishing to be churlish about the local heroism on display, there seemed almost literally no point to *Our Finest Hours* besides conflating our modern battle against infective viral matter with our previous wars against more visible adversaries.

Perhaps this offered a hint as to why Britain was so reluctant to involve itself in pan-European schemes for sourcing PPE or ventilators. This was a battle that, for some obscure reason of collective national psychology, we felt we needed to fight alone. It would, after all, be entirely consistent with the recent direction of British politics. Indeed, this exceptionalism might offer a clue about the underpinnings of Britain's inadequate response: as Italy suffered horrendously at the hands of the virus in early March, the UK carried on with arena rock shows and large sporting events. It was possible to discern a certain arrogance; an assumption of superiority, a confidence that it couldn't happen here. Sadly, coronaviruses seem to have little respect for British pluck.

Of course, the figure at the heart of both Britain's Covid-19 response and its plunge into sentimental, irrational exceptionalism has been our very own cosplay Churchill, Boris Johnson. Johnson spent the first few months of 2020 luxuriating in the free hand apparently gifted to him by the election result. But his fundamental lack of seriousness was brutally exposed by the pandemic, even before it had really got under way. He seemed unable to grasp the basic medical advice, boasting of visiting hospitals and shaking hands with Covid-19 patients as late as 27 March. And his tone was catastrophically off-key too: in early April, he reportedly made a tasteless quip, referring to Britain's disgracefully tardy attempts to remedy its shortage of ventilators as 'Operation Last Gasp'.

And yet remarkably, until his shambolic and staggeringly hypocritical defence of his special adviser Dominic Cummings' breach of the lockdown – Cummings drove 260 miles to the north of England to share childcare duties with family members – Johnson maintained a consistently high level of support. Progressives remain mystified by Johnson's continuing popularity. Perhaps what they fail to understand is that his appeal is self-reflexive. The very act of criticising him is to fall into his trap and delight his supporters. Like a pantomime villain, the criticism he attracts is part of the fun – and the more po-faced and sanctimonious, the better. Johnson is banter made political flesh; an endless Bank Holiday weekend; a pub crawl without a hangover. His elastic relationship with the truth, his laziness, his flippancy and his inconstancy are weaknesses as far as his critics are concerned. But to his supporters, they're actively part of the appeal. Because, crucially, they are underpinned by his uncanny ability to avoid consequences. Getting away with things is a guiltily seductive fantasy and it helps explain why nothing seems to stick to Boris Johnson – for him to face consequences would break the spell. He is British exceptionalism personified.

But could this giddy state of grace survive sustained contact with the grimmest reality facing any British Prime Minister since the Second World War? Shows like *Our Finest Hours* worked well for Johnson, making implicit visual and emotional connections between him and Churchill. He utilised the televised national address shamelessly – every populist's favourite trick is to commandeer the airwaves and speak directly to the people, bypassing awkward institutions like parliaments and opposition parties. Remarkably, the Scottish First Minister Nicola Sturgeon found out about his plans to relax England's strict lockdown conditions at roughly the same time as the rest of the population – Johnson hadn't seen fit to confirm it with her first.

But soon, things got tricky. The first sign of trouble was that demotic and reliable barometer of contemporary British opinion, *Gogglebox*. This Channel 4 staple acquired extra resonance during the crisis – partly because it didn't need to change its living-room format in any way and therefore offered a subliminal callback to the reality we used to know. The verdict on his crisis management was brutal. 'A shambles'. 'A shitshow'. 'Where the fuck did it all go wrong?' This personality politician, with his telegenic shtick designed and honed on panel shows, hardwired to bumble and obfuscate amusingly, suddenly had nowhere to hide. This was populism curdling before our very eyes. Boris wasn't funny any more.

In the light of these developments, the controversy over Johnson's blind loyalty to the lockdown-breaking Dominic Cummings felt like a reckoning that had been approaching for some time. The outrage it elicited was likely less to do with Cummings' offence than with the arrogance, rudeness, disingenuousness and sheer entitlement with which the Conservative leadership handled the aftermath. The days immediately after the *Guardian* and *Mirror* newspapers broke the story were genuinely disturbing – an ever more bewildering exercise in national gaslighting. We were being asked to believe things that made us doubt our own sanity – for example, cabinet member Michael Gove appeared to suggest that not only was driving thirty miles to test your eyesight a good idea but it was something he himself might have done.

It was in that context that the 26 May episode of *Newsnight* rolled out forty minutes of immaculate public service broadcasting. Lewis Goodall's report carefully and soberly drove a tank through Cummings' defence. And Emily Maitlis delivered a spectacular opening monologue, stating baldly that 'Dominic Cummings broke the rules', excoriating Johnson's 'blind loyalty' to him and describing the public's 'fury, contempt and anguish' at the official line. It was a moment of sheer relief, for both supporters of the BBC and supporters of honest governance. Here, finally, the BBC appeared to be identifying a moral position and laying claim to it. Whatever the journalist quoted in *The Economist* might have thought, here was 'a big bust up' and here were 'journalistic values' perfectly serving the needs of the nation in response.

But this wasn't quite the end of the story. As with Naga Munchetty's comments about Donald Trump, the BBC didn't have the courage of its convictions and, over the following twenty-four hours, proceeded to tie itself in knots. Amid reports of Downing Street fury, the corporation issued a pitifully mealy-mouthed apology suggesting that Maitlis's introduction didn't meet their 'standards of due impartiality'. A stronger, more self-possessed national broadcaster might have insisted that the government first identify factual errors in the programme and publicly clarify them once and for all. It might further have pointed out that the government could simply have put a minister forward to defend its position on the show and that it chose not to. Instead, it threw one of its best and bravest journalists under the bus. To put it generously, the BBC's 'journalistic values' were clearly still up for negotiation in the face of government pressure.

Nevertheless, the sense persisted of a spell being broken, albeit gradually. The BBC gamely continued with Boris Johnson's television alma mater *Have I Got News For You?* during lockdown. It didn't really work. It turned out that the audience was more important than anyone realised. The unavoidable two-second time delay created by the video-link app the show was using opened up a gaping chasm of silence into which punchlines plunged like lemmings. Around the same time, something uncannily similar and wonderfully symbolic was happening to Boris Johnson in his new stomping ground. The House of Commons observed social distancing rules and embraced video conferencing during the pandemic. This left Johnson without a gallery to play to. In this newly sombre setting, discussing the horrors of the pandemic without the support of raucous back-benchers, his antithesis, Labour's calm, relentlessly logical and intellectually accomplished new leader Keir Starmer toyed with him, surgically revealing his inability to grasp detail, his lack of substance; his basic unfitness for purpose. Without an audience, Johnson was nothing. There was nowhere left to hide.

As June approached, it seemed that the endless bank holiday might just be coming to an end. Consequences could finally be looming. Even if he recovers his footing over time, Boris Johnson suddenly appeared reduced; deflated; a little chastened. Accordingly, it could well be that we never quite see him in the same way again. Step by step, television had shown us this process as it unfolded.

The two small-screen hits of early lockdown were ITV's *Quiz* and Netflix's *Tiger King*. On the face of it, *Quiz*'s story of a couple allegedly cheating on a big-money game show and *Tiger King*'s journey into the bizarre hinterland of American underground big cat breeding didn't have much in common. All they shared, it seems, was a sense of detachment – perhaps a nostalgia for our recent past, certainly a sense that the stories they told were utterly differentiated from current circumstances. In this, they worked perfectly.

Many people began lockdown earnestly proclaiming their intention to finally learn Spanish or read the complete works of James Joyce or become an expert breadmaker. But no one was quite prepared for the jittery, distracted psychological terrain it would open up. So lots of us have simply opted to slump listlessly on the couch in front of *Masterchef* instead. Television has become a form of palliative care. But the longer the pandemic continues, the more we'll need from the screen in the corner. Television will start to change us and we will start to change television. In an amazingly prophetic coincidence, a Netflix dating show called *Too Hot to Handle* launched around the start of the lockdown. The premise was built around what we'd now think of as social distancing – touch was taboo, sexual contact between contestants reduced the prize money. Was it a taste of things to come?

It seems possible. But might it be that instead, we'll want to move away from reality TV as this period develops? The idea of watching a group of people confined to a circumscribed space and unable to leave while you're confined to a circumscribed space and unable to leave feels too meta to satisfy for long. Like whole nations of *Big Brother* housemates, our lives have become formatted by Covid-19 – the daily walks and runs, the silent supermarket queues, the weekly claps for carers, the Friday night virtual pub quiz or catch-up with friends. At times, it feels like we're trapped in our own personal reality TV shows.

Often, we're watching TV coming directly from the rooms in which other people watch TV. It's establishing a weird new intimacy that, paradoxically, stems from a loss of literal physical proximity in our own lives. Critics have anguished over the vicarious nature of reality TV for years – is this deeply isolated intimacy where we've been heading all along? Suddenly, in our isolation, we're all performing: much has been written about how tiring and alienating Zoom conversations are, even (and perhaps, particularly) between friends. It's to do with observing oneself at the same time as others: to engage in a long Zoom conversation is an uncomfortably self-conscious experience, to be simultaneously consuming and creating. All the same, formats will emerge and be accommodated within the schedules surprisingly quickly – ITV did a remarkable job of getting their drama *Isolation Stories* to air just one and a half months after lockdown began. Some tropes will, however, never die; in defiance of the fact that our current situation is part of a worldwide phenomenon, ITV were startlingly quick to lay a claim to the inevitable title *A Very British Lockdown*.

As with any of the other themes of this book, the realities of the pandemic will infect TV, and TV will infect our understanding and experience of the pandemic. For example, when *Good Morning Britain* presenter Eamonn Holmes gave credence on breakfast television to an absurd conspiracy theory surrounding 5G mobile phone masts, he was simply demonstrating a current of modern thought that, through an inexorable build-up of pressure, had found itself bursting into the mainstream. Everything ends up on television in the end – it's how, as a culture, we process our ideas; how we develop them or discard them.

This book has explored everything from reality TV's intersection with politics to national identity; from poverty and inequality to the role of the BBC. In some ways, the Covid-19 pandemic has brought all of these underlying issues to a head, has sharpened our sense of confusion about what might be next. Britain and the world will be changed for ever by the virus – politically and culturally; economically and socially. But television will continue to tell us where we've been and point to where we're going.

In early June, as the lockdown eased, many Britons hit the streets. They were out in force, in solidarity with Americans protesting about the death of George Floyd, a black Minnesotan killed by police. In Bristol, a long-loathed statue celebrating slave owner Edward Colston was yanked from its plinth, rolled the short distance to Avon Lake and dumped into the water. Britain, like America, was confronting the uncomfortable intersection of its past and present. By remarkable, almost uncanny coincidence, the following night, the BBC broadcast *Sitting In Limbo*. This drama explored the experience of Anthony Bryan, a black Briton whose attempt in 2015 to acquire a passport very nearly led to his deportation to Jamaica, though he had lived and worked in the UK since 1965. He wasn't the only one – hundreds of black Britons were detained between 2012 and 2017 as a result of the government's 'hostile environment' policy, which aimed to answer ever-present political questions about immigration by removing people without leave to remain in the UK.

Once again, TV was interrogating the gap between the two competing visions of Britain which have dominated this book. Earlier in the year, the BBC had broadcast *The Windermere Children*, the remarkable story of the Jewish refugees who arrived in Britain after the Second World War. This was Britain at its noblest, offering humanitarian sanctuary to the vulnerable and traumatised even in the midst of the country's own faltering attempts to rebuild. The drama was plush and idealised; harrowing but comforting too, depicting Britain as the good guy, a place of refuge and safety.

There's an irony here. This post-war period is often invoked by the nostalgists of the neo-nativist, Brexit-supporting British right. It's a Britain of purpose: tired but victorious; morally justified. But *Sitting In Limbo* dramatised and personalised the version of Britain now underpinned by the politics of Brexit. It documented a mean-spirited, bureaucratic nightmare, deliberately prepared by the British state, for certain of its own citizens by a government pandering to the nation's worst, most isolationist instincts. British exceptionalism is part of our post-war myth but it also led us to this snide, nasty, suspicious, frankly racist place. People who had been told they were wholly British were suddenly and brutally reminded that in the eyes of the government, their status was, and therefore perhaps always had been, negotiable.

Both *The Windermere Children* and *Sitting In Limbo* are dramas of identity. Both collective and individual identity; exploring the past and the present; certainty and doubt. What *Sitting In Limbo* managed to show wasn't simply how Anthony Bryan's physical status was threatened. It also illuminated the way in which his treatment undermined his sense of self; his understanding of his own personal history, his place in the world. And in a wider sense, this identity crisis is where Britain as a whole continues to flounder. We aren't quite sure who we are. There are, for now, two Britains. One is trying to confront its own history in order to learn lessons and move on. The other is hanging on to an identity that, in the context of modernity, is essentially both a dead weight and a dead end. Via television, this book has explored the country's gathering turmoil.

In 2020, there's confusion and trepidation about what might be next. But one thing seems clear: television has never been more important. One of the most unsettling aspects of the Covid-19 pandemic has been its amorphous, undefined quality. No one knows when, or even if, it might be over. Theatres are closed. Cinemas, music venues and comedy clubs are in mothballs. Many may never reopen. Even the act of imagining possible futures feels hopeless – disconcertingly out of range and reach. How, in this context, will we talk to each other, access inspiration, process ideas? Television comes to us. It's the art form that naturally insinuates itself into our homes; enters our quarantined lives. As a creative outlet, it's still able to thrive as other doors slam shut. Television's role in explaining modern Britain may have only just begun.

ENDNOTES

1 - REALITY TV REALITY

1. https://www.referendumanalysis.eu/eu-referendum-analysis-2016/section-8-voters/the-emotional-politics-of-the-eu-referendum-bregrexit-and-beyond/

2. https://www.independent.co.uk/arts-entertainment/tv/news/katie-hopkins-branded-an-insufferable-snob-after-this-morning-debate-on-childrens-names-8690468.html

3. https://metro.co.uk/2015/01/02/15-very-katie-hopkins-moments-from-katie-hopkins-my-fat-story-5007748/

4. https://www.theguardian.com/commentisfree/2015/apr/19/katie-hopkins-migrants-vermin-darkest-history-drownings

5. https://www.theguardian.com/media/2017/may/26/katie-hopkins-leaves-lbc-radio-final-solution-tweet-manchester-attack

6. https://www.bbc.co.uk/news/uk-17310557

7. https://www.theguardian.com/politics/2012/feb/09/a4e-welfare-to-work-contract

8. https://www.theguardian.com/uk/2012/dec/02/emma-harrison-dividend-payment

9. https://www.theguardian.com/politics/shortcuts/2016/oct/03/tony-blaie-the-master-cameron-osborne-nickname

10. https://www.theguardian.com/politics/2010/apr/29/gordon-brown-gillian-duffy-bigot

11. https://www.theguardian.com/politics/2016/oct/16/secret-boris-johnson-column-favoured-uk-remaining-in-eu

12. https://www.theguardian.com/politics/2018/nov/25/why-wont-nigel-farage-answer-my-brexit-questions

13. https://www.theguardian.com/media/2002/jul/19/broadcasting.bigbrother1

2 - HOW THE OTHER HALF LIVE

14. https://www.hollywoodreporter.com/news/british-tv-writer-paul-abbott-239117

15. *Shameless* series 1, episode 2.

16. https://www.independent.co.uk/voices/comment/why-has-david-cameron-decided-to-bring-up-the-right-to-buy-scheme-during-the-help-to-buy-debate-8877356.html

17. https://www.theguardian.com/society/2016/jan/04/end-of-council-housing-bill-secure-tenancies-pay-to-stay

18. https://www.theguardian.com/media/2009/aug/03/location-location-location-kirstie-allsopp-ofcom

19. https://www.theguardian.com/money/2017/mar/02/home-ownership-in-england-at-a-30-year-low-official-figures-show

20. https://www.ons.gov.uk/employmentandlabourmarket/peopleinwork/earningsandworkinghours/bulletins/annualsurveyofhoursandearnings/2018

21. https://assets.publishing.service.gov.uk/government/uploads/system/uploads/attachment_data/file/781567/Rough_Sleeping_Statistics_2018_release.pdf

22. https://www.theguardian.com/education/2006/sep/20/schoolmeals.schools and https://www.mirror.co.uk/news/uk-news/kids-of-mum-who-defied-jamie-150132

23. https://www.theguardian.com/education/2006/sep/20/schoolmeals.schools

24. https://www.radiotimes.com/news/2015-09-03/jamie-oliver-on-his-new-campaign-we-need-a-sugar-tax/2/

25. https://www.youtube.com/watch?v=YwY211QeEnU

26. https://www.telegraph.co.uk/culture/tvandradio/5280545/Secret-Millionaire-cash-given-back-over-Barrow-in-Furness-smear.html

27. https://www.coventrytelegraph.net/news/coventry-news/tvs-secret-millionaire-told-your-3042784

28. https://metro.co.uk/2019/05/27/time-channel-4s-jeremy-kyle-special-9698196/

29. https://www.independent.co.uk/arts-entertainment/tv/news/jeremy-kyle-show-dispatches-tv-trial-drugs-cannabis-itv-response-a8932566.html

30. https://www.newworldencyclopedia.org/entry/Polygraph

31. https://www.theguardian.com/media/2007/sep/24/television

32. https://www.theguardian.com/commentisfree/2014/jan/08/channel-4-betrayed-residents-benefits-street

33. https://www.nytimes.com/2003/10/12/magazine/ghetto-miasma-enough-to-make-you-sick.html

34. http://createlondon.org/wp-content/uploads/2018/04/Panic-Social-Class-Taste-and-Inequalities-in-the-Creative-Industries1.pdf

3 - CULTURE WAR

35. https://www.theguardian.com/media/2015/mar/20/jeremy-clarkson-foul-mouthed-rant-bbc-top-gear

36. https://www.telegraph.co.uk/news/earth/environment/climatechange/6233221/Jeremy-Clarkson-People-are-bored-of-climate-change.html

37. https://www.digitalspy.com/tv/a813745/jeremy-clarkson-is-happy-donald-trump-won-the-us-election/

38. https://www.independent.co.uk/news/people/jeremy-clarkson-announces-he-wants-britain-to-stay-in-the-eu-to-create-a-united-states-of-europe-a6928556.html

39. https://www.bbc.co.uk/news/uk-england-oxfordshire-25793358; https://www.theguardian.com/politics/2014/apr/27/ukip-farage-racism-lenny-henry-politics-europe

40. https://metro.co.uk/2016/05/12/please-spare-a-thought-for-the-tories-our-most-oppressed-minority-5878466/

41. https://www.theguardian.com/media/2016/feb/24/jeremy-clarkson-top-gear-producer-bbc-oisin-tymon

42. https://www.theguardian.com/media/1999/oct/11/channel4.bbc

43. http://news.bbc.co.uk/1/hi/uk/1709708.stm

44. ibid.

45. https://www.google.com/search?q=charlotte+church+she%27s+a+big+girl+now&source=lnms&tbm=isch&sa=X&ved=0ahUKEwjWudGGyLnjAhUrQ0EAHWH3C1YQ_AUIESgC&biw=1313&bih=592#imgrc=F5ox5RbGxtP3aM:

46. https://www.mumsnet.com/Talk/in_the_news/1859485-Heidi-Klums-8-year-old-daughter-described-as-a-leggy-beauty; https://grcade.co.uk/t:daily-mail-promotes-8-year-old-girl-as-a-leggy-beauty

47. https://www.ofcom.org.uk/__data/assets/pdf_file/0030/45489/issue114.pdf

48. https://www.telegraph.co.uk/news/earth/earthnews/3308930/Al-Gores-An-Inconvenient-Truth-can-be-shown-to-schools.html

49. https://www.theguardian.com/commentisfree/2018/dec/07/us-billionaires-hard-right-britain-spiked-magazine-charles-david-koch-foundation; https://libcom.org/blog/unsurprising-reason-jonathan-pie-rants-sound-straight-out-spiked-06022018

50. https://www.ft.com/content/3be49734-29cb-11e6-83e4-abc22d5d108c

51. https://www.theguardian.com/uk-news/2014/sep/29/peter-nunn-jailed-abusive-tweets-mp-stella-creasy

4 – HOW THE BBC BECAME THE STORY

52. https://www.dailyrecord.co.uk/news/uk-world-news/jimmy-saviles-autobiography-shock-as-pages-1359536

53. https://www.youtube.com/watch?v=kpDdVq6pi7U; http://downloads.bbc.co.uk/bbctrust/assets/files/pdf/our_work/pollard_review/pollard_review.pdf; https://www.pressgazette.co.uk/pollard-review-decision-drop-newsnights-savile-probe-was-flawed-taken-good-faith/; https://www.theguardian.com/media/2015/jul/29/bbc-savile-expose-newsnight-meirion-jones; https://www.pressgazette.co.uk/meirion-jones-speaks-out-everyone-who-was-right-side-savile-argument-has-been-forced-out-bbc/

54. https://www.commonspace.scot/articles/10001/bbc-reprimands-question-time-producer-over-far-right-social-media-posts

55. https://publications.parliament.uk/pa/cm201012/cmselect/cmpubacc/1284/1284.pdf

56. *The Times*, 14 January 1985.

57. https://www.bbc.co.uk/news/entertainment-arts-23501137

58. https://www.opendemocracy.net/en/opendemocracyuk/vote-leave-trying-to-bury-bad-news/
59. https://inews.co.uk/news/politics/theresa-may-brexit-compromise-nick-boles-robbie-gibb-hard-brexit/
60. https://www.theguardian.com/technology/2016/dec/04/google-democracy-truth-internet-search-facebook

5 - A VERY BRITISH IDENTITY CRISIS

61. https://www.theguardian.com/books/2016/jan/08/keep-calm-and-carry-on-posters-austerity-ubiquity-sinister-implications
62. https://www.radiotimes.com/news/2011-03-16/exclusive-hear-controversial-midsomer-murders-interview/
63. https://www.theguardian.com/politics/2015/may/20/metropolitan-elite-britains-new-pariah-class
64. https://www.theguardian.com/cities/2018/jan/23/battle-grimsby-great-again
65. https://www.newstatesman.com/culture/tv-radio/2017/11/detectorists-series-3-mackenzie-crook-toby-jones-interview

EPILOGUE - CRADLE TO GRAVE

66. https://www.theguardian.com/politics/2019/may/26/dominic-raab-defends-calling-feminists-obnoxious-bigots
67. https://www.independent.co.uk/news/uk/politics/michael-gove-brexit-hate-crime-vote-leave-immigration-referendum-turkey-a8954006.html
68. https://twitter.com/PaulBrandITV/status/1138878344496369664?s=20

POSTSCRIPT - VIRAL CONTENT

69. https://advanced-television.com/2020/05/20/report-94-uk-adults-accessing-bbc-during-crisis/

BIBLIOGRAPHY

Andress, David – *Cultural Dementia: How the West has Lost its History and Risks Losing Everything Else* (2018)

Banks, Arron – *The Bad Boys of Brexit: Tales of Mischief, Mayhem & Guerrilla Warfare in the EU Referendum Campaign* (2016)

Beckett, Andy – *Promised You a Miracle: Why 1980–82 Made Modern Britain* (2015)

Byers, Sam – *Perfidious Albion* (2018)

Fisher, Mark – *Capitalist Realism: Is There No Alternative* (2009)

Hanley, Lynsey – *Estates: An Intimate History* (2017)

Hatherley, Owen – *The Ministry of Nostalgia* (2016)

Higgins, Charlotte – *This New Noise: The Extraordinary Birth and Troubled Life of the BBC* (2015)

Higgs, John – *The KLF: Chaos, Magic and the Band who Burned a Million Pounds* (2013)

Higgs, John – *Watling Street: Travels Through Britain and Its Ever-Present Past* (2017)

Jones, Owen – *Chavs: The Demonization of the Working Class* (2011)

Jukes, Peter – *The Fall of the House of Murdoch: Fourteen Days that Ended a Media Dynasty* (2012)

Lanchester, John – *Whoops!: Why Everyone Owes Everyone and No-One Can Pay* (2010)

Mills, Tom – The BBC: Myth of a Public Service (2016)

Moran, Joe – *Armchair Nation: An Intimate History of Britain in Front of the TV* (2013)

Pickett, Kate and Wilkinson, Richard – *The Spirit Level: Why Equality is Better for Everyone* (2009)

Randall, Lucian – *Disgusting Bliss: The Brass Eye of Chris Morris* (2010)

Robin, Corey – *The Reactionary Mind: Conservatism from Edmund Burke to Sarah Palin* (2011)

Sahlins, Marshall – *Stone Age Economics* (2017)

Stubbs, David – *1996 and the End of History* (2016)

Trilling, Daniel – *Bloody Nasty People: The Rise of Britain's Far Right* (2012)

Westen, Drew – *The Political Brain: The Role of Emotion in Deciding the Fate of the Nation* (2007)

Young, Rob – *Electric Eden: Unearthing Britain's Visionary Music* (2011)

ACKNOWLEDGEMENTS

THANKS TO all the editors who've commissioned me. Particular gratitude to Alkarim Jivani and Emma Perry at *Time Out* who gave me my first break, and to John Doran and Luke Turner at *The Quietus* who commissioned some longer, more discursive pieces which I've drawn on in parts of this book.

Thanks to Tom Clayton at Melville House.

Thanks to Steve Gove for the edit and Luke Bird for the cover design.

Thanks to early readers and patient pub listeners; particularly Ali Catterall, Steve Downes and Sophie Harris.

All Selectadisc and Brooke Road crew, particularly Tracy Pratten and Dave Moreton for swapping all those shifts at short notice!

Much love to Amanda, Steve, Tom, Ffion, Ed and Luke.

And to Mum and Dad, who probably won't agree with large chunks of this book but will, I hope, be proud that I've written it!

ABOUT THE AUTHOR

PHIL HARRISON is a television writer and cultural critic whose work has appeared in *The Guardian*, *The Telegraph* and *The Quietus*. He was formerly Deputy TV Editor for *Time Out*, and has interviewed and profiled many famous figures including Jon Hamm, William H. Macy, Jonathan Ross and Mark E. Smith. *The Age of Static* is his first book.